CO-ATQ-356

WITHDRAWN

WITHDRAWN

Beyond Understanding

American University Studies

Series XXIV
American Literature

Vol. 65

PETER LANG
New York • Washington, D.C./Baltimore
Bern • Frankfurt am Main • Berlin • Vienna • Paris

Martha L. Henning

Beyond Understanding

Appeals to the Imagination, Passions, and Will in Mid-Nineteenth-Century American Women's Fiction

PETER LANG
New York • Washington, D.C./Baltimore
Bern • Frankfurt am Main • Berlin • Vienna • Paris

Library of Congress Cataloging-in-Publication Data

Henning, Martha L.
Beyond understanding: appeals to the imagination, passions, and will in mid-nineteenth-century American women's fiction / Martha L. Henning.
p. cm. — (American university studies.
Series XXIV, American literature; vol. 65)
Includes bibliographical references and index.
1. American fiction—Women authors—History and criticism. 2. Literature and society—United States—History—19th century. 3. Women and literature—United States—History—19th century. 4. American fiction—19th century—History and criticism. 5. Campbell, George, 1719–1796. Philosophy of rhetoric. 6. Individuality in literature. 7. Psychology and literature.
8. Imagination in literature. 9. Emotions in literature. 10. Narration (Rhetoric). 11. Self in literature. 12. Will in literature. I. Title. II. Series.
PS374.W6H44 813'.3099287—dc20 95-21018
ISBN 0-8204-2861-2
ISSN 0895-0512

Die Deutsche Bibliothek-CIP-Einheitsaufnahme

Henning, Martha L.:
Beyond understanding: appeals to the imagination, passions, and will in mid-nineteenth-century American women's fiction / Martha L. Henning.–
New York; Washington, D.C./Baltimore; Bern;
Frankfurt am Main; Berlin; Vienna; Paris: Lang.
(American university studies: Ser. 24, American literature; Vol. 65)
ISBN 0-8204-2861-2
NE: American university studies / 24

Cover design by James F. Brisson.
Author photo by Kendra Cott.

The paper in this book meets the guidelines for permanence and durability of the Committee on Production Guidelines for Book Longevity of the Council of Library Resources.

© 1996 Martha L. Henning

All rights reserved.
Reprint or reproduction, even partially, in all forms such as microfilm, xerography, microfiche, microcard, and offset strictly prohibited.

Printed in the United States of America.

3996-6

In memory of

my childhood companion, Claudia Minor,
who taught me to venture beyond understanding
before she was taken by the Big Sur coast.

THE COVER

As this book explains, nineteenth-century fiction often spoke in a language of flowers. Accordingly, the illustrated cover speaks in terms explained by such keys as Sarah Josepha Hale's *Flora's Interpreter, and Fortuna Flora* (1865). The Holly-hock, reminescent of the "ambition of the scholar" (86), brings to mind the faculty of understanding. White or red Periwinkles reflect the powers of the imagination to recall "pleasures of memory" (149). The Scarlet Lily announces the "high souled" (116) sense of the passions. Finally, the Mountain Pink proclaims the "aspiring" (156) nature of the will. "Reading" the cover as signified by its floral coding thus adds further dimension to the title.

ACKNOWLEDGMENTS

Many have helped and encouraged me as I have worked on *Beyond Understanding*. Influencing me as a child, my grandmother, Louise Udden, early taught me to look beyond foregrounded images to foundational backgrounds, while she and her sister, my Great Aunt Ruth (Middlebrook), instilled in me the powers of "elbow grease." Meanwhile, my mother, Ruth Henning, challenged me to make sense of the tensions she felt amid various aspects of art and the cognitive domain.

Lively prodding to conclude this work has come from my father, Robert J. Henning, and his wife, Gibora. Ideological discussions with my son, Nathan C. Hamilton, have helped sharpen and extend my thinking on several issues; daughter Sarah L. Hamilton has shown me consistently the joys of perseverance, be it in research or in field studies. Those directly influencing this project include Lucy Freibert, whose steadfast wisdom and numerous readings helped shape the original manuscript. Jane L. Polsky contributed both hospitality and insight as Chapter V materialized. Lang editor Heidi Burns has since saved me from many stylistic faux pas and colleague Susan Dobra has generously pointed out aberrations of thought and wording. Artists Allison Gildersleeve and Jeri Hise have done a remarkable job of bringing author portraits to life.

Librarians and archivists have been a tremendous help: Iain Beavan of the Aberdeen University Library of King's College, Aberdeen, Scotland, supplied the image of George Campbell from which the artists drew. Likewise, the Stowe-Day Foundation of Hartford, CT, supplied the model prints of Harriet Beecher Stowe. For their assistance in directing me to historical materials of the Wyoming Valley, 1770s, I thank Elsie B. Russell of the Memorial Library, Montour Falls, NY; The Wyoming Valley Historical Society, Wilkes-Barre, PA; and the Newberry Library, Chicago. Ljiljana Kuftinec of the University of Louisville, Margaret English of Monterey Peninsula College, and Joan Hyer of The Untamed Shrew, Rare Books, have worked wonders to provide original sources for this study. Finally, for sustaining my spirit, humor, and relative sanity through three summers of writing, I am especially grateful to my mate, Peter Stock, who has generously afforded me time by sacrificing his own.

CONTENTS

ILLUSTRATIONS

INTRODUCTION

Until recently, twentieth-century literary scholars have had difficulty recognizing as "proper literature" those works by nineteenth-century American women that drove their contemporary Nathaniel Hawthorne to lament, "I should have no chance of success while the public taste is occupied with their trash . . ." (I: 75). Most twentieth-century critics have busied themselves discussing the quaintness or failure of works coming from the 1850s, an era in which women clearly dominated the nation's literary tastes and market.[1] Typically, twentieth-century critics have all but laughed at Susan Warner's (1851) "aristocratic little Ellen" who is "constantly being orphaned and adopted," have condemned as "carelessly written . . . loosely constructed, faulty" Harriet Beecher Stowe's *Uncle Tom's Cabin* (1852), have scorned as "sensational effects" Ann S. Stephens's (1858) use of historical sources, or have tired of E.D.E.N. Southworth's "conventional trappings" in all her books.[2]

Fortunately, however, recent theorists[3] have sought to shift these views. Implicitly rejecting current culture's domination by elements of individualism and competition, feminist critics are re-evaluating and "re-valuing" works situated in a cultural agenda of domesticity, communality, and attention to the general welfare. Gayle Greene, for example, writes that in the nineteenth-century novel "we find the fullest rendering of individual in relation to collective, of the social dimensions of personality" (4). Greene's statement sheds a positive light on elements of nineteenth-century American prose that until recently had met with indictments. "In the sentimental novels, such as *Uncle Tom's Cabin*, stereotypes were often turned into powerful symbols," writes Kristin Herzog (xx). Scholars are beginning to appreciate the literary conventions that once "rang certain bells in the average reader's mind" (Herzog xx) and reconsider the once maligned "cover story"[4] that the various authors do not so much retell as participate in. Drawing readers into a community of assent, these stock elements contrast with those elements of later literature that portray "man as 'solitary, asocial, unable to enter into relationships with other human beings'" (Greene 4), appealing to that sense of isolation within the reader, and implicitly fostering the same. Considering "conventional trappings" not "cliché," but indicative of "an extraordinarily high degree of social cohesion, of shared values and world view" between the author and readership (Harris, *19th-Century* 32) opens possibilities for new readings of mid-nineteenth-century American women's writing.

Traditionally, twentieth-century literary scholars sought to designate this literature as a window into past culture: "I shall consider the book only as it throws light upon the characteristics of the 1850s," writes Fred Louis Pattee (130). Shifting this paradigm, several scholars turn from considering "the book as a representation of or statement about the world" (as Jerome Bruner observes of Tzvetan Todorov's Marxist views) to considering the world "as the origin of the book" (157). Accordingly, authors create textual clues borne of their cultural habits. Acknowledging this latter perspective can nudge the contemporary reader to seek a literary experience more closely approximating the one that brought these works to influence 1850s culture and monopolize the country's first bestseller list. Reading within the rhetorical context that spawned mid-nineteenth-century American women's works also allows contemporary readers a view of how authors propelled their works. But, as Kenneth Elliot observes, "one must be enculturated as to what the clues, as clues, mean." A reader attempting such "enculturing" him- or herself could probably use some assistance.

One valuable guide, overlooked until now, comes from the eighteenth-century rhetorician, Reverend Dr. George Campbell. Born in Aberdeen, Scotland, on Christmas Day, 1719, "philosopher, disputant, and defender of religion" Campbell served Aberdeen as a minister, the Principal of Marischal College, and Professor of Divinity (Bitzer ix). In his cornerstone of the Scottish New Rhetoric, *The Philosophy of Rhetoric* (1776), Campbell weaves his era's fascination with inductive reasoning together with theology and principles of faculty psychology to examine how discourse embodies and reflects persuasion and human interconnectedness.

As set forth in *The Philosophy of Rhetoric* (reprinted in America in 1818), Campbell's philosophy permeated the rhetorical world in which 1850s American women's books originated:[5]

> Nineteenth-century thinking on rhetoric in America was completely dominated by Campbell . . . (Berlin 19)

> Campbell's . . . accomplishment . . . shaped the philosophical context in which rhetoric would be defined throughout the nineteenth century. Nine-teenth-century theory would be indebted not only to Campbell's general re-structuring of the philosophical foundations of rhetoric but also to the reex-amination and reiteration of standard elements and principles of theory that *The Philosophy of Rhetoric* provides. (Johnson, *Nineteenth-Century* 20)

"No movement influencing early American thought so engaged the heart of the American public as the study of rhetoric," writes Janet Gabler-Hover (4). Seeking to extend the canon of traditional rhetoric, Patricia Bizzell alerts us to such historical periods when, lacking access to formal schooling, women did participate in "lively fora of popular literacy and oratory . . ." (54). American successors of the Scottish "New Rhetoricians," such as Harriet Beecher Stowe's brother Henry Ward Beecher, learned rhetoric theory expressly to preach. Book-learned rhetoric theory thus reached women as rhetorical practice. While their male counterparts engaged themselves with Campbell, Hugh Blair, and other theologian-rhetoricians in a comparatively more academic and theoretical manner, women customarily engaged themselves with theology and rhetoric in a more practical manner. They practiced the rhetoric of evangelical Christianity in their speech, journals, letters, and other writings.[6]

Together with the theoretical works of such ministers and professors of theological rhetoric as countryman Blair and American Beecher, Campbell's work influenced the era, providing a backdrop interwoven of Christian ideology and attention to the powers of language. Writing in this scene, mid-nineteenth-century American women authors influenced the community in two respects delineated by Campbell: "through the subject matter conveyed as well as through the aesthetic appeal of rhetorical form" (Johnson, *Nineteenth-Century* 230).

Gabler-Hover's study shows how the New Rhetoric of the Scottish theologians, Campbell, Blair, and Richard Whately, and their American successors, Beecher, Samuel Newman, etc., influenced

> many of the century's *great authors*—notably, Nathaniel Hawthorne, Herman Melville, Mark Twain, Charles Brockden Brown, and Henry James—and provided them a common ground of moral reference with their audience. There was, for example, a community-based concept of truth as both know-able and morally necessary—a concept that grew out of the study of rhetoric. (Gabler-Hover, flyleaf) (emphasis mine)

The rendering that follows complements the work of Gabler-Hover by stepping outside the canon of "great authors" to show how Campbell's theological philosophy of rhetoric also informed mid-nineteenth-century "prominent authors." The following chapters explore how Campbell's rhetorical appeals to a reader's four faculties—the understanding, the imagination, the passions, and the will—inform the subject matter and aesthetics of four works by prominent nineteenth-century American women authors: Warner's *The Wide, Wide World* (1851), Stowe's *Uncle Tom's Cabin* (1852), Stephens's *Mary Derwent* (1858), and Southworth's *The Hidden Hand* (1859).

Several issues need to be addressed at the outset, however. First, Campbell presents his theory and terminology of discourse primarily in terms of the orator, not of the writer. Hence, many of Campbell's quotations included here use such terms as "speaker," "orator," "listener," and "hearer." Various scholars of the history of rhetoric argue for applying the principles of oral to written discourse.[7] Addressing the issue directly in terms of Campbell's work, Albert R. Kitzhaber writes:

> . . . the book was aimed specifically at the spoken word. This did not, however, prevent much of what he said from applying equally well to written composition. It was indeed as a composition textbook that the *Philosophy* was mainly used. (52)

Nan Johnson provides a rationale for this use:

> Campbell explicitly refers to oratory throughout his treatise and implies by his frequent references to writing in his discussion of style that his discussion of the philosophical principles of rhetoric applies to both public speaking and composition . . . . (*Nineteenth-Century* 32-33)

Johnson continues, ". . . nineteenth-century theory . . . extend[s] the scope of rhetoric to include all forms of oral and written discourse . . . ." (*Nineteenth-Century* 87):

> By the late nineteenth century, rhetoricians perceived the domain of rhetoric as including public speaking, all forms of argumentative, expository, descriptive, and narrative composition, and the critical study of literature. (*Nineteenth-Century* 230)

Indeed, Johnson lists one of the four "theoretical commitments" of the "promoters of the New Rhetoric" as "the view that the study of rhetoric applies to all major forms of communication, oral and written" (*Nineteenth-Century* 19). Accordingly, I apply Campbell's philosophical principles of rhetoric to narrative composition, often referring to "speaker" and "writer" or "hearer" and "reader" interchangeably.

A second issue arises from the fact that Campbell and all his successors teaching and/or writing about theology and rhetoric through the 1850s spoke exclusively to males: "Nineteenth-century rhetoricians unfailingly characterized the practitioner of rhetoric as male" (Johnson, *Nineteenth-Century* 246). Nonetheless, matters of eloquence and morality (the bases of Campbell's work) fairly permeated 1850s discourse and literature; that is, rhetorical mores extended in the nineteenth century far beyond academe, from which women were excluded. Women found direct lessons in moral discourse and notices for reprints and reviews of rhetorics by the Scottish rhetoricians and their American successors appearing in *Godey's Lady's Book* and numerous other women's literary journals. Also, much 1850s discourse took place in theological arenas. Men who had in college studied such rhetorician/theologians as Campbell became the preachers who filled the ears and hearts of the nation's church-going women. Thus, whether or not women took advantage of available rhetorical and literary theory, they certainly became thoroughly versed in Campbellian rhetorical practice on a regular basis.

Another area of critical evolution involves the concept of intention. I counter the view that acknowledging an author's statement of intention (see, for example, Holman 242) necessarily constitutes a theoretical fallacy. As a fundamental premise, I hold, with Tompkins, that women authors of the mid-nineteenth-century had intentional "designs" on their readers. Indeed, for many of the stories about women in the middle of the nineteenth century, authorial intent is the raison d'être. Furthermore, authorial intent of message more often than not finds its main vehicle in rhetorical intent. Harris (*19th-Century*) concurs, "the concept of authorial intention is integral to the study of these novels, then, but from a rhetorical rather than a psychological point of view" (33). Campbell's theory shows rhetorical and psychological appeals of discourse to be interdependent as he situates his philosophy of rhetoric in faculty and association psychology. Johnson explains that basic to Campbell's theory, "the aims of rhetoric are linked necessarily to affective intentions" (*Nineteenth-Century* 46). Specifically, she writes:

> the aims of rhetoric and the function of particular modes and rhetorical techniques are linked directly to affective intentions (to enlighten the understanding, please the imagination, move the passions, and influence the will) (*Nineteenth-Century* 66-67).

Exploring rhetorical appeals based on principles of faculty and association psychology within mid-nineteenth-century American women's works helps explain not only the presence, but also the workings of these authors' intentions.

A small issue of note involves the term "novel." The authors whose works I explore here have varied and complex ideas regarding the term (for example, see Chapter III, note 18 on page 78). Accordingly, to honor their various objections, I avoid using a term that might be not only distasteful to those authors, but also inaccurate. When referring to critics who call these authors' works "novels," I reluctantly do likewise; elsewhere, I use a variety of alternate terms.

Finally, I should qualify the issue of the publication dates for the works I choose to explore. Literary critics traditionally have focused on the mid-nineteenth century as the era that produced America's first million sellers. Most of this popular fiction was written by women, hence the decade's fame as "the feminine fifties"—as dubbed by critic Pattee. At first glance, my choices of literature might not seem properly representative of books from the 1850s. All but *The Wide, Wide World* first appeared as serials[8] rather than books; the "story," "Mary Derwent: A Tale of the Early Settlers," first appeared (serialized) in 1838; *The Hidden Hand* was not published in book form until 1888. The choices are representative, however, considering various circumstances. "Mary Derwent's" first appearance as the "$200 Prize Article" for *The Ladies' Companion* merely told the story of Mary Derwent. Comparing the 1838 "article" to the later published full work reveals Stephens's extensive use of historical sources. She amended earlier references to Native American peoples and individuals, added large quantities of historical material, and recast several characters to align them with historical figures. In other words, Stephens corrected, expanded, and enriched her earlier "article" to complete her book, *Mary Derwent*, published in 1858.[9]

Although Southworth's *The Hidden Hand* was not seen in book form until three decades later, its popular impact came in 1859 with the first of its three serialized publications in *The New York Ledger*. Unlike *Mary Derwent*, Southworth's serial very closely resembles the later published book form. By the time *The Hidden Hand* appeared in a single volume, Southworth's hero, Capitola, was well established in America and Europe, having clothing styles, towns, and races named for her. Essentially, the authors' sense of their works' completion warrants both *Mary Derwent* and *The Hidden Hand* as representative of the 1850s, joining other best-sellers of the decade, *The Wide, Wide World* and *Uncle Tom's Cabin*.

In retrospect the decade holds interest as that time when our country's national ethos struggled between identifying with the characteristics surrounding domesticity and identifying with the characteristics surrounding the rise of the market economy. The four literary works I explore here depict a decade beginning with readers' concerns focused on attaining Christian identity. In fact, in *The Wide, Wide World* and *Uncle Tom's Cabin*, this Christian identity challenges men's earthly and patriarchal social and economic systems. Firm in their Christian convictions, orphan girls and slaves face men's earthly laws and customs with a sense of impunity. Implicit in the early decade is the sense that the culture could tilt either way. The character trait of personal economic acquisition (requisite for a market economy) was just on the edge of social acceptability; it was good to nurture one's soul and give unto others. The decade's literature progresses, however, to show not men donning skirts and becoming more generous and concerned with their souls, but women donning pants and becoming more concerned with their survival within men's evolving economic systems. The decade closes with Capitola literally thumbing her nose at cultural restrictions, but acceding to economic systems that continue to oppress women.

Initially an effort to explore issues underlying literary canonization, my work has moved toward an inquiry of literary and rhetorical contexts. Stemming from issues of gender inclusiveness, it is reasonable to reevaluate the canon in terms of its historical rhetorical context. The "positivist, materialist, and scientific-technological" cognitive bent that Cecelia Tichi observes to have "dominated later nineteenth- and twentieth-century American history" (and reading habits, one might add) should not be allowed to "conceal a mid-nineteenth-century ethos . . . much less prevent the study of it" (224). Rereading representative works of the 1850s with attention to their various rhetorical appeals demonstrates how the works grew from their cultural origins. Rereading them within the context of Campbell's rhetorical theory of multiple faculties raises issues of canon in terms of rhetorical appeals and invites the contemporary reader to experience original readings—often beyond understanding.

NOTES

[1] Helen Waite Papashvily describes how "all through the countryside the scratch of pen on paper filled their air, and the century, reaching the halfway mark, found the women who would dominate fiction for the next fifty years hard at work" (Papashvily 61).

[2] Ann Douglas so criticizes Warner's *The Wide, Wide World* (*Feminization* 64); Fred Louis Pattee so faults Stowe's popular work (132); Nina Baym so denigrates Stephens's prose (*Woman's* 181); Helen Waite Papashvily so complains of Southworth's extensive writings (133).

[3] Such as Gayle Greene, Kristin Herzog, Jane Tompkins, Susan K. Harris, and others.

[4] See Harris, *19th-Century* (32) and others.

[5] See, for example, Albert R. Kitzhaber 52.

[6] Susan Miller notes that women—whom she characterizes "The Sad Women in the Basement"—historically have practiced the teaching that "fills the time that others take to build theories" (121). Current feminist rhetoricians (such as Susan Dobra) are beginning to attribute rhetorician status to women who practiced oratory and writing as well as to those who more overtly wrote about the nature of discourse.

[7] Classical (Greek and Roman) rhetorical theory is also couched in oral terms; that theoretical tradition is commonly used as a basis for teaching contemporary written composition.

[8] Serialized literature received as much, if not more, recognition as did published books of the era.

[9] The finished text gathered so much attention that the publisher, Beadle, asked Stephens to rewrite another of her serialized tales, "Malaeska" into what would become the first "Dime Novel," a project intending to bring "the choicest work of the most popular authors" to "the million" readers (cover, *Malaeska*).

Reverend Dr. George Campbell, D.D.

I

REGARDING GEORGE CAMPBELL'S
THE PHILOSOPHY OF RHETORIC

George Campbell prefaces *The Philosophy of Rhetoric* (1776) by describing his intention to provide not

> a correct map, but a tolerable sketch of the human mind . . . and . . . to ascer-
> tain . . . the radical principles . . . whose object it is, by the use of language, to
> operate on the soul of the hearer, in the way of informing, convincing, pleas-
> ing, moving, or persuading. (xliii)

To accomplish this task, Campbell uses a methodology designed to avoid
the pitfalls he sees inherent in two philosophies of his time—the empiric
and the visionary. He criticizes the empiric method because he considers
founding knowledge on facts to be limited by both the scarcity of facts and
the misapplication of human reasoning. He criticizes the visionary
method because he feels it argues from principles having no foundation in
nature. Rather than base his work on either of these "extreme" methods,
Campbell proposes to sketch within the human mind the interplay of psychology and rhetoric by studying the mind's natural processes of perception.

Campbell describes the mind's natural ability to perceive in terms of
three general processes: receiving direct sensations, acquiring ideas of
memory, and forming ideas of imagination. Campbell calls the senses
"the original inlets of perception." Senses report the existence of objects
in the material world just as the objects of the material world produce sensations (40). Sensations resolving into consciousness cause Campbell to
say "I am certain that I see, and feel, and think, what I actually see, and
feel, and think" (41). Reality, according to Campbell, depends on a person's belief in his or her own perceptions. When two or more persons
sense or perceive phenomena similarly, communal or "common sense"
results. Recent scholars designate this concept, "the social construction of
reality" (Berger 1967).

For Campbell, sense in its initial perception acts "instantaneously" and interdependently with the memory:

> the memory becomes the sole repository of the knowledge received from the sense; . . . Memory, therefore, is the only original voucher extant of those past realities for which we had once the evidence of sense. (47)

Thus working together, these two faculties, sense and memory, produce knowledge. According to Campbell, more than one sense perception-turned-memory is requisite to generate knowledge; it takes repetition of direct circumstantial sensations to imprint knowledge on the mind. Such knowledge remains in the mind after time erodes the memory's direct circumstantial sensations. A new sense perception triggering knowledge (or recalling sensations stored in memory) Campbell terms "experience" (48). A person gains greater experience in life by contracting greater numbers of associated sensed and remembered ideas. Knowledge and experience regulate life's concerns (46).

Campbell places the mind's third process of perception, imagination, "next to the influence of the memory." He describes imagination as "the faculty of apprehending what is neither perceived by the senses, nor remembered" (81). Elsewhere, however, while discussing the use of tropes, Campbell emphasizes how strongly the imagination is "affected by what is perceived by the senses" (304). The apparent contradiction is easily resolved. The imagination works by means of the association of ideas. The mind first perceives an idea by direct sensation. This sensation joins other sensations in the mind to comprise remembered ideas. Campbell refers to the mind's power to associate the newly sensed idea with one or more sense perceptions or idea(s) stored in the memory as the association of ideas. He considers the association of ideas, in turn, as a function of the imagination. The mind can imagine or associate ideas together in several ways. Campbell explains that "connexions" naturally occur in three areas. The mind can make connections among things, between words and things, and, in language, among words (258). The associative powers of the human mind reflect these natural connections.

According to Campbell, of the mind's three means of perception—sense, memory, and imagination—sense produces the greatest vivacity, memory produces less vivacity, and imagination produces the least vivacity. Within this conceptual framework an author or rhetorician seeks to reproduce for his or her audience the experience of an idea as close as possible to the experience of an originally sensed perception. And herein lies the rub: because the author or rhetorician works through language, he or she must produce the "lively idea" within that sphere of perception that is least likely to produce vivacity—the imagination.

In a somewhat circular manner, the study of rhetoric offers insight into human nature while the ongoing study of rhetoric must be grounded in that study of human nature. Relating the art of rhetoric to the science of human nature, Campbell draws on other thinkers' psychological and philosophical theories. Contemporary scholar, Vincent M. Bevilacqua, notes Campbell's use of classical rhetoric in *The Philosophy of Rhetoric*:

> the underlying classicism of the work itself and the conspicuous reliance on classical authors indicates that Campbell was thoroughly acquainted with traditional theory and that he largely assented to it. (1-2)

To the insights of the ancients, Campbell adds further insights that he draws from or shares with Bacon, Thomas Reid, and Henry Home (Lord Kames). Combining ideas from these different eras enables Campbell to turn from such classical doctrines of invention as the syllogism and topoi to a more inductive concept of invention.

James L. Golden, Goodwin F. Berquist, and William E. Coleman note Campbell's debt to John Locke (167).[1] These contemporary scholars trace four of Campbell's concepts to Locke's 1690 *Essay on Human Understanding*: the concept of the faculties of the mind, the concept of the association of ideas (as explained above), the importance of the pathetic proof, and the rejection of the syllogism.

Locke reasons that the human mind's natural ability to "perceive and prefer" reveals its two major constituent faculties, the understanding and the will. Describing the first faculty—the understanding—Locke explores the nature of ideas. Ideas result from direct sensory experience and can be united by reason. Relating heretofore unrelated ideas or relating a sensory experience with an "associate" idea permits us to conflate the two perceptions into a single unit in the mind. Arguing that since the mind has the power to prefer one idea to another, Locke holds that the mind must include a faculty of will. The mind may understand an idea without acting upon it. In discourse, he says, the pathetic appeal determines whether or not an idea that has reached the understanding functions to activate the will (Golden, Berquist, and Coleman 168).

In addition to drawing on Locke's ideas of faculty psychology, the association of ideas, and the importance of the pathetic appeal, Campbell also joined Locke in rejecting the syllogism:

> It is long since I was first convinced, by what Mr. Locke had said on the subject, that the syllogistic art, with its figures and moods, serves more to display the ingenuity of the inventor, and to exercise the address and fluency of the learner, than to assist the diligent inquirer in his researches after truth. (61-62)

Placing the syllogistic method of arguing in contradistinction to his own "moral reasoning," Campbell explains that

> In moral reasoning we proceed by analysis, and ascend from particulars to universals; in syllogizing we proceed by synthesis, and descend from universals to particulars.[2] (62)

The eighteenth and nineteenth centuries saw a real tension between inductive and deductive methods of reason. Long-time editor of *Godey's Lady's Book* and spokesperson for her era, Sarah J. Hale (1858) cites from *Frazer's Magazine* an "interesting article written by Mr. Henry Thomas Buckle, in which he describes 'The Influence of Woman on the Progress of Knowledge.'" Hale quotes Buckle, describing the methods of reason much as Campbell does:

> "The inductive philosopher collects phenomena either by observation or by experiment, and from them rises to the general principle or law which explains and covers them. The deductive philosopher draws the principle from ideas already existing in his mind, and explains the phenomena by descending on them, instead of rising from them." (463)

Hale continues to quote Buckle who ascribes the "method" of deduction to women and that of induction to men, clearly favoring deduction:

> "Now, there are several reasons why women prefer the deductive, and if I may so say, ideal method. They are more emotional, more enthusiastic, and

more imaginative than men; they therefore live more in an ideal world; while men, with their colder, harder, and austerer organizations, are more practical and more under the dominion of facts, to which they consequently ascribe a higher importance." (463)

Although Campbell overtly favors the inductive method of reasoning to the deductive, his "philosophy of rhetoric" emphasizes the roles that the faculties—imagination, passion, and will—play in persuading a reader. Campbell's concern with these faculties shows his inclination to advocate appeals to what is "universal" in a reader's mind, despite his historical and social disposition to reject the syllogism and favor inductive to deductive reasoning.[3]

Campbell distinguishes the different occasions appropriate for syllogistic and moral reasoning. While "the analytic is the only method which we can follow, in the acquisition of natural knowledge," he writes, the synthetic method lends itself to "communicating the principles of science" and to demonstrating mathematical principles and probabilities (62-63). That Campbell considers his study rooted in the science of human nature helps to explain his synthetic method of presentation.[4]

Campbell's rejection of the syllogism[5] complements his concept of the mind's three-way ability to perceive. The mind first perceives through direct sensations of particulars. The mind then transforms these particulars into memory; particulars accumulating in the memory become generalized into knowledge. Finally, it falls to the imagination to associate each newly perceived circumstance with the mind's accumulation of gathered knowledge.

Another contemporary empiricist, David Hume, also influenced Campbell as Lloyd Bitzer clearly establishes in his "Introduction" to Campbell's *Philosophy of Rhetoric*. According to Bitzer, Hume's *Treatise on Human Nature* (1739) in part derives from Locke's psychological concepts of the mind's faculties, the association of ideas and the dependence of the understanding upon the emotions. Hume was especially influenced by Locke's recognition of the emotions as prime movers of the will. Contending that human motivation derives from and depends on human beings' fundamental emotional nature, Hume argues that discourse must appeal to the passions, especially those generating pleasure or pain, to produce in the discourse's recipient the will to act. In fact, building on Locke's concept that the understanding could be approached only through emotional stimulation, Hume claims: "reason is and ought only to be the slave of the passions, and can never pretend to any other office than to serve and obey them" (*Treatise* 195). Thirty-seven years later Campbell would recontextualize this concept within his philosophy of rhetoric:

> Knowledge, the object of the intellect, furnisheth materials for the fancy; the fancy culls, compounds, and, by her mimic art, disposes these materials so as to affect the passions; the passions are the natural spurs to volition or action, and so need only to be right directed. (2)

The statement in and of itself illustrates Campbell's agreement with Hume's premises regarding the mind's faculties ("the intellect," "the fancy," "the passions"), regarding the association of ideas ("furnisheth materials," "culls, compounds," "disposes," "to affect," "natural spurs"), and regarding the intellect's ultimate dependence on the passions. Hume's philosophical influence thus informs Campbell's work throughout.

Campbell's thinking reflects that of contemporary fellow Scottish rhetorician and psychologist Henry Home (Lord Kames), who had written extensively about the "Association of Ideas" and "The Influence of Passions with respect to our Perceptions, Opinions, and Belief" (*Elements of Criticism* 1762). Campbell joins with Home, Locke, and Hume in their rejection of the syllogism, their inquiry method of developing knowledge from direct sense experiences, and their mutual interests in faculty psychology and the association of ideas. These ideas were, in turn, shared by the physician, David Hartley, whose other ideas also influenced Campbell. In his *Observations on Man, His Frame, His Duty, and His Expectations* (1749), Hartley recognized faculties of the mind in addition to those—the understanding and will—observed by Locke. Hartley conceptualized the human mind to include faculties of memory, imagination or fancy, and affection. Drawing, in part, from Hartley, Campbell in his *The Philosophy of Rhetoric* recognizes the mental faculties of understanding, imagination, passions, and will. While Hartley observes that sense impressions proceed from "vibration" to culminate in "all human actions" in a medical context, Campbell, in a philosophical context, considers sensations as requisite to establishing the knowledge upon which people act.

Scottish philosopher Francis Hutcheson's *Short Introduction to Moral Philosophy* (1753) and Adam Smith's *Theory of Moral Sentiments* (1759) contributed the principle of sympathy to eighteenth-century Scottish intellectual thought and to Campbell's thinking in particular. Campbell writes "sympathy is one main engine by which the orator operates on the passions" (96). He elsewhere adds, "Sympathy is not a passion, but that quality of the soul which renders it susceptible of almost any passion, by communication from the bosom of another" (131). Sympathy in Campbell's view is more than a theological principle or a moral sensibility. Within Campbell's psychological and philosophical orientation sympathy becomes a vehicle for the association of ideas. As regards his theories of rhetoric, sympathy acts to stimulate the imagination and passions by associating images (as they are experienced in discourse) with images accumulated in the memory.

Campbell's philosophical and psychological beliefs and writings are thus well founded within his time's intellectual environment. In the tradition of Locke, Hume, and Hartley, Campbell rejects syllogistic reasoning to probe the science of human nature taking care to build his own knowledge by moving from particular observations and/or circumstances to generalized principles. Also in accord with these thinkers, Campbell holds that the will to action requires an impulse from human passions and/or emotions rather than from the understanding alone. Campbell likewise grounds in this tradition his tenets of faculty and association psychology—that the mind is compartmentalized into faculties of understanding, imagination, passions, and the will and that present ideas associate themselves with ideas accumulated and generalized in memory. Finally, Campbell weaves principles of sympathy drawn from Hutcheson, Smith, and his own Christian theology into the psychological principles of associationism to develop his own theory of the dynamics of human communication.

Campbell begins his treatise on rhetoric with his often quoted statement regarding the ends of discourse:

> All the ends of speaking are reducible to four; every speech being intended to enlighten the understanding, to please the imagination, to move the passions, or to influence the will (1).

He adds,

> In general it may be asserted, that each preceding species, in the order above exhibited, is preparatory to the subsequent; that each subsequent species is founded on the preceding, and that thus they ascend in a regular progression. (2)

That is, a speaker persuades a hearer by drawing him or her through a progression of appeals to the faculties.

In discussing the appeal to the listener's understanding, the first of the faculties he names, Campbell offers a speaker two methods. The first of these ways is "either to dispel ignorance or to vanquish error" (2). The speaker either provides the listener with new information or corrects the listener's old (erroneous) information. In doing so, the speaker should use language that the listener can readily understand. Campbell therefore instructs speakers to fashion their discourses to the "capacity, education, and attainments of the hearers" (73). That is, he instructs his speakers to fit their language to the various discourse communities of their respective listeners.

The speaker's second way of enlightening the understanding is to use language that is "reputable, national, and present." Campbell describes as "reputable" (or "sometimes called general use") those "modes of speech [that are] authorized as good by the writings of a great number, if not the majority, of celebrated authors" (145).[6] By "national" Campbell generally means urban and learned as opposed to rural and "vulgar." Yet, since according to Campbell, "different orders of men are different," speakers wishing to enlighten the understanding of the vulgar should address the vulgar in their own syntax, vocabulary, and dialect. Within his concept of "present usage" Campbell condemns as barbarisms the use of "new words" (172). By excluding from "present" use slang and foreign words adapted to English, Campbell essentially privileges "reputable" over "present" usage.

Keeping in mind this jumble of ideas meant to facilitate listener understanding vis-à-vis language use, Campbell instructs speakers to "enlighten the understanding" by developing discourse with "*perspicuity*" to provide the listener with "*information*." Further, Campbell instructs the discourser to compose an "*argument*" to evince the listener's "*conviction*." [Emphases Campbell's.] Information imparted through verbal perspicuity causes the listener to know something; conviction evinced by argument causes the listener to believe something. Campbell later clarifies that conviction ought not be considered the end of discourse, but rightly ought to accompany discourse's end (33). Conviction and belief within Campbell's view of humans' multifaceted nature have their limitations in discourse because they neither do much to produce any real change in the listener's life nor do they cause the listener to act in any new manner.[7]

"To please the imagination,"[8] Campbell's second end in the progression to produce some action in the listener, the speaker should attempt "to awake and fix the attention" (285) of the listener. Doing so requires the speaker to cultivate a language style that is both vivacious and elegant. Vivacious language stimulates the reader's attention by providing the pleasurable experience of discovering a resemblance between remembered sensation/s and some new sensation provided by the speaker's words. Campbell notes an exciting and sensual dimension felt by the hearer when a speaker's words touch the hearer's former sense impressions stored as ideas of memory.

Vivacity in language stimulates memory by the speaker's use of the "lively idea." Although cold historiography may successfully produce belief in the mind of the listener, the lively idea in its sensual, pleasurable play on memory commands closer attention and remains remembered longer. According to Campbell, a sentence considered perfect to the logician or grammarian may be obscure, languid, inelegant, unmusical, and/or flat to the rhetorician or general listening public. The speaker should aim, therefore, to please the imagination of the listener through an association of ideas in the listener's mind as well as through elegance in manner of speech. Elegance in speech derives, in Campbell's view, from a speaker's success in making elements of language correspond with elements of thought, a situation analogous to the natural intermingling of elements of body and soul. Summoning the hearer's imagination though language's play on memory, the speaker elicits some action on the part of the hearer.

The appeal to "move the passions," Campbell's third end of discourse, provides the means to stimulate such action. Awakening in the listener a passion useful to the design of the orator results from "communicating lively ideas of the object." Like the imagination, the passions can be excited by the impact of language's sensation on the memory. Campbell names seven circumstances by which language might operate on the listener's facility for passion: probability, plausibility, importance, proximity of time, "connexion" of place, relation of the actors or sufferers to the hearers, and interest of the hearers or speaker in the consequences. Campbell discusses probability and plausibility in relation to each other. Probability, the first circumstance stimulating passion in the listener, energizes passion when the speaker provides evidence for an argument that produces belief. Plausibility, the second circumstance, results from a natural and feasible consistency in the narration. While probability derives from proofs, plausibility derives from "a native lustre issuing directly from the object" (82). Campbell makes an exception, however, in urging speakers to speak with plausibility. An orator may move his or her hearer's passion by utilizing various means of narrative and rhetorical devices to astonish the hearer with the implausible. The challenge to the orator lies in astonishing while sustaining the hearer's capacity for belief. The orator should seek to create narrative comprising both reason and fancy and so both instruct and entertain the hearer.

Importance, the third circumstance affecting the passions, adds "brightness and strength to the ideas" (86). According to Campbell, an action (or for the purposes of this study, a literary circumstance) derives its importance from its own nature, from the concern of its characters, or from its consequence. That is, a literary circumstance affects a listener's or reader's faculty of passion by the degree to which the circumstance departs from the ordinary, by the quantity of characters or importance of the single character involved in the circumstance, or by the impact of the action's consequence.

An action's "proximity of time" similarly affects the listener's (or reader's) passions because a person is more likely to be moved by an action taking place in the present than one taking place in the past or future. An action taking place in the past, however, does have the advantage of moving the passions through evidence. Campbell allows that literary evidence is able to bring a past action up to date, thereby pushing its proximity of time closer to the present and, so, moving the listener's passion.

"Connexion" of place, Campbell's fifth circumstance to move the passions, can also bring a past action up to date and, so, move the listener's passions. Campbell notes how listeners and readers are naturally curious to know what past actions have affected the present circumstances of their identity space. Familial, cultural, gender-related, etc. connections to a narrative's characters move the listener's or reader's passion even more strongly.

Finally, a listener's interest in a circumstance's consequences can move a listener's sympathy and so move the passions. The effective lively idea that causes a listener to identify with a character's circumstance can blur the distinction between the character's interest and that of the narrative's recipient. Campbell's "lively idea" is, thus, important both to pleasing the imagination and to moving the passions. Specifically, the lively idea results from rhetorical figures. Eloquence, in the form of rhetorical figures, stimulates the imagination, making ideas ". . . resemble the impressions of sense and traces of memory" (94).[9] Campbell concedes, "It were endless to enumerate all the rhetorical figures that . . ." can be used to please the imagination and move the passions (94). The focus for the contemporary student lies in Campbell's basic principle that discourse, from both writer and reader's vantages, is not only to be understood, command attention, and be remembered, " . . . but, which is the chief point of all, [it should] interest the heart" (94).

Through interesting the heart, the speaker, according to Campbell, attains the last end of discourse—influencing the hearer's will. Campbell calls on Greek and Roman rhetoricians to support his contention that persuasion or influencing the will "makes a man master of his hearers"(4). After exciting "some desire or passion in the hearers," a speaker must connect that passion with "the action to which he would persuade them" (77-78). For Campbell, the "argumentative" lies in "presenting the best and most forcible arguments which the nature of the subject admits" (78). Establishing persuasion as the proper end of discourse, Campbell posits, " . . . we do not argue to gain barely the assent of the understanding, but, which is infinitely more important, the consent of the will" (6). Consequently Campbell instructs writers to appeal to the understanding , whose object is truth, and to the passions to show "that acting thus is the sure way to procure such [truth as] an object" (78). Appeals to the various faculties combine to bring the audience to the object of the will—good.

Moving in time and region from Scotland, 1776, to America, 1850s, such concepts as "imagination" and "passion" translate much more consistently than they translate between the 1850s and current usage. The British-written and American-published *A Dictionary of Science, Literature, and Art* (1850)[10] discusses "imagination" as a metaphysical term "denoting that faculty of the mind . . . [which produces] new combinations of ideas from materials stored up in the memory." The dictionary declines to elaborate: "it would be vain to enumerate the various definitions of this term, or to attempt to give even an abstract of the diversity of views entertained by philosophers respecting the nature and extent of its operations," but uses such Cambellian sounding descriptions as "*lively conception* of the object of sight" and, like Campbell, states "in many philosophical disquisitions imagination is used as nearly synonymous with *fancy*" (591). The 1850 definition of "passions" operative both in Britain and in America similarly reflects the concept's roots in philosophy and psychology, speculating "whether the precise situation of the impetus of the passions be in the spiritual or material part of man." Admitting that "the theories and conjectures of philosophers upon this subject are almost boundless; but to pursue them would be of little advantage," the editors refer the reader to the tradition from which Campbell's works derive: "we shall merely refer the reader for ample particulars to the works of Hume, Reid, Hartley, Locke, Lord Kames, &c." (905).

By the end of the twentieth century, usage commonly denigrates "imagination," "passions," and even the term "rhetoric" itself: "it's all in your imagination," "stop venting your passions," "cut the rhetoric," etc. Fresh from classrooms and therapists who consciously seek to engender self-esteem, current readers approach fiction poised to analyze and to judge. We do not ask that a book change us or influence our will; conversely, we deconstruct the work; we work our will on the book in question. Whereas current readers want to judge a book "a good read" or not, 1850s readers sought constructive or instructive reading. Our predecessors approached books as "spurs to volition or action"—tales to grow by. Of the four faculties that Campbell would have discourse influence, only understanding remains to the current reader a legitimate arbitrator of meaning.

Several contemporary literary scholars recognize the difference between nineteenth-century and current readers' stances toward works. Jane Tompkins, for example, informs current readers that mid-nineteenth-century American women authors often had real "designs"[11] to gain their readers' "consent of the will." A look at Campbell's philosophy of rhetoric as it informs mid-nineteenth-century readers' and writers' stance can demonstrate why this body of popular literature seems antiquated; its authors appeal to faculties that as current readers, we no longer sanction as elements of reason. Admitting "lost" works into the canon of nineteenth-century literature should derive not only from current scholars' self-assured literary judgment. Questions of canonizing "lost" works should reflect on lost reader capabilities as well. Campbell restores our lost faculties to us. His legacy of discourse urges us to change our minds, enabling us to reread more holistically the American women writers of the 1850s.

NOTES

[1] See also Hagaman 146.

[2] See also Chapters IV and VII.

[3] Like Hale and Buckle, nineteenth-century philosopher, Ralph Waldo Emerson, also criticizes Locke's method of reason:

> . . . The highest species of reasoning upon divine subjects is rather the fruit of a sort of moral imagination, than of the "reasoning Machine," such as Locke (80).

That is, Emerson poses "moral imagination" against Locke's method of reason; conversely, Campbell explains Locke's method of reason in terms of "moral reasoning."

[4] Interestingly, current astronomer-theorists grapple with the same dilemma. Speaking of inductive and deductive reasoning, Allan Sandage notes that the inductive method leaves us with no way to know where to turn for data and no way to know what data will prove relevant to particular inquiry. The deductive method, though, leaves us dependent on the products of human inquiry, isolating us from nature and experiment. Discussing these "problems raised by the hermeneutical circularity," like Campbell, Sandage proposes not only to avoid the pitfalls inherent in the extremes of induction and deduction, but also argues for a third method to knowledge: imagination. Calling on a nineteenth-century author, Sandage writes, "[Edgar Allan] Poe dismissed the methods of both Bacon and Aristotle as the paths to certain knowledge. He argued for a third method to knowledge which he called imagination . . . ." Sandage concludes that in attempting to discover "true order in nature, if it exists," current thinkers should "like Poe, trust in the imagination" (1: 2,3).

[5] "George Campbell rejected syllogistic reasoning," observes Janet Gabler-Hover, "as inadequate to the description of the way one really lives and makes decisions. Campbell relied on the power of the memory as a decision-making tool" (55), she adds.

[6] Questioning "celebrated by whom?" contemporary historian of rhetoric, Olivia Smith, points out that Campbell implicitly directs speakers to couch their language within the discourse habits of those authors celebrated by the elite. At the same time, however, Campbell urges speakers to tailor their language to its intended particular listeners.

[7] The work of Brazilian educator, Paulo Freire, affirms Campbell's idea that understanding is but a first step "to [spur] volition or action" (Campbell 2). Freire sees that within "the word" (or discourse) there are "two dimensions, reflection and action" (75). Both action and reflection are necessary to produce "praxis," the work of

renaming the world (76). According to Freire, the word (understanding) without action is mere "verbalism" or "idle chatter." Freire teaches that any transformation of the self or the world requires both commitment and action (76). Campbell would agree that such volition and resultant action are the proper ends of discourse.

[8] Gabler-Hover discusses Campbell's influence on nineteenth-century American rhetoric and philosophy generally and specifically on that of Henry Ward Beecher, Harriet Beecher Stowe's brother, two years her junior, whom Kathryn Kish Sklar (1991) describes as "the closest companion of Stowe's childhood and youth" (in Stowe, *Uncle* 521). Gabler-Hover attributes Beecher's sense that "spiritual evolution occurred through the imagination" (57) in part to Campbell's influence (55, 57).

[9] Contemporary scholars discuss this concept in terms of hermeneutic and symbolic codes. See Susan K. Harris (*19th-Century*) and chapters V and VI of this study.

[10] Harper & Brothers, New York, published

A

DICTIONARY

OF

SCIENCE, LITERATURE, AND ART:

COMPRISING THE

HISTORY, DESCRIPTION, AND SCIENTIFIC PRINCIPLES

OF EVERY BRANCH OF

HUMAN KNOWLEDGE;

WITH

THE DERIVATION AND DEFINITION OF ALL THE TERMS IN GENERAL USE.

[11] Jane Tompkins explains her term "design" in her book, *Sensational Designs*, 1985.

"Do n't be disagreeable, Smith, I'm just getting inspired!"

The Blue Stocking

An original design by Fred. M. Coffin in Fanny Fern's
Fern Leaves from Fanny's Port-Folio (1854): 101.

II

AMERICAN WOMEN WRITERS OF THE 1850S, THEIR CRITICS, AND GEORGE CAMPBELL

Reviewing the mid-1850s American literary scene as it has been perceived through twentieth-century critical lenses reveals the need for a heuristic appropriate to the nineteenth-century rhetorical climate. George Campbell's rhetorical theory of quadripartite ends of discourse provides such a guide. Recognizing in nineteenth-century works Campbell's suggestion that authors "enlighten the understanding, . . . please the imagination, . . . move the passions, or . . . influence the will" (1), can help current readers and critics appreciate (rather than denigrate) those works' rhetorical ploys.

Several twentieth-century scholars have recognized the impact that Campbell's morally based theory had on nineteenth-century American ideology and culture. Observing the study of the "New Rhetoric"[1] to extend beyond American universities and their texts, Janet Gabler-Hover writes,

> The love of rhetorical study from the end of the eighteenth century into the final decades of the nineteenth century engrossed Americans of all sorts, those people intellectually and philosophically inclined but also those literate and perhaps not so literate within the popular culture. (35)

Nan Johnson (*Nineteenth-Century*) connects the influence of rhetorical theory, largely derived from Campbell, to the evolution of a nineteenth-century ethos:

> Whenever the speaker or writer informs others, moves them to action, or provides them with insight into the literary experience, the rhetorician affects the intellectual and moral constitution of the community. (230)

Based significantly on Campbell's *The Philosophy of Rhetoric*,[2] the nineteenth-century American rhetorical climate helped foster, as Winifred Bryan Horner (*Nineteenth-Century Scottish*) puts it, a "strong sense of nationalism and morality and the idea that good literature was morally uplifting" (182).

In the mid-1850s, women writers and readers fairly well dominated the literary market. Critic Alfred Habegger concedes, "the fifties was the one decade in American history in which women wrote practically all the popular books" (ix). Writing a century closer to the period, Phebe A. Hanaford (1882) quoted the *North American Review* to assure readers of her voluminous *Daughters of America or Women of the Century* that nineteenth-century American women authors would long retain their firm grip on the country's literature:

> "It is a fortunate thing for any country, that a portion of its literature should fall into the hands of the female sex; because their influence in every walk of letters is almost sure to be powerful and good." Such has surely been the influence of our American women, who have written books the world will not soon stop reading. (196)

Despite Hanaford's nineteenth-century assurance, however, contemporary literary critics may now join John Cawelti in asking, "who outside of dedicated literary scholars reads today the enormously successful nineteenth-century social melodramas of Mrs. E.D.E.N. Southworth or Susan Warner?" (263). Indeed, although they may be taught in women's studies courses, the women authors who dominated the American literary scene just 150 years ago currently appear only rarely in mainstream English department curricula.

A partial explanation for this discrepancy may stem from the different ways nineteenth- and twentieth-century readers comprehend these works. Nineteenth-century authors often had "designs" on their readers as Jane Tompkins shows in her study *Sensational Designs*. Whereas twentieth-century readers tend to consider books as objects of study or objects of art, nineteenth-century readers tended to consider books as agents of change.[3] In this respect the books' ontology has evolved through time.

These designs[4] on the reader took shape in various ways. Some 1850s women authors wrote to educate the young reader to moral, Christian, and domestic values. Others sought to encourage the reader to play an active role in shaping his or her own life and/or the developing (and volatile) American culture. Still others sought to reevaluate and reconstruct (for the reader) notions of the American frontier and its native inhabitants. To augment these obvious intentions regarding subject matter, authors utilized less obvious, but not necessarily less powerful, rhetorical ploys.

Notable among writers who intended their works to educate the young reader to moral, Christian, and domestic values were Susan Warner (*The Wide, Wide World* 1850), Maria Cummins (*The Lamplighter* 1854), and Martha Finley, who based her later Elsie Dinsmore series on Warner's big seller.[5]   Authors who wished to enlist the reader's help in developing cultural mores wrote about the issues of abolition, prohibition, and women's rights.   Encouraging abolition, for example, were Lydia Maria Child [*An Appeal in Favor of that Class of Americans Called Africans* (1833)],[6] Harriet Beecher Stowe [*Uncle Tom's Cabin* (1851) and *Dred, a Tale of the Great Dismal Swamp* (1856)], Harriet Wilson [*Our Nig* (1859)], and Harriet Jacob [*Incidents in the Life of a Slave Girl* (1860)].[7]   Other authors such as Sarah Josepha Hale [*Liberia* (1853)], Caroline Lee Hentz [*The Planter's Northern Bride* (1854)], and Augusta Evans Wilson [*Macaria* (1863)] approached the issue of slavery variously.

Depicting how alcohol in their contemporary economy created hardship for women and children were writers such as Hale [*Boarding Out* (1846)], Metta Fuller Victor [*The Senator's Son* (1853)], and S.A. Southworth[8] [*Lawrence Monroe* (1856)].   Encouraging their readers to consider women's rights were authors such as Maria McIntosh [*Two Lives* (1847) and *Charms and Counter-Charms* (1848)], Caroline Chesebro' [*Isa, A Pilgrimage* (1852) and *The Children of Light*, 1853)], Fanny Fern (Sara Willis Parton) [*Ruth Hall* (1855)], E.D.E.N. Southworth [*The Hidden Hand* (1859)], and Augusta Evans Wilson [*Beulah* (1859)].

Women authors working in diverse genres encouraged readers to reevaluate and reconstruct notions of the American frontier and its native inhabitants.   Elizabeth F. Ellet's non-fiction *Pioneer Women of the West* (1852) documented and implicitly legitimated women's place in the western wilderness.   Close friends, poet, Lydia H. Sigourney [*The Western Home and Other Poems* (1854)] and editor, poet, and fiction-writer, Ann S. Stephens [*Mary Derwent* (1858)] drew from history to show women's rightful place in creating an American culture that included the frontier. Authors such as Cummins and E.D.E.N. Southworth provided a vision of taking eastern culture west intact (Kolodny 203-26); Sigourney and Stephens gave the reader a vision of America enriched by mixing the refinement of European culture with the vitality of Native American culture.   In these various ways, nineteenth-century women authors reached a market

of women readers yearning for education (at a time when college enroll-
ment was limited to men), empowerment (in the face of legislated economic paternalism), and participation in creating a national ethic.

So fully did women writers then inundate the publishing world that male
writers of the period, today recognized as progenitors of American literature, typically had difficulty getting their works published. Habegger
comments,

> . . . Women's fiction posed a challenge to men . . . [who] established them-
> selves against, (*sic*) the maternal tradition of Anglo-American women's fic-
> tion. (ix)

Writer, editor, publisher, and jealous brother of the period's celebrated
Fanny Fern, Nathaniel Willis, "recognized that 'the republic of letters'
was 'fast coming under female dominion'" and referred to *Godey's* as a
"'powerful gynocracy'"[9] (Ann Douglas, "The 'Scribbling'" 16). Illustrat-
ing men's frustration at the time, Nathaniel Hawthorne complained from
Liverpool to his American publisher, "America is now wholly given over
to a d____d mob of scribbling women, and I should have no chance of
success while the public taste is occupied with their trash—" (*Letters* 56).
Also writing from England, critic and novelist George Henry Lews issued
the ironic "A Gentle Hint to Writing Women"[10] in *The Leader* (1850):

> It will never do. We are overrun. . . . It's a melancholy fact, and against all
> Political Economy, that the group of female authors is becoming every year
> more multitudinous and more successful. Women write the best novels, the
> best travels, the best reviews, the best leaders, and the best cookery-books. . .
> they are ruining our profession. Wherever we carry our skillful pens, we find
> the place preoccupied by a woman . . . now I starve. What am I to do . . .
> (Helsinger et al. 4)

In New York, referring to the flood of women's works, *Knickerbocker's
Magazine* (1855), lamented, "still they come" (525).

Three waves of twentieth-century literary scholars have examined this
"flood" of nineteenth-century American women writers. Very generally,
the scholars of the first wave base their critical assessments of nineteenth-
century literature on twentieth-century cultural and literary assumptions
and so explain (and affirm) the literature's failure in terms of not meeting
anachronistic reader expectations. This group includes Herbert Ross

THE WRITERS, THEIR CRITICS, AND CAMPBELL   31

Brown (1940), Fred Lewis Pattee (1940), Frank L. Mott (1947), James D. Hart (1950), Helen Waite Papashvily (1956), Carl Bode (1959), and Ann Douglas (Wood) (1971, 1977). A second wave begins to look not only at the literature itself, but also at the criteria on which the canon that excludes it is based. These scholars include Kathryn Kish Sklar (1973); John G. Cawelti (1976); Nancy F. Cott and Elizabeth H. Pleck (1977, 1979); Sandra Gilbert and Susan Gubar (1979); Nina Baym (1978, 1981, 1984); Elizabeth K. Helsinger, Robin Lauterbach Sheets, and William Veeder (1983); Kristin Herzog (1983); Mary Kelley (1984); Annette Kolodny (1984); Janice Radway (1984); Elaine Showalter (1985); Judith Fetterley (1985), Lucy M. Freibert and Barbara A. White (1985), Jane Tompkins (1985), and Eric J. Sundquist (1986). Going beyond issues of canon to explore alternative reading strategies are several scholars from the previous list together with Cathy N. Davidson (1986, 1989), Janet Gabler-Hover (1990), Susan K. Harris (1990), and Susan Coultrap-McQuin (1990).

The earliest twentieth-century scholars of nineteenth-century American women's novels, Brown, Pattee, Mott, Hart, Papashvily, Bode, and Douglas, generally assume that social conditions, changing through time, render this body of literature inaccessible or irrelevant to twentieth-century readers and critics. Brown criticizes the body of work for its "limitation of scope to . . . comparatively narrow domestic interests" (105). He argues that as the interests of readers broadened beyond domesticity, the literature, so limited, lost its relevancy. Pattee, stating that a novel "must be examined against the background of its times" (57), similarly points to an excessive emotionalism and "effeminacy" generally characterizing the 1850s and its literature:

> The decade was fatuous. The nerves of the nation, stimulated by the intensity
> of the times, began to crave added emotional stimulants: circuses, melo-
> drama, "shilling-shocker" fiction. Religious emotion, always in America un-
> der loose control, expressed itself in a tearful flood of poems and novels and
> betterment movements. (8)

Also concerned "with the mass impact of so much reading matter upon the public" (5), Mott anticipates Baym (*Novels* 24-25), by contrasting "vox populi,"—the best-seller reading public[11]—to the "professional literary critic," who forms the

> exasperated conclusion that the great popular audience seldom or never rec-
> ognizes first-class literature, has no conception of good taste, and never agrees
> with their own judgments. (2)

Similarly addressing the contradiction between "the ladies" and "the lite-
rati," Hart traces how the popular novel, "Like the nation, . . . dreamed
and sentimentalized" (104) and so succumbed to

> Eastern centralism, organized for acquisition . . . a predatory class of capital-
> ists . . . that made and owned the machines . . . that set standards . . . moved
> men into the cities; it controlled working hours, pay, and living conditions; it
> dictated what crops could be grown and how they could be marketed; it even
> established a national code of ethics and new standards of culture. (157)

Ironically, in retrospect, this so described class control[12] contributed, in
part, to the demise of 1850s women's literature at the same time that
women authors designed to educate readers to their own powers of shaping American culture.

Papashvily creates what has since become a recurring reading: mid-
nineteenth-century women's literature was subversive. Together with
those critics who follow her lead, she points out strong subversive messages lurking beneath the works' more overt contents:

> To maim the male, to deprive him of the privilege of slavery and the pleasure
> of alcohol was not, of course, enough. Female superiority at the same time
> had to be established and maintained. (95)

Papashvily sees the literature's greatest success as the positive economic
consequences it brought for the authors—significant in a culture where
women were economically dependent on men by law and by custom.[13]
Because these authors subversively[14] emasculated their male characters
and presented female models who "took their turn at being selfish, domi-
neering, inconstant, intemperate, ruthless . . ." (212), Papashvily argues,
"the domestic novel had served its purpose and the time had come for
common sense in the household" (209). Further, like Hart, she points to
the economics of industrialization as the force that overpowered both
women's literature and women's power to shape the nation (197).

Bode explains the demise of 1850s women's literature in terms of gender issues. He points to the "altered audience" between centuries: nine-

teenth-century literature was originally read by both men and women, whereas the appeal of sentimentality[15] in the twentieth century (Bode claims) is limited to "housewives"[16] and also limited by "the diminished role of religion" in current culture (170).[17]

Douglas applies concepts of the market economy to mid-nineteenth-century American women's novels, but does so differently from Hart:

> sentimental "domestic novels" written largely by women for women [that] dominated the literary market in America from the 1840s through the 1880s
> . . . . [were] courses in the shopping mentality, exercises in euphemism essential to the system of flattery which served as the rationale for the American women's economic position. (*Feminization* 62)

Douglas recognizes in the literature Papashvily's sense of its subversiveness, but argues that the struggles of mid-nineteenth-century women and their literature were "doomed to failure" because of women writers' reliance on subversive messages in place of a soteriological ideology for protest[18] (167).

When Douglas continues her indictment, important by virtue of its foundational position in nineteenth-century American women's literary studies—"Indeed, this literature seems today both ludicrous and painful" (63)[19]—she presents a very basic literary critical assumption. Like many scholars, she feels quite comfortable reading and judging the literature of one age by the cultural suppositions of another. Indeed, Douglas legitimatizes removing the whole body of nineteenth-century women's literature from the American canon on this basis.

The next wave of scholars (notably Cawelti; Cott; Helsinger, Sheets, and Veeder; Baym; Kelley; Kolodny; Radway; Fetterley; Freibert and White; and Tompkins) moves from documenting the fact of nineteenth-century American literature's demise to looking at the theories that account for excluding and/or including the literature from the canon. As Baym says, "theories account for the inclusion and exclusion of texts in anthologies, and theories account for the way we read them" ("Melodramas" 123). Some of these second-wave scholars confront theories that exclude nineteenth-century women authors from the canon; others offer theories that could lead to expanding the canon.

Helsinger, Sheets, and Veeder show how nineteenth-century women authors' contemporaneous critics used a concept of realism to judge a work's seriousness. Citing various reviews of the time, they show how presumptions about women authors' limited experiences of "actual knowledge" (54) were said to limit their works' measure of realism. Along these same lines, Baym (*Novels*) traces the roots of what she recognizes as current polarized theories to varied criteria for literary judgment among nineteenth-century readers and reviewers. According to Baym, scholars have always tended to judge "serious" literature favorably:

> "Seriousness" has become the justification for our enterprises of academic literary criticism and literary pedagogy and is the source of their tension with the general public. (Novels 24)

Further, she points out that scholars who sanction literary "seriousness," usually assume "the dynamic principle of plot as the novel's formal essence" (*Novels* 24).

Baym continues her argument showing the power of critics and scholars to establish the canon. Nineteenth-century critics, she says, measured literature's value as superior when it presented "a vision of a morally governed universe" (*Novels* 24). Nonetheless, twentieth-century theory-making scholars have left "these books, and these authors, out of the picture" ("Melodramas" 124). Of twentieth-century readers she says, "we never read American literature directly or freely, but always through the perspective allowed by theories" ("Melodramas" 123). Thus, the power of canonization falls not to the nineteenth-century novels themselves nor to their lay readers, but to readers who are scholars and critics. To correct this situation, Baym invites twentieth-century readers and scholars alike to focus on how the works might have been read within their nineteenth-century context and so experience the literature beyond "doomed to failure."

Similarly, Tompkins (*Sensational*), calls the tendency to read and judge the literature of one age by the cultural suppositions of another "presentist"[20] (xiii) and argues for "a new kind of historical criticism," that would read nineteenth-century works "as sympathetically as possible" within a recreation of their own cultural context. Questioning their ideological foundations, Tompkins points out that twentieth-century critics' "assumptions about the nature and function of literature" produce an inability "to appreciate the complexity and scope of a novel like Stowe's, or to account for its enormous popular success" (125).

While other critics explore the various ways in which changing social conditions—economic, political, religious, cultural, etc.—changed the way readers have read the mid-nineteenth-century novel, Tompkins shows the reverse to be true as well. That is, Tompkins claims that literature has a hand in directing history, affecting "the way people understand their lives" and "defining historical conditions" (*Sensational* 195). She asks current literary scholars to reevaluate and rename the canon of nineteenth-century literature to reflect nineteenth- rather than twentieth-century criteria of literary judgment. Thus Baym and Tompkins alter the criteria for critical judgment; they create the critical situation that allows nineteenth-century American women's literature entry into the canon.

In addition to scholars who confront theories that exclude nineteenth-century women's literature from the canon, scholars (in addition to Baym and Tompkins) broach issues of canon that advocate inclusion. And they do so in various ways. One way involves reevaluating theories of genre. Freibert and White challenge those critics who conflate the varied aspects of nineteenth-century American women's writing into a single characterization.[21] For example, while Cawelti patly characterizes the works of Southworth, Stowe, and Warner as formulaic[22] social melodramas, Freibert and White describe E.D.E.N. Southworth's works as belonging to the genre, melodrama, but extend the scope of her work beyond formula. They characterize Stowe's and Warner's novels not as melodramas at all, but the former as polemic and the later as a novel of education. Cawelti's examination of the Romantic Western omits references to women's novels altogether, whereas Freibert and White devote a whole section of their anthology to early Frontier Romances written by women, and Kolodny supplies a whole book about early American women writers and the frontier.

Fetterley advocates expanding the canon to include nineteenth-century American women's works from another angle. She suggests that women writers before 1865 exhibit "a considerable degree of self-consciousness toward the act of writing" (5). Fetterley thus counters Douglas, who describes these authors' denial "of writing while in fact engaged in the act of writing" (5), and Gilbert and Gubar, who describe an "anxiety of authorship" attending the work of nineteenth-century English women writers—a description that Kelley likewise sees as "informing the work of nineteenth-century American 'literary domestics'" (5). Citing Baym's (*Woman's*) argument that women writers saw themselves as professionals with satisfying and productive work to do (6), Fetterley asks that the work of these authors be taken seriously. That is, while Baym questions "seriousness" as a criterion by which to judge literature, Fetterley accepts "seriousness" as a critical element and, accordingly, so proceeds to discuss nineteenth-century American women's writing favorably.

In their studies that advocate canon inclusiveness, Kelley and Radway analyze reading method. On the one hand, Kelley shows how nineteenth-century women writers have been denigrated as "sentimentalists" or "scribbling women" or, in another extreme, "as subversives, as promulgators of quasi-revolutionary manifestos with the expressed purpose of liberating women from their domestic captivity" (viii). On the other hand, Kelley presents the literature as it reveals nineteenth-century women's daily lives. She asks readers to change their stance from reading nineteenth-century American women authors as diminished to reading them as "historical figures in the social and cultural context of the nineteenth century" (viii, ix).

Radway, too, presents "reading the romance" from an angle of reading method. Noting how discourse communities vary across space and over time, she connects texts with the communities that produced and consumed them "to specify how the individuals involved actually constructed those texts as meaningful semiotic structures" (4). Doing so, Radway hopes to fulfill American studies' need for ethnographies of reading.

Writing from a similar impulse, Kolodny places her study outside social and literary history, focusing on "the sequences of fantasies through which generations of women came to know and act upon the westward-moving frontier" (xii). Like Kelley, Kolodny concerns herself with women's both private and public responses. As historians, Kelley, Radway, and Kolodny use nineteenth-century women's literature as a source from which to reconstruct women's ethnography.[23]

Extending the studies of others, scholars of the most recent wave—such as Davidson, Coultrap-McQuin, and Harris—explore various hermeneutics or strategies for reading nineteenth-century American women's novels. In her approach to issues of canon, Davidson challenges an assumed institutional control over the canon and the concept of canon itself (*Reading* 162). She cites Mikhail Bakhtin's argument that the novel

"... has no canon of its own. It is, by its nature, not canonic. It is plasticity itself. It is a genre that is ever questing, ever examining itself and subjecting its established forms to review," [39] an enterprise that can also encourage the reader to subject other or all established forms of authority to review. (162)

Davidson delimits traditional constraints on the novel even further:

> The distinctive feature of the novel as a genre may not be its formal qualities, its verbal artistry, its realistic or sensational plot lines, nor even its paraphrasable content, but rather the "dialogue" that it enters into with the reader . . . This active apprehension of text can be psychically liberating for the individual reader in ways that are threatening to those who perceive themselves as the arbiters (or former arbiters) of cultural work. (*Reading* 162)

Exploding the concept of canon as myth, Davidson (*Reading* 162 and *Revolution* 52) implicitly takes the power of judgment that Baym confers on academics, scholars, and critics and gives it to the individual reader.[24] Thus diffusing the concept of canon, Davidson melds studies in history with studies in literature to produce a feminist literary politics.

Continuing Papashvily's argument that characterizes the nineteenth-century American women's novel as subversive, Davidson (*Revolution*) explains how the novel's soteriological nature threatened ministerial authority and how it seduced its readers to confront other authorities as well. She sees the novel's subversiveness to lie in the reader's activity "because the complex intellectual and emotional activity of reading fiction empowers the hitherto powerless individual . . ." (*Reading* 162). Davidson thus hints that a work's subversiveness might hinge on whether readers consider it an object of art or an agent of change.

Coultrap-McQuin moves from studies of characters' and authors' private lives to examine nineteenth-century American women's professional careers. She sides with Fetterley in denying evidence of women's anxiety about authorship and views mid-century women writers as competent literary professionals. She also joins with Freibert and White in refusing to lump women's works together.

Using "approaches to literary analysis that emphasize language and textual structure" (*19th-Century* 12), Harris offers strategies for reading the works of another culture. She takes issue with Papashvily's theme of subversiveness and refuses to read these novels as "a war between female demons and male victims" (*19th-Century* 13). Like Kelley, she does so with reference to women's voices, both private and public. Lifting from the novels "the overplot [that] functions to disguise multiple hermeneutic possibilities" (*19th-Century* 13), Harris combines insights from modern formalist studies with recent scholars' interpretive conventions to increase reader appreciation of the texts.

Very generally, the earliest twentieth-century scholars examined and judged nineteenth-century women's literature against their own post-industrial values, mores, beliefs, and agendas. Writing during the 1970s and into the mid-1980s, the second-wave twentieth-century scholars, also examined these works in light of evolving twentieth-century literary, cultural, and political concepts, and began to look at nineteenth-century women's literature more consciously within a historical context.

Recently, some literary scholars, such as Harris, seem to be moving away from earlier academics' inclinations to classify, analyze, and so objectify mid-nineteenth-century women's literature. Delimiting criticism that focuses on the works' social/sexual context and encouraging "access to the novels' verbal, structural, and thematic adventures" (*19th-Century* 20), Harris invites the reader to explore (a term she favors) these novels rhetorically. Specifically, she extends the study of nineteenth-century narratives to explore these works' "multitude of codes" (*19th-Century* 78). Offering the reader insight into hermeneutic codes, familiar to the nineteenth-century reader, but generally lost to the twentieth-century reader, she uncovers an enriched complexity of text.[25] Employing current literary theoretical assistance, she seeks "to recreate readers' responses to literature of a past century" and so "be able to retrieve their complete experience" (*19th-Century* 79).[26]

In sum, twentieth-century scholars have paved the way for the study at hand in several respects. Foremost, they have introduced and legitimated the field of mid-nineteenth-century American women writers within English studies. Further, current scholars have dispelled as simplistic earlier stereotyping of the genre and have begun to question certain literary-critical conventions as "presentist" (Tompkins). Moreover, current scholars are recognizing the legitimacy of authorial intent and supplying reading strategies that might help twentieth-century readers "reread" these novels more responsively to those intentions. Harris writes:

> The concept of authorial intention is integral to the study of these novels, then, but from a rhetorical rather than a psychological point of view. (*19th-Century* 33)

Explaining nineteenth-century authors' success at fulfilling their intentions, Harris points out these texts' power to evoke reader response in order "to change readers' social and literary horizons, and therefore, ultimately, to change both literature and society" (*19th-Century* 32).[27] She encourages other scholars to explore these novels in terms of intent beyond the simply didactic to discover interesting and complex thematic and structural tensions.

Campbell's *The Philosophy of Rhetoric* offers a comprehensive, systematic, and contemporaneous heuristic by which to explore just how nineteenth-century women's texts evoke reader response. Nan Johnson's study, *Nineteenth-century Rhetoric in North America*[28] explains how Campbell's philosophy, central to the Scottish New Rhetoric tradition, pre-dated and came to permeate nineteenth-century American rhetoric. Tracing Campbell's philosophy of rhetoric from its roots in eighteenth-century Scottish theological oratory to its flowering in nineteenth-century North America, she puts Campbell's theory into the time and culture of mid-nineteenth-century authors:

> Nineteenth-century rhetoricians . . . focused on how the writer (as well as the speaker) can utilize rhetorical strategies to appeal to the readers' understanding, emotions, will, and imagination. (173)

Whereas Johnson shows how Campbell's four ends of discourse in large part informed the rhetorical background of the age, other scholars show more directly how "The New Rhetoric" informed women's writing. For example, Pattee writes that Susan and Anna Warner's father, Henry W. Warner, educated his daughters at home where among other things they read Blair's *Rhetoric* (55).

The New Rhetoric informed women's writings not only in terms of discourse, but also thematically. Gabler-Hover, linking rhetoric with idealism in nineteenth-century novels, describes rhetoric's theological element as deriving from such rhetoricians/preachers as Campbell and Henry Ward Beecher, "who perpetuated the notion that truthfulness was tantamount to virtue, and imperative" (39). Gabler-Hover documents that Harriet Beecher Stowe's father, "was required to study Campbell . . . "

(48). For such nineteenth-century students, Campbell's *The Philosophy of Rhetoric* was, according to Gabler-Hover, "an undisguised moral treatise that emphasized the necessary relationship between rhetorical eloquence and sincerity" (191). Campbell's philosophy thus both affected the culture at large and reflected nineteenth-century women writers' obvious concerns with Christian themes and rhetorical eloquence.

Although I cannot contend that 1850s authors used Campbell's actual *Rhetoric* to accomplish their stated ends, I do argue that writings of these authors parallel Campbell's teachings and that an appreciation of Campbell can enrich a twentieth-century rereading of these works. Recalling Harris's statement of authorial intention as "integral to the study of these novels, then, but from a rhetorical" (33) stance, contemporary readers can profitably observe how these authors lead the reader through Campbell's ends of discourse, which they render "conducive to that which is the primary intention" (Campbell 1). Studying the works' progressions as mirrored by Campbell's ends of discourse provides readings that reflect the authors' intentions to affect both the individual reader and society.

These intentions apply in two respects. Campbell describes the rhetorical effects that an author can create for a reader as the effects of association psychology. He prefaces his remarks about how language conveys knowledge with a sense of metaphysical curiosity:

> That mere sounds, which are used only as signs, and have no natural connexion with the things whereof they are signs, should convey knowledge to the mind, even when they excite no idea of the things signified, must appear at first extremely mysterious. (258)

He then posits three "connexions" by which an author can affect a reader's response:[29] the connection that exists among things, the connection that exists between words and things, and the connection that exists among words. The following chapters explain the psychological connections that an author can create in a reader by using words—that is, those connections an author can create in the reader's mind between words and things and those connections an author can create in a reader's mind among words.[30]

Campbell describes the association of words and things in a reader's mind:

For having often had occasion to observe particular words used as signs of particular things, we hence contract a habit of associating the sign with the thing signified, insomuch that either, being presented to the mind, frequently introduces or occasions the apprehension of the other. . . . Thus . . . the ideas of things . . . come to be as strongly linked in our conceptions, as the ideas of things naturally related to one another. (258)

Here Campbell explains that an author can, through associating the sign with the thing signified in the reader's mind, move the reader.

Of Campbell's rhetorical connections between things and words and between words and words, Johnson observes that authors affected nineteenth-century American culture both " . . . through the subject matter conveyed as well as through the aesthetic appeal of rhetorical form" (230). Accordingly, when applicable, I point out the appeal an author makes via subject matter through the example of a heroine.

Privileging the understanding to other faculties, current readers may not immediately recognize "the aesthetic appeal of rhetorical form" of a bygone era. Mid-nineteenth-century authors sought to educate by appealing to the reader's whole being. In Campbell's terms the reader comes to more than a simple "understanding" of moral, Christian, and domestic values and their real-life possibilities; through appealing to the reader's "imagination" and "passions," the author brings the reader to a belief or a change of mind. In this manner, the author is able to influence the reader's "will." In terms of its subject matter, the book thus acts as an agent for the reader's growth and change. The "connexion" between idea and word occurs in mid-nineteenth-century American women's novels more in terms of their appeals to the understanding and will. The following chapters about Warner's *The Wide, Wide World* and Stowe's *Uncle Tom's Cabin* focus more closely on this sort of "connexion" than do the later chapters.[31]

Of the "connexion" among words Campbell means,

solely that connexion or relation which comes gradually to subsist among the different words of a language, in the minds of those who speak it . . . that those words are employed as signs of connected or related things . . . . ideas associated by the same idea will associate with one another. (258-59)

Here Campbell moves from discussing language in terms of its subject's impact (by association) on the reader to discussing language in terms of its rhetorical impact (by association) on the reader.[32]   This aspect of Campbell's philosophy proves very helpful in explaining how mid-nineteenth-century women authors use hermeneutic signs and codes: signs,[33] Campbell shows, "insensibly become connected in the imagination" (259-60). The later chapters, concerning Stephens's *Mary Derwent* and Southworth's *The Hidden Hand*, focus more closely on how authors use floral and architectural codes that by "conception, habit, or tendency of the mind" (Campbell 259) become "connected in the imagination."

The following chapters demonstrate how Campbell's theory—that a discourse intends to enlighten the understanding, to please the imagination, to move the passions, or to influence the will—informs readings of mid-nineteenth-century popular literature. This demonstration, directed to popular women's fiction, offsets Johnson's statement concerning academic rhetoric of the same period:

> In Campbell's philosophy of rhetoric, the aims of enlightening the understanding, pleasing the imagination, moving the passions, and influencing the will *constrain* the nature of rhetorical proof, shape the substance of types of discourse, and *constrain* the stylistic process of rhetoric. (*Nineteenth-Century* 22) (emphasis mine)

Campbell's four appeals may well have "constrained" rhetorical proof and style within the nineteenth-century academic setting. As nineteenth-century academic rhetoric filtered into the period's popular literature, however, use (conscious or not) of Campbell's four appeals "informed" the nature of rhetorical proof, "inspired" the stylistic process of rhetoric, and necessitated certain rhetorical elements. A mid-nineteenth-century author seeking to influence a mid-nineteenth-century reader's will had to appeal to the reader's multiple faculties.

The impulse to reread mid-nineteenth-century American women's texts as informed by Campbell's quadripartite ends of discourse is indebted to and grows out of earlier scholarship of these works. Harris's exploration of hermeneutic codes, for example, opens various textual paths to investigate. Campbell's theory offers a unified and contemporaneous heuristic by which to continue investigating rhetorical aspects of mid-nineteenth-century women's fiction. Reading these works as informed by Campbell's quadripartite ends of discourse should increase the literature's value for casual and scholarly readers alike.

NOTES

[1] Defining the late eighteenth-century English tradition known as the "New Rhetoric," Johnson writes,

> The New Rhetoric evolved from the efforts of theorists such as George Campbell (*The Philosophy of Rhetoric*) and Hugh Blair . . . to reconcile the principles and practices of rhetoric with theories of the mind, logic, and language . . . . (19)

[2] Albert R. Kitzhaber traces the publication of Campbell's *The Philosophy of Rhetoric* to America:

> George Campbell's *Philosophy of Rhetoric* was first printed in 1776 in Edinburgh, and though copies found their way to America in the 1780s it seems not to have been reprinted here until 1818. (52)

[3] Tompkins's study presents the period's literature similarly: "It sees literary texts not as works of art . . . but as attempts to redefine the social order" (xi).

[4] This sense of the mid-nineteenth-century American woman author's "designs" on her reader differs from the concept of didacticism. Nina Baym describes didactic works: "They meant readers to take away something from their reading that would help them in their lives" (*Woman's* 16-17). Lucy Freibert and Barbara White later elaborate, "The didactic fiction of the mid nineteenth century . . . strives to educate women in preparing themselves for marriage, building a home and family, and developing religious principles" (219). This sense of overt didacticism differs from the more covert "designs" on the reader that Tompkins describes: "For the novel functions . . . as a means of changing [the social world] . . . and . . . recommends a strategy for dealing with cultural conflict [as] an agent of that strategy" (135). After all, "literary texts have the power to change readers' social and literary horizons, adds Susan K. Harris, "and therefore, ultimately, to change both literature and society" (*19th-Century* 32).

[5] Helen Waite Papashvily calls Finley the "most popular of all Susan Warner's imitators" (170).

[6] Although Child may be remembered best for her literary fame, she was well re spected by contemporaries for her

> philanthropic spirit. The exercise of this noble spirit caused her books to fall into sudden obscurity. She anticipated this when she wrote her "Appeal" in behalf of the poor slave. (Hanaford 148)

[7] Although Jacob's *Incidents* is a biography, its style brings it close to fiction. Cathy N. Davidson comments, "Metahistorians have suggested that every work of history is essentially an imaginative work, a narrative little different from a novel" (vii).

[8] Papashvily remarks that "at least two other Southworths traded on the magic name" of E.D.E.N. Southworth (180-1).

[9] Willis's sense of nineteenth-century literacy as "under female dominion" sharply contradicts the views of later critics such as Leslie Fielder who (as Baym points out) hold "that the matter of American experience is inherently male" ("Melodramas" 70).

[10] *Leader*, 1 (1850) 189. This amusing article is easily accessible in Helsinger, Sheets, and Veeder, vol. 2, 4-5.

[11] Mott stresses that lumping all readers together as "vox populi" is a misconception as is lumping together all popular literature by virtue of its popularity. Baym, Tompkins, and others later show how the antithesis between "vox populi" and "vox dei" (Mott's terms) led to the demise of popular literature, as the nineteenth century, becoming increasingly more class-structured, allotted more clout to the professional literary critics.

[12] Hart's terms are later taken up by Isabelle White in her treatment of Susan Warner's *The Wide, Wide World.*

[13] Davidson (*Reading*) warns that one should not rely on the argument that commercial success spells literary success because "mass culture is often dismissed as commodity, inflicted by a ruling class upon a mindless proletariat" (168).

[14] Radway, commenting from the perspective of popular culture, sees two strains of thought regarding nineteenth-century novels' subversive messages. She sees that readers can consider the act of romance reading (as opposed to the literature itself) to be subversive: an activity of protest in reaction to cultural institutions' failures "to satisfy the emotional needs of women" (213). At the same time, she holds that the act of reading can disarm the impulse to protest the failures of cultural institutions by vicariously meeting "those very needs and requirements that might otherwise be formulated as demands in the real world and lead to the potential restructuring of sexual relations" (213).

     Cott continues along this line, posing social change against the "cult of domesticity" proffered by "opinion-makers such as Hale and Catharine Beecher . . ." (*Root of Bitterness* 12). Elsewhere (*The Bonds of Womanhood* 197), Cott traces views of domesticity as they derive from twentieth-century historians' views of nineteenth-century women's letters.

[15] The idea of sentimentality has not always had its current negative associations. Apologizing for using such a modern term, Campbell defines "sentimental" as "what is addressed solely to the moral powers of the mind." He explains that the term "occupies, so to speak, the middle place between the pathetic and that which is addressed to the imagination, and partakes of both, adding to the warmth of the former and grace and attractions of the latter" (80). Baym points out that currently "'sentimental' is often a term of judgment rather than of description, and the judgment it conveys is of course adverse. . . . Such adverse judgments are culture-bound, in my view" she adds (*Woman's* 24).

[16] In her analysis of nineteenth-century culture as one "of separate spheres" (12-33), Janet Wolff challenges Bode's assumptions.

[17] Interestingly, Bode's Jungian analysis of the literature, predicts that the domestic novel should span cultural and time changes. Because the domestic novel (as he calls it) appeals powerfully to both *anima* and *animus*, and provides views of both the wise old man and the earth mother, it spans gender expectations and needs. Thus, he argues that the domestic novel should withstand cultural and time changes (171-2).

[18] Harris later shows how Papashvily "extends the contradictory critical situation Brown's text initiates" (*19th-Century* 5).

[19] Various critics currently dismiss such statements.

[20] I prefer to call this concept "chronocentric" to parallel the spirit of "ethnocentric,"—"a tendency to view alien groups or culture in terms of one's own,"—emphasizing time instead of ethnicity.

[21] Brown groups "sentimental romances" together according to their "same facile sentimental formula," to which he juxtaposes the work of "authentic artists like Nathaniel Hawthorne" (322). Mott later notes "the tendency of the literary critic to lump all books that seem to him beneath notice . . . into one group and label them 'the best sellers'" (4). Mott calls this tendency a "mistake."

[22] Mott earlier declares "there is no formula which may be depended upon to produce a best seller" (285). Despite denying such a formula, he lists and explains certain elements he finds common to best-sellers.

[23] The list of literary scholars concerned with nineteenth-century American women's literature continues beyond those mentioned here. Henri Petter offers a descriptive and critical survey of the American novel up to the year 1820; although a bit early for the study at hand, Petter lays foundations from which other scholars must work. Gilbert and Gubar's classic study and Anita Levy's *Other Women, the Writing of Class, Race, and Gender, 1832-1898* (1991) focus primarily on British authors and culture. Eric Sundquist [*New Essays on Uncle Tom's Cabin* (1986)] and Elaine

Showalter [*The New Feminist Criticism, Essays on Women, Literature, and Theory* (1985)] provide collections of essays, several of which have enhanced this study. Teresa Toulouse (1987) reveals a basic paradox within the concept, "art of prophesying": "prophecy" denotes passive spiritual inspiration whereas "art" denotes writing's activity. Frances B. Cogan [*All-American Girl, The Ideal of Real Womanhood in Mid-Nineteenth-Century America* (1989)], Cott (1977 and 1986), Kathryn Kish Sklar (1973), and Janet Wolff [*Feminine Sentences*, (1990)] approach the subject at hand from the perspective of social history. So does Kristin Herzog, who in *Women, Ethnics, and Exotics, Images of Power in Mid-Nineteenth-Century American Fiction* (1983) states

> Wherever women and other classes and races really count, individual human beings have balanced primitive instinct and guiding reason, and human societies have balanced the rights and responsibilities of different sexes, races, and nationalities. (xxvi)

[24] Indeed, the individual reader may be any combination of reader, academic, scholar, and/or critic.

[25] Richard M. Weaver (1953) treats what scholars now call hermeneutic codes in terms of a "homogeneity of belief" that was the nineteenth-century orator's or writer's "capital" (167). Still other scholars (notably Baym and Tompkins) offer soteriological hermeneutic codes, but contextualized within limits of social or cultural statements.

[26] Harris devotes herself to this feat despite her sense of its ultimate futility. No approach can be entirely free of a reader's cultural assumptions and concerns.

[27] Harris draws from both Jauss and Barthes here.

[28] This work now supersedes Winifred Bryan Horner's *The Present State of Scholarship in Historical and Contemporary Rhetoric* (1983) and James A. Berlin's *Writing Instruction in Nineteenth-Century American Colleges* (1984). It is complemented by Horner's *Nineteenth-Century Scottish Rhetoric: The American Connection* (1993).

[29] I present Campbell's theory of association within the context and parlance of twentieth-century reader-response theory to emphasize Campbell's relevancy for current study.

[30] Campbell's concept of "resemblance" is relevant here, again as part of his discussion of the appeal to the imagination (74, 215, 285, 304).

[31] I do not mean here to place any formulaic limits on nineteenth-century works that educate the reader to the individual author's intention. Rather, I intend to show

how, through association of the literary word and the thing it represents, an author can effectively appeal to a reader's understanding.

[32] Naturally, the concept, association of ideas, could have come to nineteenth-century American authors from various sources. This study means only to show the usefulness of that heuristic to a contemporary reading of mid-nineteenth-century works.

[33] Campbell uses the terms "sign," "idea," and "word" somewhat interchangeably:

I have hitherto, in conformity to what is now become general and inveterate custom, and in order to avoid tiresome circumlocutions, used the terms sign and idea as exactly correlative. . . . All words are signs   . . . (260)

Susan Warner

III

SUSAN WARNER'S *THE WIDE, WIDE WORLD*: BECOMING THE CHRISTIAN MODEL

That so many of America's early best-sellers were written by women seems to have rankled certain twentieth-century literary scholars. James D. Hart, for example, generalizes: ". . . these novels of rural life became soggy with happiness when women began to try their hands at the new genre" (208). Specifically attacking *ad feminam* America's first million-seller author, Susan Warner, Hart editorializes, "One look at her spare equine face distinguished by a pair of eyes set not quite evenly in her head, a thin determined mouth, and hair brushed tightly behind large ears proclaimed her a spinster by nature" (95). Referring to both women readers and writers, Hart's "scholarly survey"[1] instructs,

> Women have always been the great readers of fiction in America and nearly every novel has had to appeal to them to be successful, but in only a few periods have the popular novels been written mainly by women and for women. Syrupy pathos, sentiment, and optimism then flourish until the reader is drowned in tears or scorched in the sunshine of gladness. (208)

Such critical decrees to oust from the canon of American literature those works written for and by women rest on firm assumptions that privilege logos to pathos and privilege the faculty of understanding to those of the imagination, passions, and will. Arguing to admit 1850s women's literature to the canon by virtue of gender equality—rejecting such sexist "criticism" as Hart's—is, of course, important. Going further, however, critics might begin to question rhetorical assumptions that ask readers and writers to engage in discourse rejecting holistic human responses stemming from appeals to faculties in addition to understanding. Rather than women limiting themselves to the critical cognitive methods traditionally claimed by men, perhaps both men and women might revalue the multiple cognitive faculties as outlined by Campbell.

Reading Susan Warner's *The Wide, Wide World* (1851) against the background of New Rhetorician George Campbell's rhetorical theory (*The

Philosophy of Rhetoric, 1776) enables current readers to understand more clearly Warner's tremendous impact on her contemporary readers, to appreciate *The Wide, Wide World*'s nineteenth-century critical responses, and to challenge twentieth-century negative criticism of the book. Reviewing *The Wide, Wide World* in terms of Campbell's four ends of discourse and appropriate nineteenth-century reviews helps explain twentieth-century criticism and provides the reader with a guide by which to read more holistically a narrative appealing to a reader's several faculties.

The Wide, Wide World traces Ellen Montgomery's childhood from her abandonment by her cold, unfeeling father, through her education in domestic economy and humility at the hands of her cruel aunt, Miss Fortune, and her theological nurturing by her "adoptive" sister and brother, Alice and John Humphreys, to her struggle to attain personal and Christian autonomy under the guardianship of her uncle, Mr. Lindsay. The story begins with Ellen at home, respectfully caring for her mother who offers constant soteriologic instruction. When Mrs. Montgomery's doctors decide that her only possible chance for survival lies in an extended rest in Europe, Ellen, who must stay behind, begins her own journey to attain for herself Warner's model of womanhood through a process of Christian education.

From the moment of her departure for her aunt's country home, Ellen encounters a variety of characters whose intentions toward her range from evil to benevolent. Most notable among Ellen's nemeses are the characters of Mr. Saunders, Mrs. Dunscombe, Miss Fortune, Nancy, and the taunting children at Ventnor. Ellen must struggle against evils on two levels: she must deal with her nemeses as she encounters them, and she must vanquish her "instinctive human" reactions to such evils. Through the sympathy Warner develops in the reader toward Ellen and the words of both Mrs. Montgomery (21) and Alice (270), Warner challenges her reader to work as Ellen must to develop patience and to "overcome evil with good."

Warner balances those characters who threaten Ellen with other characters who help her, notably Alice and John Humphreys, whom Ellen encounters while she resides with Miss Fortune. Alice becomes a Christian mother figure for Ellen, and both Alice and John stimulate Ellen's natural curiosity, providing her with insight into Christian values, the sciences, visual and equestrian arts, history, music, and literature. With her natural mother and Alice both fated to die during the story, Ellen eventually must look to herself for the intellectual, emotional, and spiritual direction that her maternal and Christian role models have provided.

By keeping her characters uninformed of each other's activities, Warner offers her reader a sense of privileged discovery by which to enter her tale. She begins her narrative revealing the various circumstances that will challenge her characters. From the very start, the reader learns first hand from Mrs. Montgomery's doctor what no other character knows: that Mrs. Montgomery has no hope of recovery from her illness (19). An investigation of *The Wide, Wide World*, then, should not ignore the reader, for whom Warner provides an overview of the book's action and whom she frequently addresses directly.

Three months after *The Wide, Wide World*'s publication, the highly respected nineteenth-century critic and editor of the popular *Godey's Lady's Book*, Sarah Josepha Hale, described it as "carefully and naturally written, manifesting in every page the anxiety of the author . . . to inculcate profitable lessons in real life . . . " (March, 1851). A year later, professor, editor, biographer, and bibliographer, John S. Hart (1852), in his well reviewed[2] *Female Prose Writers of America* (sixty-one "sketches" of American women writers) described Warner's book as "the only professed novel in which real religion, at least as understood by evangelical Christians, is exhibited with truth" (387). Even the conservatively opinioned anti-abolitionist *Southern Literary Messenger* reports positively after a customary misogynist dig at women writers:

> We were first tempted to read this work by an advertisement which stated it to be from the pen of Mrs. Browning, the elegant authoress of the "Drama of Exile." The authoress, or rather *author*, as the fair knights of the Pen are fond of styling themselves in these latter days, is not Mrs. Browning, but Mrs. Elizabeth Wetherell.[3]
> The work appears highly entertaining and in the heading, to the chapters, we were particularly struck with the tact and skill of the writer. Chapters under such delightful curiosity-prompting titles must needs be engrossing. (189)

The positive critical acclaim that *The Wide, Wide World* received during the early 1850s derives largely from the rhetorical context in which the book was first received. Recent histories of nineteenth-century American rhetoric[4] depict that context as largely informed by the Scottish theological writers of the New Rhetoric and their American successors.[5] Reading *The Wide, Wide World* in light of Campbell's multidimensional rhetorical context helps explain more than the rhetorical power Warner wielded with her readers. Reading in light of Reverend Campbell's multi-dimensional philosophy also answers some of the current feminist outrage at a book that literally preaches submission to patriarchal systems. In her "Afterword" to the Feminist Press reissue of the work, Tompkins succinctly describes current arguments for the work's dismissal:

> Its ideology of duty, humility, and submission to circumstance, and its insistence on the imperative of self-sacrifice, are infuriating to some readers, for these doctrines challenge everything the twentieth century has stood for in politics, psychology, and morals. The novel's ethic of submission violates everything the feminist movement has taught women about the need for self-assertion. It negates modern psychology's emphasis on the dangers of repressed anger. It rejects totally the liberal belief in self-determination and faith in individual enterprise, and implicitly denies the Marxist claim that collective action to reshape economic structures can improve the lives of the exploited. (585)

Sanctioning rhetorical appeals to the imagination, passions, and will to the same extent that current readers commonly sanction intellection, readers can move beyond such "bottom-line" readings as—through submission, orphan girl makes good. Sanctioning intellection to the exclusion of the other faculties allows for the individualism requisite to the competitive marketplace. Bereft of passion and sympathy, the self-assertive individual can without qualms accumulate material goods, regardless of their source. Clearly lacking sympathy for Ellen, for example, Miss Fortune provides Warner with a conduit for appealing to readers' understanding regarding the chemistry and economics of the prosperous, self-sufficient, and cold-hearted land-owner. The hoarding Miss Fortune epitomizes the entrepreneurial woman who would exploit others—men, women, and children—to her own inurement. Readers with the ability to share Ellen's tears cannot self-determinedly create such a Newt Gingrich/Miss Fortune-ate world nor join in the "cold austerer" systems that assent to and perpetuate those systems.

Campbell teaches that the first step necessary to appeal to a listener (or, for the purpose here, to a reader) is to enlighten the understanding by dispelling ignorance and vanquishing error (2). An author achieves this goal by using language that is reputable (141), national (145), and present (147); by writing with "perspicuity" so as to provide the listener with information; and by communicating "conviction" so as ultimately to provide the listener with argument (2-3). Accordingly, Warner uses language easily accessible to readers of all ages. With unprecedented popularity and many imitators (G. M. Goshgarian 1-2), *The Wide, Wide World* became a prototype for language that is reputable, national, and present.[6] Warner's learned and often biblical language frequently sacrifices subtlety for clarity: she means to be understood. As Warner presents Christian and domestic information using episodes, parables,[7] and examples, her "perspicuity" provides the reader with knowledge as her "conviction" provides argument.

In her story, Warner makes rhetorical appeals in terms of both her subject matter and her psychology of language. Johnson explains this duality of nineteenth-century rhetoric:

> Because nineteenth-century theorists conflated the acquisition of rhetorical skills with the development of taste, they assumed that the orator and the writer influence the community through the subject matter conveyed as well as through the aesthetic appeal of rhetorical form. (230)

Working with both subject matter and rhetorical form, Warner associates the idea of Ellen's challenges and growth with possibilities for the same in the reader. Protagonist Ellen must widen her own understanding by degree: she must begin by understanding her own nature and move step-by-step toward understanding herself as a Christian. Thus, a reader might gain enlightened understanding either directly from the author or by imitating the protagonist. Ellen's first task is to dispel her own ignorance: she must learn both Christian moral principles and the lessons of secular texts. Using the circumstances of Ellen's education "to enlighten the understanding" of her readers, Warner writes with "perspicuity" to provide the reader with this same information.

Warner constructs her supporting female characters so that they instruct Ellen in an informal manner. Before the story opens, Ellen had been receiving a Christian education from her mother. Ellen had already begun to learn the stories of the Bible, but her distress at her mother's illness and their separation provokes Ellen to begin to understand the biblical parables more fully. Warner uses the words of Mrs. Montgomery to make clear that education is crucial to a person's development:

> "I wish to have the comfort of thinking, when I am away, that I have left you with everything necessary to the keeping up of good habits . . . . I wish you to . . . improve yourself by every means . . . ." (31-32)

Ellen's mentor, Alice Humphreys, continues Mrs. Montgomery's efforts to educate Ellen:

> "Ellen, are you as well versed in the other common branches of education as you are in your mother tongue?" . . . "Geography, for instance; do you know it well?" . . . "Would you like to go over the Atlas again, talking about all these matters, as well as the mere outlines of the countries you have studied before?" (172)

Alice enriches Ellen's lessons in geography with visits to a Swiss woman, Mrs. Vawse, so that Ellen can learn French. On such a trip, Alice urges Ellen to ask about the botanical functions of leaves (185-6). The botany lesson that Alice provides for Ellen also serves to inform Warner's reader in the specifics of botany.[8] Similarly, Warner's readers learn lessons in dairying, home economics, and the chemistry of cheese-making from the practical Miss Fortune.

The young clergyman, John Humphreys, whom Ellen encounters midway through the story, and Ellen's Scottish guardian, Mr. Lindsay, whom she meets later, provide Ellen a more formal education. Their pedagogical styles, however, differ greatly. Assuming the role of Ellen's principal teacher in riding and traditional academic subjects, John encourages Ellen to explore new fields of knowledge and to delight in "the felt exercise and enlargement of her own powers" (519):

French gave her now no trouble; she was a clever arithmetician; she knew geography admirably, and was tolerably at home in both English and American
history . . . . He [John] put her into Latin; carried on the study of natural
philosophy they had begun the year before, and which with his instructions
was perfectly delightful to Ellen; he gave her some works of stronger reading
than she had yet tried, besides histories in French and English, and higher
branches of arithmetic. These things were not crowded together so as to fa-
tigue, nor hurried through so as to overload. Carefully and thoroughly she
was obliged to put her mind through every subject they entered upon; and just
at that age, opening as her understanding was, it grappled eagerly with all that
he gave her . . . . (463-64)

John provides information for Ellen, but he skillfully uses Ellen's own
questions to draw her attention from one topic to the next in a manner that
resembles Cambell's method. Campbell describes the principles of association psychology:

When a number of ideas relating to any fact or event are successively introduced into my mind by a speaker; if the train he deduceth coincide with the
general current of my experience; . . . my mind accompanies him with facility, glides along from one idea to another, and admits the whole with pleasure. (83)

Warner's dialogue between John and Ellen explains similarly:

"When two things have been in the mind together, and made any impression,
the mind *associates* them; and you cannot see or think of the one without
bringing back the remembrance or the feeling of the other."

"And in that way you would heap associations upon associations?"

"Yes, until our storehouse of pleasure was very full." (479-80)

In a like manner Warner uses association psychology to instruct her
reader while creating pleasure for her reader with her instructive story.[9]

Eventually Ellen becomes able to function at an intellectual level she
otherwise might never have attained. The education John gives Ellen duly
impresses her uncle and guardian, Mr. Lindsay, who builds on that beginning by providing Ellen with "masters for the piano and singing and
different branches of knowledge" (535). He provides her with riding lessons and sends her to a scholar-tutor, Mr. Muller, twice a week. Despite

Mr. Lindsay's ample resources for Ellen's education and although he recognizes in Ellen "a face of uncommon intelligence" (521), he fails to use John's methodology of association of ideas and questioning:

> Mr. Lindsay, to be sure, had answered her questions with abundant kindness and sufficient ability; but his answers did not, as those of her brother often did, skilfully [sic] draw her on from one thing to another, till a train of thought was opened which at the setting out she never dreamed of . . . . Mr. Lindsay told her what she asked, and there left her. (519)

Mr. Lindsay dispels Ellen's ignorance in a kind and forthright manner, but ignores the principles of association psychology that Warner both uses in her writing and would have her reader learn to use. Despite his generally positive attitude, Mr. Lindsay seeks to enlighten Ellen's understanding with an education that reifies knowledge; his method focuses on developing Ellen's informational base even at the expense of her inquisitive mind. Warner thus "enlightens" her reader's "understanding" by "dispelling ignorance" as John, Mr. Lindsay, Mrs. Montgomery, Alice, and Miss Fortune do for Ellen.[10] By using principles of association psychology on her reader, Warner creates circumstances in which her reader "glides along from one idea to another, and admits the whole with pleasure" (Campbell 83)—offering both immediate instruction and a method of continuing self-education.

Warner's distinction between the pedagogical styles of John and Mr. Lindsay incorporates Campbell's other element of understanding: to evince "conviction" in the reader through the rhetorical quality, "argument" (2-3). On the one hand, the less sympathetically portrayed of Ellen's two male teachers, Mr. Lindsay, defies Campbell's and Warner's shared dictum of encouraging personal conviction. Mr. Lindsay's interest lies in teaching Ellen what *he* would have her learn. John, on the other hand, leads Ellen until she no longer needs a leader. Using her lessons as guides to help meet various challenges produces conviction.

Although Ellen's developing perspicuity (in Campbell's sense; see 18 above) might dispel her natural childhood ignorance, she must utilize her life trials to bring conviction to her understanding. Near the end of the story, Warner explicitly articulates "enlargement of her own powers" (519) as an important element of understanding. When John has helped Ellen become intellectually free, Ellen becomes his intellectual equal.[11]

By combining the contrasting pedagogical methods of John and Mr. Lindsay, Warner unifies Campbell's requirements by which the understanding may be enlightened.

Warner also combines Ellen's religious and secular education with various challenging incidents to produce Ellen's enlightened understanding. Where education acts to "dispel ignorance" (Campbell 2-3), incidents that test Ellen's ability to direct her behavior according to her education act to "vanquish error." For example, in order to deal with the several challenges posed by her abrasive aunt, Miss Fortune, Ellen must dispel ignorance by studying scripture and vanquish error by applying the practical lessons she has learned from her scriptural studies.

From the beginning of their relationship, Ellen develops a realistic understanding of Miss Fortune's character and attitude, an "understanding" that Warner extends to the reader. Rather than pitting Ellen's will against that of her cold and unfeeling aunt, Warner makes Ellen's struggle an internal one: she must strive to subdue her pride. When Miss Fortune withholds a letter sent to Ellen by her dying mother, Ellen responds with furious anger. Disobeying Miss Fortune's order to remain inside the house, Ellen rushes out into the woods where she feels as if nature itself might soothe her anger. Even "amid the sweet influences of nature" (148), however, Ellen is unable to calm herself.

At this point in the story begins Ellen's real conquest of error (Campbell's prerequisite for enlightening the understanding), which, through creating sympathy for Ellen, Warner offers her reader. In the forest, Warner first makes Ellen aware of Alice, the woman whose Christian teachings will augment and reinforce those of Mrs. Montgomery. Ellen, recognizing her own error in dealing with the instance of the concealed letter, tells Alice about the incident. Ellen understands she has

> ". . . never been so bad in my life as I have been since then. Instead of feeling right I have felt wrong all the time, almost,—and I can't help it. I have been passionate and cross, and bad feelings keep coming, and I know it's wrong, and it makes me miserable. And yet, oh! ma'am, I haven't changed my mind a bit,—I think just the same as I did that day; I want to be a Christian more than anything else in the world but I am not,—and what shall I do!" (151)

Through Ellen's experience, Warner makes clear to her reader that "enlightening the understanding" (Campbell) entails more than mere "book learning." To come to real understanding, Ellen must use her biblical lessons to "vanquish" the error of her behavior. To take effect, these two elements of understanding—to dispel ignorance and to vanquish error—must act in harmony. Such incidents reveal Warner's Christian attitudes; self-command and submission to God's will can free one from earthly problems.[12] Only by resigning one's will to God can one triumph unscathed over one's earthly trials. Through actions and language that produce sympathy in the reader for Ellen, Warner extends to the reader Ellen's Christian lessons: we must all forgive our "misfortunes" if we are to find peace. If Warner is finally to influence her reader's will, she must augment her reader's understanding with appeals to her reader's other faculties—such as the imagination.

Of the second of Campbell's four ends of discourse, the appeal to the imagination, Campbell writes,

> The second thing requisite is that his reasoning be attended to: for this purpose the imagination must be engaged. Attention is prerequisite to every effect of speaking, and without some gratification in hearing, there will be no attention, at least of any continuance. (73)

Campbell argues that a writer should address a reader's imagination "by exhibiting to it a lively and beautiful representation of suitable object" (3). As a contemporary writes of Warner's work, "she is always real and vivid in her imagination of places and scenes, as if she wrote from a ready and keen observation" (Chapman 335-36). Chapman here reveals the nineteenth-century sense of imagination as dependent on close observation. This requisite connection between the real and the imaginary differs from the twentieth-century sense that the imaginary is "not real."[13]

Using the word "fancy" interchangeably with the word "imagination," Campbell explains the transition from the appeal to the understanding, to that of the imagination: "knowledge, the object of the intellect, furnisheth materials for the fancy" (2). Warner's words approach those of Campbell when she says, "how profitable this kind of musing is,—where memory furnishes material which imagination takes" (Mary Kelley 220). According to Campbell, at the same time that effective language should enlighten the understanding with its message, it should also provoke the fancy with such characteristics as vivacity, beauty, sublimity, and novelty.

A writer creates vivacity in language by offering the reader "striking resemblances in the imagery, which convey, besides, an additional pleasure of their own" (Campbell 73). Much like the "lively idea," vivacious language involves a pleasurable play on the reader's memory that stems from an association of ideas. Warner uses the Twenty-Third Psalm, for example, to open the book. Using the Twenty-Third Psalm as a sign immediately recognizable to the nineteenth-century general reader, Warner stimulates her reader's experience of what Campbell calls rhetorical "resemblance" (215, 285, 304). The reader experiences a direct identification between the Twenty-Third Psalm as stored in memory and an immediate sensation of Ellen's recitation. Thus, from the very beginning of her book, Warner uses Campbell's principle of "resemblance" to awaken her reader's attention.

Campbell explains different ways by which an author can create vivacity and so capture a reader's attention.[14] During the nineteenth century, it was commonly assumed that discourse could gain "its object by means of splendid images and sublime expressions" (295), writes Elizabeth Starling in her short article, "Female Eloquence," in *Godey's Lady's Book* (1852). Thus, according to Campbell, vivacious language may both attract the reader's attention and provide impact to a message. An author can use "The Less for the more General" (Campbell 299) to imply a likeness by association and so produce linguistic vivacity. Warner uses the Twenty-Third Psalm at the very beginning of *The Wide, Wide World* thus to foreshadow the very nature of Ellen's future trials. Warner shares information rhetorically with her reader, securing the reader's attention by playing on the imagination, while she keeps Ellen mercifully unaware of her future. Similarly, Warner uses a relationship between "the part and the whole" (Campbell 294) when she presents woodland botanical specifics

> . . . the white wind-flower, and pretty little hang-head Uvularia, and delicate
> bloodroot, and the wild geranium and columbine; and many others the names
> of which she did not know. They were like friends to Ellen; she . . . seemed
> to purify herself in their pure companionship. (336)

The wild flowers stand for all nature and so show that all nature itself is Ellen's friend, so creating a sense of vivacity and sublimity for the reader.

Beauty, the second linguistic characteristic meant to please the imagination, similarly appeals to the reader. Campbell explains with a description of resemblance: "the mind receives a considerable pleasure from the discovery of resemblance" (74). Metaphor, an aesthetically pleasing sort of resemblance (294), brings intellection and beauty together in an appeal to the imagination. Warner uses floral metaphors to provide her readers with explicit lessons. For example, in the Marshman's greenhouse, John asks Ellen what associations she makes with the white camellia. Ellen replies that the flower "seemed to speak to her," reminding her of "what I ought to be—and of what I shall be if I ever see heaven; it seems to me the emblem of a sinless pure spirit,—looking up in fearless spotlessness." Warner uses the camellia to bring another association to the reader, that of a parable:

> ". . . Do you remember what was said to the old Church of Sardis?—'Thou hast a few names that have not defiled their garments; and they shall walk with me in white, for they are worth.'" (325)

Here Warner combines metaphor with a Christian parable that the nineteenth-century reader would easily and comfortably recognize. The "Literary Notice" for Mrs. E. W. Wirt's *Flora's Dictionary* (1856) shows the religious connection to floral metaphors that was generally assumed in the nineteenth century: "To foster a love of flowers is to awaken the heart to the veneration and the love of God" (*Godey's* 87).

The "Literary Notice" for Henrietta Dumont's *The Floral Offering* (1852)[15] ties the language of flowers directly to the faculty of imagination:

> We know of no more beautiful idea than the construction of a language of flowers. How fitted to become the types of the hues of passion, and the bud, bloom, and decay of hopes, feelings, and even life itself. . . . the language of flowers is an important . . . new field for the exercise of . . . the imagination. (*Godey's* 165)

"The language of flowers" was used in nineteenth-century American women's discourse to appeal to the imagination in two ways. Authors sometimes used floral metaphors, providing explanations for the reader as Warner does with the camellia above. Authors could also use floral metaphors without supplying explanation, however, because various flowers had specific referents in the nineteenth-century rhetorical context.

Discussing this idea in terms of Warner's book *Queechy*, Susan K. Harris explains:

> By the nineteenth century, the association of specific flowers with specific meanings had become a symbolic code, in large part reflecting liberal Protestantism's assumption that nature reflects God's intentions (in other words, it is a symbolic system compounded of other codes characteristic of a specific subculture). (80)

Several reference books from the era provide current readers with insight into the now largely forgotten code. For example, in her *Flora's Interpreter, and Fortuna Flora*,[16] published both before and after the heyday of *The Wide, Wide World*, Sarah Josepha Hale "reads" the camellia just as Warner does:

> UNPRETENDING EXCELLENCE.
> The chaste *Camellia's* pure and spotless bloom,
> That boasts no fragrance, and conceals no thorn
>   William Roscoe (38)

Campbell and various mid-nineteenth-century women writers thus provide bases for Harris's later theoretical work in hermeneutics and semiology—Campbell providing a psychological and rhetorical explanation for the use of words as signs (258-59) and Wirt, Hale, Dumont, and others providing volumes of specific illustrations.

Campbell explains "the sublime," the third linguistic characteristic meant to provoke the fancy and so please the imagination, as language that "raiseth admiration" (3). Admiration, according to Campbell, pleasurably

> ariseth on the perception of magnitude, or of whatever is great and stupendous in its kind . . . For there is a greatness in the degrees of quality in spiritual subjects . . . (3).

Ellen's response to John's question about the camellia (above) reflects Campbell's notion of admiration. Associating the purity of the camellia with spiritual subjects through Ellen's admiration, Warner appeals to the reader's imagination. With Ellen's admiration of the camellia, Warner also exemplifies Campbell's concept that effective language should provoke the fancy with sublimity; Warner's language provokes the reader's fancy to such "magnitude" that as Ellen is overcome with tears, so is the reader, a response commonly acknowledged by reviewers.[17]

Warner's use of "novel" language, the fourth characteristic by which a writer might please his or her reader's imagination, reflects Campbell's own near contradiction in advocating language that is, on the one hand, "reputable, national, and present" (139-51), and is, on the other hand, "novel." The tremendous popularity of *The Wide, Wide World* established Warner as a reputable writer, allowing her to have a hand in setting the standard for what was considered reputable language in the mid-nineteenth century. Her language, thus popularly established, could hardly be considered "novel" to her later readers. Her language did, however, have a catchiness that piqued her earlier readers' imaginations. The very title of her best-selling book, for example, *"The Wide, Wide World,"* became a national idiom, perhaps because of its initial novelty.[18] In Campbell's terms, Warner's appeals to her reader's imagination gratify the fancy more by her language's vivacity, beauty, and sublimity, than by its novelty.

That the critics of Warner's day recognized her emphasis on the imagination is beyond question. Devoting an entire "Editors' Table"[19] feature to Warner's *The Wide, Wide World*, the editors of *Godey's Lady's Book* (1851) focus on the appeal to the imagination:

> God has implanted the imaginative faculty deeply in our nature . . . . He never intended that we should crush out this faculty more than any other with which He has endowed us.

Acknowledgment of *The Wide, Wide World*'s positive impact on the reader's imagination came from English critics as well as American. Reviewing jointly *The Wide, Wide World* and Amy Lothrop's (pseudonym of Anna Warner, Susan Warner's sister) *Glen Luna* for *The Prospective Review*, John Chapman describes: "None could read them without benefit. They move the heart and charm the imagination . . . " (314).

Campbell's third appeal—to the passions—proceeds from his appeals to the understanding and the imagination. Just as Warner imparts understanding both to Ellen and to the reader, and just as she stimulates both Ellen's and the reader's imaginations, so she both shows the reader Ellen's passions moved and, through sympathy, moves the reader's passions. To Campbell, moving the passions takes the reader from a rational understanding of something to the motivation to do something with that under-standing: "thus passion is the mover to action, reason is the guide" (78). Appealing to the understanding "without the pathetic, the speaker is as far from his purpose as before" (78).

Campbell saw sympathy as one "main engine" of passion's motion. "Sympathy is not a passion, but that quality of the soul which renders it susceptible of almost any passion, by communication from the bosom of another" (131). Throughout *The Wide, Wide World*, sympathy functions as a principal "engine" of motion, as Ellen expresses her passion, alter-nately weeping, then rejoicing, then weeping again only to rejoice again and then to weep. Campbell characterizes sympathy as a definite process of mind, which communicates passion from one person to another: "It is by sympathy we rejoice with them that rejoice, and weep with them that weep" (131). Without sympathy, one becomes an object, just as Ellen without sympathy feels herself ". . . a thing to be cared for, taught, gov-erned, disposed of . . . " (538). Without Warner's efforts to gain the reader's sympathy for her story and her ideology, the reader, too, would consider Ellen (and most probably the book itself) an object. Feeling sympathy with Ellen might embarrass a twentieth-century reader bent on critical analysis; critics contemporary to Warner, however, praised her use of sympathy to identify the reader with Ellen: ". . . we have felt during [our] . . . perusal . . . carried away by a sympathy as young and enthusi-astic as Ellen Montgomery's" (Chapman 314). More recent reviewers observe that *The Wide, Wide World* was "read with the most heartfelt sympathy . . ." (Pattee 57).

Campbell maintains that readers are taught to respond not just by rea-soning, but by feeling. The reader "carried away by a sympathy," re-sponds to Ellen's expression of passion. Describing the phenomenon, Campbell (96) says in verse:

> With them who mourn, we sympathize in tears;
> If you would have me weep, begin the strain,
> Then I shall feel your sorrows, feel your pain.
> Francis.

Ellen weeps constantly; she weeps in the presence of the reader while she fights weeping in the presence of the other characters in the story:

"I will *not* trouble mother—I will not—I will not," she resolved to herself as she got out of bed, though the tears fell faster as she said so. . . . "I'll not go down 'till papa is gone," she thought, "he'll ask me what's the matter with my eyes." . . . and tears fell from the eyes of each that the other did not see. (15-17)

Ellen seeks to control her passions so as to spare herself sympathy from other characters; yet, in many cases, it is with these same scenes of Ellen's struggles for self-control that Warner effectively engages the sympathy of her readers. During these scenes Warner portrays Ellen by herself, alone with her struggles. Away from other characters, Ellen is alone with the reader; in such privacy the reader feels free to share Ellen's tears.

Campbell specifies the vehicles for moving the passions as "probability, plausibility, importance, proximity in time, connexion of place, relation of the actors or sufferers to the hearers or speaker, interest of the hearers or speaker in the consequences" (81). Warner uses these rhetorical vehicles in varying degrees in *The Wide, Wide World*. Of them, the reader finds particularly striking attention to "importance" and "relation of the actors or sufferers to the hearers or speaker."[20]

As Campbell defines it, "importance" adds brightness and strength to an idea by its own nature: by how much the circumstance departs from the ordinary, by how much concern the author develops in the reader for the characters (either in their number or in their significance to the story), and by how much the actions and circumstances of the story affect the reader. Warner attends to such rhetorical importance by interweaving events with the lessons learned from those events. For example, when Ellen finds a letter on her bed, the event's importance derives from "how much the circumstance departs from the ordinary" and from the "significance to the story" of both Ellen and her mother. Since the letter is Ellen's reward for having been kind to another child (Nancy) who had been mistreating her, the event becomes a vehicle that teaches about the rewards of kindness.

Campbell's rhetorical "importance" is a major element in Warner's presentation of Ellen's discovery of her mother's death. Warner has already developed in her reader a sense of Mrs. Montgomery's importance to Ellen; Ellen loves her mother and believes that she needs her mother to teach her the moral and spiritual requirements for the "good" life for which she yearns. More practically, Mrs. Montgomery's fate will determine where Ellen will finally live and with whom. Finally, through the sympathy Warner develops in her reader for Ellen, Mrs. Montgomery's death strengthens Warner's Christian message. It forces her reader to consider Christian behavior as presented in the story and the story's personal impact.

Through the incident of Mrs. Montgomery's death, Warner also moves the reader's passions because of the "relation of the actors or sufferers to the hearers or speaker." Through the sympathy that Warner has already established in the reader for Ellen, the incident of Mrs. Montgomery's death takes on greater importance. The event means Ellen must become a better Christian because she must rely more heavily on her own strengths. Mrs. Montgomery's death also affects Ellen's future by putting her at the mercy of various relatives who may act as her custodians. Because of the reader's sympathy for Ellen, Warner can move the reader's passions when at Mrs. Montgomery's death the reader becomes concerned where Ellen will live, and with whom. Through sympathy for Ellen, the reader is moved to feel bereft, burdened, and worried.

Warner moves her reader's passions also toward the joy and eventual salvation that she sees as the ends of Christian suffering:

> Ellen's cup of enjoyment was running over. . . . from one joy to another her thoughts went,—till her full heart filled and fixed on the God who had made and given them all, and that Redeemer whose blood had been their purchase-money. . . . she thought of the one dearer yet from whom death had separated her;—yet living still,—and to whom death would restore her, thanks to Him who had burst the bonds of death . . . . And the thought of Him was the joyfullest of all! (405)

With the vehicle, sympathy, Warner moves the reader to feel Christian passion. In addition to being moved to tears, the reader is moved to Christian joy.

Although Campbell's and Warner's rhetorical methods for moving the passions resemble each other, the two authors do not agree on the nature of passion itself. For Campbell, passion plays an integral part in the psychology of human nature. Warner, however, demonstrates a basic contradiction regarding passion. On the one hand, she seems quite comfortable using rhetorical devices to move her reader's passions for Christian ends. On the other hand, however, apart from recognizing Christian joy, Warner generally views human passion as ungodly and a stumbling-block to relinquishing one's will to God. On the one hand, Campbell finds an appeal to the passions necessary if an author is to transform a reader's understanding into the will to act. On the other hand, Warner asserts that one must obliterate earthly passion in order to resign his or her will to God's will.

The difference between Campbell's and Warner's views of the nature of passion seems to lie in their readings of Christianity. Considering Warner's rhetorical position apart from her theological stance, however, one can see that her views regarding passion as a rhetorical appeal are not far from those of Campbell. *The Philosophy of Rhetoric* teaches the writer to use the passionate appeal to cause a reader to alter his or her will. Warner's rhetorical method reflects Campbell's theory in that she enlightens her reader's understanding, pleases the imagination, and moves the passion in order to influence her reader's will to subjugate his or her passions and will to God. Warner has little problem appealing to the reader's passion to her own ends.

Campbell's fourth and final end of discourse, influencing the will, results when an author artfully combines convincing the reader's judgment with interesting the reader's passions. One must mix the argumentative with the impassioned to produce vehemence of contention. *The Wide, Wide World* focuses on Ellen's efforts to gain control of her own will, "to overcome evil with good." By establishing sympathy in the reader for Ellen's persona and the trials she undergoes to control her will, Warner encourages the reader to improve as a person and come closer to God, so that, by extension, the world will become a better place. Thus, Warner's two levels of operation, her manipulation of the story and her manipulation of the reader through rhetorical technique, reflect Campbell's strictures for the four ends of discourse. Within the book itself, Warner mixes reason and Christian passion in Ellen's experience to enable Ellen finally to control her will. By establishing her reader's sympathy for Ellen, Warner convinces her reader's judgment and arouses her reader's passions and so influences her reader's will.

A writer influences the reader's will by mixing appeals to the reason with appeals to various passions. To "stimulate to action" a reader's will, the writer combines appeals to the reader's reason with appeals to passions of hope, patriotism, ambition, emulation, and/or anger (5). Combining appeals to the reader's reason with appeals to passions of sorrow, fear, shame, and/or humility may result in dissuading the reader from action (5). To persuade or dissuade a reader, the writer should combine an appeal to reason with an appeal to passions of joy, love, esteem, and/or compassion (5). Whereas justness in reasoning roots passion more deeply, mingling reason with carefully selected other elements should ultimately influence the will of the reader as the author desires (5).

According to Campbell, the interplay of reason and the passion of hope, patriotism, ambition, emulation, and/or anger stimulates a reader's will to action. This interplay occurs in an episode of *The Wide, Wide World* in which children playing on a Sunday (against Ellen's religious tenets) shun Ellen after she refuses to join them in play on the Lord's day. Later that evening, John directs Ellen to read a particular passage from the Bible, which gives her comfort. As a result, Ellen goes to bed happy, despite her mistreatment by the children earlier in the day (305-14). Ellen's ability to read the passage logically, when combined with the passage's message that appeals to her sense of the rightness of emulation, serves to move Ellen toward continued emulation of biblical precepts. Similarly, the reader who comprehends the logic of this episode and combines it with a sense of emulation (of Ellen) is influenced to act accordingly.

Campbell says that mixing reason with passions of shame and humiliation acts to dissuade the reader from action (5). Warner uses this combination to dissuade her reader from such evil behaviors as cause a person not to "feel right" in an episode in which several children are making Christmas presents at Ventnor. They draw lots to determine which materials will go to which child, but when Ellen's turn comes to pick from the materials, she peeks at the available scraps and takes the most desirable one for herself. Almost immediately, she experiences shame, sorrow, and humiliation for what she has done. That night, John teaches her about "man's weakness." These two events that combine reason and a passion of shame, etc. influence Ellen to recognize and regret her error (296). Ellen resolves not to repeat cheating; Warner, through the sympathy she has created in the reader toward Ellen, implicitly asks the reader to follow suit.

Warner combines an appeal to the reader's reason with an appeal to passions of joy, love, esteem, and/or compassion in her depiction of Alice's death. After Ellen's mother dies, her mother/sister/Christian mentor figure, Alice, dies. Ellen is bereaved, but she has learned the importance of placing good before personal sorrow, and so applies her reasoning (that through doing good comes reward) to thoughts of the love and esteem she felt for Alice, thereby adding compassion for Alice's final suffering. Again, Warner appeals to the reader to rethink his or her own behavior in such a circumstance. The episode combines appeals to the reader's reason and passion through the love and esteem Warner has developed in the reader for the character, Alice. Warner thus influences the reader's will to consider the needs of others before indulging in one's own self-pity.

Warner defines the challenge of Christianity as attaining self-command or self-will. When the exemplary Christian's (Alice's) will leaves her, then "Alice was gone." As Alice dies, Warner describes her arms: "The will and the power that had sustained them were gone" (441). Will, according to Warner, stands as the one human faculty that a person striving to be a Christian cultivates through and above understanding (education), imagination (appreciation of art and nature), and passion (controlling those impulses that might inhibit one's journey toward Christ). For the Christian who has attained the ability to command his or her own will, that will remains the last of these four faculties to depart the mortal body. The passion that Warner elicits both in Ellen and in her reader through the event of Alice's death serves to transform Alice from friend and mentor into a figure emblematic of the complete Christian. Warner uses the very sorrow over Alice's death to reinforce all the Christian principles that Alice personified in her life.

By the end of the nineteenth-century version of the book, Ellen exhibits a firmly established will:

> To Mr. Lindsay and his mother she was the idol of life, except when, by chance, her will might cross theirs. She had what she wished and did what she pleased . . . .
> "I will do what I think right come what may." (538-41)

The end of the story as republished in the twentieth century (1987) and including an originally unpublished final chapter (see note 11) similarly shows a respect on the part of the supporting characters for Ellen's will. Ellen's new husband John spares no effort or expense to satisfy Ellen. The newly published final chapter describes the care John has taken to respect Ellen's will for privacy and study. Ellen responds with gratitude as she explores the "easy circumstances and refined habits, . . . the appliances of comfort and ease and literary and studious wants" (574) of her new living situation with John, a situation that includes her own private room with access to John's study: "'That door is always open,' said he,—'except when you choose to lock it'" (577). The potentially confining[21] physical arrangement of Ellen's rooms requires Ellen to continue to exercise her will; Ellen (and so the reader) can not relax her will on earth even to such benign paternalism as John offers.

Either with or without the recently supplied final chapter, Warner's subject matter progresses in a logical manner. Ellen has accomplished what her mother and Alice had taught her; she has purposely willed herself to God. She has done so through a lifelong journey, beginning with the understanding that she receives from her mother as set out in the early chapters. Her journey continues through the imagination, so that resemblances and images draw her attention to her mother's motto enabling Ellen to reinforce academic lessons with experiential ones. She journeys further, and learns to accept the joys of Christian passion and to reject those passions that might mar her Christian behavior. Finally, as an adult she completes her life's mission: she attains the self-control to submit her will to that of God.

"The sole and ultimate end of logic," such as that presented by Warner's subject matter, "is the eviction of truth" says Campbell, but "pure logic regards only the subject, which is examined solely for the sake of information. Truth, as such, is the proper aim of the examiner (33). "To convince the hearers . . . to influence the will, and persuade to a certain conduct" is the proper end of eloquence (33). It is Warner's use of language that effects conviction in the reader of the book's truth(s).

As Ellen moves through the book and so exercises her faculties, so does the reader. Warner first attends to the reader's understanding of the Christian's challenge: each of God's creatures faces major obstacles in the struggle to overcome evil with good. The reader experiences appeals to imagination with the author's appeal to what is general[22] in the nineteenth-century memory. For example, Warner presents biblical verses and floral coding with which her reader is probably familiar. Next, Warner moves the reader's passions through the vehicle of sympathy, identifying Ellen's feelings with those of the reader. Finally, Warner succeeds in influencing the reader's will by combining the reason or understanding presented at the outset—how to overcome evil with good—with the passion the reader experiences through sympathy with Ellen throughout the book's episodes.

In addition to providing the current reader with an experience closer to that of *The Wide, Wide World*'s contemporaries, reading the book in light of George Campbell's four ends of discourse also illuminates the differences in critical responses to the work that occur between the nineteenth and twentieth centuries. Differences in cultural assumptions between the centuries generate differences in critical responses—especially regarding issues of whether the book's elements are realistic; whether its language is pious, over-blown, and/or trite; and whether its plot is formulaic, predictable, and/or too unlikely.

Some twentieth-century critics judge a book's worth by examining whether the book's characters, scenes, plot, etc. seem realistic. Alfred Habegger, for example, wrote *Gender, Fantasy, and Realism in American Literature* "to make a case for seeing realism[23] as the central and pre-eminent literary type in democratic society" (vii).[24] He separates "works of realism" from "popular literature," stipulating that realism can "correct" the "cartoon cut-outs" produced by the "scribbling women" of the nineteenth century and states that "many works of realism were written as conscious corrections of a large body of popular literature" (vii).[25] Speaking of Warner in particular, Habegger notes that she "had her head in a rosy dream of fiction half the time" (4). Another twentieth-century critic, Russel B. Nye, faults domestic fiction for its lack of probability:

> we may find their complicated plots and preposterous characterizations, the melodramatic devices of missing wills, lost heirs, identifying birthmarks, and improbable coincidences [risible] . . . (4).

In an article that treats these works as "useful historical materials" (2), Nye considers them to be far-fetched.

Offsetting such negative criticism as that of Habegger and Nye,[26] Jerome Bruner reminds his reader that language functions to construct "realities" (8)—a concept that differs widely from "realism." Delimiting current literary and cognitive mores can illuminate realities of Warner's own construction: social, theological, and generally instructive in ways limited neither to "homely details" (Habegger ix) nor to an unembellished reflection of its heroine's life. Whereas some critics have panned *The Wide, Wide World* (and mid-nineteenth-century American women's literature in general) for its failure to portray its subjects realistically, especially in terms of the protagonist's, Ellen's, characteristic (silly and unrealistic) tendency to burst into tears, Baym, Tompkins, Harris, and others seek to redeem these works from such allegations. Baym chronicles the flow and ebb of criticism regarding "nonrealism"—judged a fault in American fiction by the influential Lionel Trilling ("Melodramas" 131). Tompkins challenges critics who characterize women authors as "generally thought to have traded in false stereotypes, dishing out weak-minded pap . . . as manipulators of . . . self-justifying clichés" (*Sensational* 124). In her chapter discussing Warner, Harris explains that twentieth-century professional readers who "reject religious pieties as well as emotional expression, . . . have tended to lambaste nineteenth-century women's novels as 'pious' in addition to being 'sentimental'" (*19th-Century American* 79). For example, Mott writes, "*The Wide, Wide World*, is, at best, mawkish in its sentimentality and pious to a repulsive degree" (123). Bode speaks of Warner's appeal "through various means, including elements so divers as ostentatious piety" (179). Douglas describes the period's literature as "sentimental heresy" (*The Feminization* 11). Affirming Harris, however, more recently Tichi writes,

> if a positivist, materialist, and scientific-technological bent dominated later nineteenth- and twentieth-century American history, feminist criticism argues, that direction nonetheless must not conceal a mid-nineteenth-century ethos of evangelistic piety. (224)

Reading *The Wide, Wide World* in the light of Campbell's philosophy helps a twentieth-century reader bring more to the work than the need and/or expectation for realism. A twentieth-century reader-critic can use Campbell's theory of the quadripartite ends of discourse to appreciate the rhetorical appeals appropriate to the era in which the work was presented rather than judge it by anachronistic standards.

Another literary critical assumption that varies from nineteenth to twentieth centuries has to do with language use. Warner uses language that often causes readers to draw on commonalties within their discourse communities, thus drawing them together into a community of belief. Richard Weaver[27] explains: "It is now a truism that the homogeneity of belief which obtained three generations ago has largely disappeared" (167).[28] Warner's language, which often depends on her readers' community of meaning or knowledge of cultural codes, advocates a cultural cohesiveness contrasting the individualism requisite for the nineteenth-century's developing market economy.

Although language such as Warner's may use "terms which scandalize the modern reader with their generality" (Weaver 166), that language, ringing familiar to her contemporary reader, appealed to the reader's imagination and passions. Nineteenth-century critic John Hart praises the author and her work: "No living writer has such power to open the fountains of tears, or to warm the heart with thoughts and instances of goodness" (387). Although twentieth-century readers may consider mid-nineteenth century American language that evokes such reader responses to be "spread-eagle," "high-flown" (Weaver 165), "tear-jerking," overused, trite, pious, and/or sentimental, Warner's contemporary readers appreciated such use.[29]

Harris, reflecting Weaver, writes that such language "reveals an extraordinarily high degree of social cohesion, of shared values and worldview" (32). Harris adds, "mid-nineteenth-century American women's novels . . . rooted in institutional conventions [and] need only nod toward them for their readers to 'fill in' the outline they have sketched" (32). Warner's "spacious language" plays on a reader's imagination through association in terms of hermeneutic codes—symbolic and cultural codes (such as floral or biblical) that she could rightly assume were accessible to her readers.[30] Thus Warner uses language to invite the reader to participate in the text in a manner that, as Bruner stipulates, "must recruit the reader's imagination" or encourages "the reader to 'write' his own virtual text" (25).[31]

In addition to differences between the centuries' cultural assumptions and expectations regarding what is realistic and what is "good" language, literary critical assumptions regarding plot also vary from nineteenth to twentieth centuries. Warner creates action in *The Wide, Wide World* primarily to show the protagonist's inner growth. Twentieth-century critics looking for plot are usually disappointed.[32] Mott recognizes a plot, which he derisively calls the "Home-and-Jesus formula": an orphan growing up in an alien family (123). More specific to the text, Helen Waite Papashvily writes, "The book, almost devoid of plot, told the story of Ellen Montgomery, a lachrymose, pious, hypersensitive orphan sent to live with unknown relatives in the country" (3-4). Nina Baym (*Woman's*) generalizes, "the genre that I am calling woman's fiction" features an "overplot" formula that

> tell[s] one particular story about women . . . a heroine who, beset with hardships, finds within herself the qualities of intelligence, will, resourcefulness, and courage sufficient to overcome them. (22)

Tompkins (*Sensational* xi-xix) argues against evaluating any nineteenth-century woman's fiction by criteria of twentieth-century conventions—especially the criterion, plot:

> the function of these scenarios is heuristic and didactic rather than mimetic, they do not attempt to transcribe in detail a parabola of events as they "actually happen" in society; rather, they provide a basis for remaking the social and political order in which events take place. (xvii)

Tompkins later asks her readers

> to set aside some familiar categories for evaluating fiction . . . to see the sentimental novel not as an artifice of eternity answerable to certain formal criteria . . . but as a political enterprise, halfway between sermon and social theory.

Because the work comprises various instructive scenarios, each of which functions as its own parable—a story and lesson, often linked by transition scenes of horseback or boat ride—it seems more appropriate to read *The Wide, Wide World* as a series of biblical parables than as a linear narrative with a unified plot. Tompkins points out that Warner herself "never referred to her books as 'novels,' but called them stories, because, in her eyes, they functioned in the same way as Biblical parables" (*Sensational* 149).[33] That is, events in *The Wide, Wide World* proceed "as variations of a single ideological proposition" (Tompkins, *Sensational* 61), reminiscent of how the Bible presents parables.

Where the twentieth-century reader may find such reiteration tedious, the nineteenth-century reader may have found comfort in a familiarity that motivated him or her to identify with the protagonist's daily challenges, lessons, and, finally, triumphs. Sharing Ellen's lessons in submission, education, discipline, and self-reliance, receiving "profitable lessons in real life" (Hale, *Godey's*) through a montage of scenarios or Bible-like parables, would have been common among Warner's nineteenth-century audience; a reader of either century can sense a thematic unity or focus without regard to plot.

Tompkins reconceptualizes for twentieth-century readers what 1850s American women's literary texts were and how they functioned:

> When literary texts are conceived as agents of cultural formation rather than as objects of interpretation and appraisal, what counts as a "good" character or a logical sequence of events changes accordingly. (*Sensational* xvii)

Tompkins reverses critics' negative judgments regarding an "overplot" in such texts as *The Wide, Wide World*, arguing "for the positive value of stereotyped, . . . formulaic plots." Tompkins seems to understand the formulaic plot in a light similar to what Harris later calls a hermeneutic code—the formulaic plot does not lack originality, but, like familiar language, draws readers into a community of belief. In response to the problems that arise when one applies twentieth-century assumptions to mid-nineteenth-century fiction, Harris, noting the limits of Baym's (1978) notion of "overplot," laments such critical "entrapment in the interpretive conventions of the American academic literary establishment" (*19th-Century American* 10). Her message is clear: one should neither reduce such literary texts to linear narrative nor mold them to fit twentieth-century academic "interpretive conventions" that may not be those of nineteenth-century readers.

Contemporary critic, Isabelle White, reads *The Wide, Wide World* within a nineteenth-century cultural context. Describing the 1850s as a period when "competing interests struggled to shape a definition of America" (31), White pictures Ellen's task as using the good values of "domesticity and evangelical Christianity" to overcome the evil values stemming from "the individualism and materialism basic to an expanding market economy" (31).[34] Although White reads the subject matter of *The Wide, Wide World* within a nineteenth-century cultural and economic context, she does not read the work within a nineteenth-century rhetorical context. She does not appreciate the rhetorical aspects of *The Wide, Wide*

World that counter such individualism, aspects such as Warner's use of "spacious" language, hermeneutic codes, recognizable "plot," and Biblical-like montage of scenes (or parables) that draw readers together as they share lessons in personal growth and self-reliance.

Considering *The Wide, Wide World* in terms of Campbell's theoretical four ends of discourse adds a rhetorical dimension to the book's historical, economic, cultural, and feminist readings to date. Using Campbell's theory as a heuristic device, a reader can gain awareness of appeals that progress from simple understanding through resemblance and sympathy to will. Campbell's theoretical four ends of discourse encourage readers to respond in multiple ways without privileging one faculty over another. Readers can subordinate arguments about which reading is best to admit various readings that enrich each other and thus the experience of the book. Finally, an awareness of Warner's rhetorical appeals to the reader's multiple faculties may not only help put *The Wide, Wide World* into the canon of American literature, but also nudge the criteria for admission toward reading experiences beyond understanding.

NOTES

[1] *The Nation* so endorses Hart's views (back cover).

[2] Reviews of Hart's *Female Prose Writers of America* (1852) appear in "Literary Notices," *Godey's Lady's Book*, 44 (January 1852): 91 and later in 49 (December 1854): 554. This "splendid gallery of distinguished literary women" is also reviewed in "Literary Notices," *Ladies' Repository* 15 (April, 1855): 251.

[3] Susan Warner began writing and publishing under the name, Elizabeth Wetherell.

[4] Janet Gabler-Hover, *Truth in American Fiction: The Legacy of Rhetorical Idealism*; Nan Johnson, *Nineteenth-Century Rhetoric in North America*; and Winifred Bryan Horner *Nineteenth-Century Scottish Rhetoric: The American Connection* describe the nineteenth-century American rhetorical context.

[5] Johnson examines Campbell's influence on the nineteenth-century rhetorical climate:

> Campbell's redesign of the aims and procedures of rhetoric proved to be one of the most powerful accomplishments of the New Rhetoric, an accomplishment that shaped the philosophical context in which rhetoric would be defined throughout the nineteenth century. (20)

[6] Tompkins's "Afterword" to The Feminist Press's 1987 edition of *The Wide, Wide World* describes its popularity: "No novel written in the United States had ever sold so well. It went through fourteen editions in two years and became one of the best-selling novels of the nineteenth century both in this country and in England" (584). Tompkins elsewhere (*Sensational*) names *The Wide, Wide World* as a model for subsequent popular books, citing Maria Cummins's *The Lamplighter* its "direct literary descendant" (148). Goshgarian prefaces her chapter about *The Wide, Wide World* with remarks about this successor (76-79).

[7] Although the twentieth-century reader may feel more comfortable referring to *The Wide, Wide World* in terms of plot, referring to the text as a compilation of parables reflects its structure and the author's stated purpose more accurately.

[8] Elizabeth B. Keeney's *The Botanizers: Amateur Scientists in Nineteenth-Century America* discusses the importance of nature study in nineteenth-century American culture.

[9] Further, Warner educates her reader (enlightens the reader's understanding) to principles of association psychology with such explicit explanations.

[10] By directly educating her reader—both through Ellen's example and by association sharing Ellen's lessons with the reader—Warner distinguishes her work from the genre she disavows, the dangerously mindless romance novel.

[11] *Godey's* reports, "Both love and matrimony are insinuated in the concluding pages" ("Editors'" 186). In last chapter, published in 1987, John and Ellen marry, thereby reinforcing the argument that the free intellectual course is the most desirable intellectual course. "A Note on the Text" (8) preceding the 1987 edition, edited by Tompkins, explains that the final chapter was not available to the nineteenth-century reader. Presumably, the original editors felt the omitted chapter would have added unnecessary length to the book.

[12] Tompkins elaborates this theme (162-3). Reading Warner differently from Tompkins, Isabelle White begins her argument by calling Ellen's work to subdue her anger "sacrifices made in this world [that] would be more than compensated for in the next" (33). Later in her article, however, White's reading reflects that of Tompkins: "at the end of the novel Ellen is no longer in a hierarchical arrangement in which she is always subjected to external authority. She has internalized authority . . ." (36). Further, "submitting to religious authority began to approach learning to rely on oneself" (37).

[13] *The Random House College Dictionary.* Ed. Jess Stein. Revised ed. New York: Random House, 1975: 663.

[14] Nineteenth-century readers, writers, and scholars valued rhetorical figures and tropes whereas some twentieth-century scholars consider them (in Richard Lanham's terms) "difficult ornaments" (130).

[15] The subtitle reads, *A Token of Affection and Esteem. Comprising the Language and Poetry of Flowers.*

[16] Sarah Josepha Hale's *Flora's Interpreter, and Fortuna Flora* (1832, 1860, and 1865) explicitly shows how floral metaphors derive from nature and Christianity and also draw on both intellection and beauty (Campbell) in language. She first stimulates her reader's intellect with scientifically oriented sections of botanical information: "Hints to the Lovers of Nature," "Botanical Explanations," "Inflorescence; or, Manner of Flowering," "Classes and Orders," and "Poisonous Plants." She then provides "Flora's Interpreter"—a book length illustration of Harris's later observations in hermeneutics. Hale introduces her work:

> Flowers have always been symbols of the affections, probably ever since our first parents tended theirs in the garden of God's own planting. They seem hallowed from that association, and intended, naturally, to represent pure, tender, and devoted thoughts and feelings. The expression of these

feelings has been, in the ages, the province of poetry; therefore we must refer to the poets in order to settle the philology of flowers. (iii)

This book is just one of many nineteenth-century studies connecting flowers to theological and/or everyday ideas.

[17] Helen Waite Papashvily refers to the "tremendous audience who wept over the pages (of *The Wide, Wide World*) for more than half a century" (10-11).

[18] Campbell felt novel language should please the imagination. Yet, perhaps because "the novel's novelty, precisely, challenges 'real religion's' timelessness" (Goshgarian 113), Warner expressed antipathy toward the genre, "novel." Preferring to have her works read as "stories," Warner claimed "to have written a fiction non-novel" (Goshgarian 113). The sermon-like quality of *The Wide, Wide World* reflects her belief that reading should be instructive rather than fictional (*Godey's* first announcement of the work attests to this characteristic). Warner, through John, specifically prescribes that a young woman's reading should lack fiction. John supplies Ellen with " . . . two or three new English periodicals . . . . There was no fiction in them either; they were as full of instruction as of interest" (464). Even more directly, near the end of her story, Warner, again through John, directs Ellen (and implicitly directs the reader) to "read no novels" (564).

[19] As was customary, *Godey's* uses the plural here, making it unclear whether the article was written by Hale alone or by others or collaboratively.

[20] Twentieth-century critic Baym points out the identification of the heroine with readers in nineteenth-century American women's fiction. (*Woman's*, 16-17). Campbell offers a rhetorical appreciation of how authors accomplish this identification of interests between characters and a reader.

[21] Referring to a "disconcerting image of woman's confinement," Freibert points out

The house arrangement says it all. Ellen's room is "between" John's rooms, having, as Ellen remarks, "no entrance but through other rooms where no one can intrude." Later she remarks that her door is "for you [John] to walk in here. Not for me to walk in there." "Both," he protests, but the reader senses that in her "heaven on earth" Ellen is less than free" (68).

[22] "Rhetoric, as was observed already," Campbell reminds his reader, "not only considers the subject, but also the hearers and the speaker. The hearers must be considered in a twofold view, as men in general, and as such men in particular" (71).

[23] Habegger uses the terms "realistic" and "realism" interchangeably: "My own volume . . . regard[s] the realistic novel as a principal type of American fiction" (vii).

[23] Habegger uses the terms "realistic" and "realism" interchangeably: "My own volume . . . regard[s] the realistic novel as a principal type of American fiction" (vii).

[24] Habegger differentiates "realistic fiction" from "homely detail":

> The popular women-authored books of the 1850's all purveyed a certain complicated fantasy, . . . that they embodied . . . in homely detail . . . Women's fiction posed a challenge to men, a challenge taken up in a definitive way in realistic fiction. (ix)

Habegger thus ostensibly diminishes efforts of such critics as Papashvily who touts Warner's depictions of women's daily life—"rich, poor and middle class, in town and in the country"—as so realistic as to elicit requests from readers for "'the receipts [recipes] for the biscuit on which the cat set his paw'; for 'splitter,' 'for the cake Alice made,'" (7) and the like.

[25] Habegger's full quotation humorously bemoans

> the fact that many works of realism were written as conscious corrections of a large body of popular literature in the background leaves us with the unwelcome burden of reading that literature. (vii)

[26] Although William Rose Benét's *Reader's Encyclopedia* declares that realism began with certain eighteenth-century English novelists, the reference attributes the literary trend's rise to the later advance in science (910). C. Hugh Holman's *A Handbook to Literature* explains,

> The realist eschews the traditional patterns of the novel. In part the rise of *realism* came as a protest against the falseness and sentimentality which the realist thought he saw in romantic fiction" (398).

Freibert and White state "realism did not become a literary movement in America until the 1880's, nor was the term realism in use during the period," (183).

[27] Weaver devotes a full chapter, "The Spaciousness of Old Rhetoric" (164-185), to explaining and documenting this principle.

[28] The use of language to draw readers together directly contrasts twentieth-century Stephen Toulmin's concept that in a pluralist (or fragmented) culture, language should specify all premises, a gesture that reinforces each individual's right to his or her own private discourse.

twentieth-century valuation of discourse that comes from and provokes "thinking for one's self" (172).

[31] Bruner cites Wolfgang Iser's claim here.

[32]

HE DIDN'T KNOW HOW TO APPRECIATE NATURE.

Drawing by Bruce Eric Kaplan; © 1992
The New Yorker Magazine, Inc.

[33] Professor of Divinity and preacher, Campbell, in his *The Philosophy of Rhetoric*, presents a prescriptive approach for writing religious sermons. His combination of moral philosophy and rhetorical appeals are especially appropriate to Warner's sermon-like writing. I do not argue that Warner (or any of her contemporaries) specifically used Campbell's approach to theological writing; rather, I argue that viewing Warner's work within Campbell's rhetorical context can provide the current reader with an enriched experience of the book that more closely approximates that enjoyed by the nineteenth-century reader.

[34] Extrapolating from White's thesis, one can see that Warner poses the values of domesticity and Christianity against capitalism's "possessive individualism" (C. B. Macpherson) in two respects. Ellen's domesticity must overcome a rising middle-class capitalist economy as represented by Miss Fortune's rural production as well as

with an enriched experience of the book that more closely approximates that enjoyed by the nineteenth-century reader.

[34] Extrapolating from White's thesis, one can see that Warner poses the values of domesticity and Christianity against capitalism's "possessive individualism" (C. B. Macpherson) in two respects. Ellen's domesticity must overcome a rising middle-class capitalist economy as represented by Miss Fortune's rural production as well as overcome a landed corporate capitalism as represented by the aristocratic Lindsays. The story concludes that Ellen's domesticity and Christian values can overpower both.

White notes that Warner's act of writing implicitly promotes an individualism attendant on the economic ideology against which *The Wide, Wide World* argues. That is, Warner's individualistic activity, writing, placed her in the very market economy her book seeks to malign. White's reading extends that of Douglas, who sees Warner's heroine, Ellen, as a willing pawn of the market system: "Ellen feels the quintessential pleasure of the consumer" (64). Although the criticism of Douglas and White might be justified, Warner's claim "that she wrote *The Wide, Wide World* on her knees" (Douglas 109), diminishes the author's image as a willful contender in the market economy.

Harriet Beecher Stowe

IV

HARRIET BEECHER STOWE'S *UNCLE TOM'S CABIN:* MODELING COMMUNAL WILLFULNESS

In a letter discussing Harriet Beecher Stowe's *Uncle Tom's Cabin* (1852),[1] "Famous abolitionist[2] and anthologist,"[3] Lydia Maria Child, remarks: "Mrs. Stowe's truly Great work, 'Uncle Tom's Cabin,' has done much to command respect for the faculties of woman" (69). *Uncle Tom's Cabin* not only reflects the faculties of its author, but also plays upon those of its reader.[4] Describing the faculty psychology of Scottish rhetorician, George Campbell, so popularized in the first half of the nineteenth century in America, Nan Johnson writes: "Campbell's concept of the human mind as comprising the discreet faculties of the will, the imagination, the understanding, and the passions . . . [shows how] language links empirical knowledge with the mental faculties" (5). Applying Campbell's *Philosophy of Rhetoric* (1776) to Stowe's *Uncle Tom's Cabin* does just that. The rhetorical analysis reveals how Stowe uses language to link arguments against The Fugitive Slave Law of 1850 with her readers' mental faculties (beyond understanding alone) to effect personal and social change.

As described in the Introduction above (3) and elsewhere (Berlin 19, Gabler-Hover 4, Johnson, *Nineteenth-Century* 20, Kitzhaber 52), the theories of the Scottish New Rhetoricians fairly permeated the rhetorical atmosphere of mid-nineteenth-century America. In addition to the moral preoccupation and aesthetic theories engendered by The New Rhetoric that informed nineteenth-century discourse in general, Stowe's family situation offers a possibility of her even more direct contact with Campbell's theory. Her brother, only two years her junior, Henry Ward Beecher, studied and taught rhetoric, including the principles of George Campbell: "At Amherst, Beecher was required to study Campbell, Blair, Whately . . . " (Gabler-Hover 48). "The eighteenth- and nineteenth-century rhetorical renaissance was impelled by ministers such as Hugh Blair, George Campbell, and Henry Ward Beecher" (5), Gabler-Hover continues. She also shows that the influence of rhetorical study and of Campbell's *Philosophy of Rhetoric*, in particular, extended beyond the confines of the university and into "a cultural life that lasted well into the final decades of nineteenth-century America" (4). More specifically, the "movement in rhetoric . . . directly touched many of the century's great American authors" (4-5).[5] Whether Stowe consciously applied Campbell's principles while writing *Uncle Tom's Cabin*, or whether Campbell's rhetoric so permeated mid-nineteenth-century discourse that it could not help but permeate the time's fiction, the twentieth-century reader enriches his or her experience of the book by appreciating its appeals to various faculties.

Referring to her book as "these sketches" (9), Stowe weaves her tale almost wholly of incident and episode. Jane Tompkins describes the book's structure as "typological narrative":

> the plot abounds with incidents that mirror one another. . . . It is this tradition rather than that of the English novel that *Uncle Tom's Cabin* reproduces and extends; for this novel does not simply quote the Bible, it rewrites the Bible as the story of a Negro slave. (*Sensational* 134)

The book's arrangement thus resembles biblical parables;[6] in fact, describing her own purpose and form, Stowe (1856) explains that her work should be "understood to be a parable—a story told in illustration of a truth or fact" (Kelley 250). Elaine Showalter likens the book's organization to a quilt:

> Stowe continued to think of her writing as the stitching together of scenes. Uncle Tom's log cabin . . . is a metanarrative marker of the Log Cabin quilt, which in its symbolic deployment of boundaries, is particularly apt for Stowe's novel of the borders and conflicts between the states, the races, and the sexes. In the novel, Uncle Tom's cabin becomes the iconographic center upon which narrative blocks are built up. . . . The novel does not obey the rules which dictate a unity of action leading to a denouement, but rather operates through the cumulative effect of blocks of events structured on a parallel design. (*Sister's* 155)

Discussing certain "white" authors such as Stowe, Kristin Herzog describes a nineteenth-century narrative arrangement pattern that does not simply

> move "from point A to point B to point C," but . . . spin[s] "something like a
> spider's web—with many little threads radiating from a center, criss-crossing
> each other" until finally "the structure will emerge . . . and . . . meaning will
> be made."[7] (177)

These images of nineteenth-century narrative arrangement patterns[8] answer those twentieth-century critics who would denigrate fiction refusing to present a unified and linear plot. One such critic, C. Hugh Holman, defining "plot" in his *A Handbook to Literature*, writes, "The one great weakness good writers of fiction avoid is the use of incident and episode which are extraneous to the essential purposes of the plot pattern" (358). Critics of the 1850s, however, praised such arrangement: *"Uncle Tom's Cabin* . . . was a work of high literary art. . . . the tale developed through a series of incidents and dialogue, which constantly arose in interest and dignity" ("Editor's" 551). Focusing on action to the exclusion of unifying mandates may obscure the complexities an author offers his or her reader.

Stowe's "sketches" present interrelated mandates: abolishing slavery, establishing evangelical Christianity, and promoting a nineteenth-century feminist responsibility for righting the world's wrongs. These mandates reflect a fundamental ideology, the importance of which easily overrides her bifurcated "plot."[9] Although Tompkins, Showalter, and Herzog demonstrate that *Uncle Tom's Cabin*, like Susan Warner's *The Wide, Wide World* (1851), focuses more directly on ideology than on plot, an overview of the plot provides a background for examining Stowe's work in the light of Campbell's theory.

The action in *Uncle Tom's Cabin* moves back and forth, following the separate ordeals of two slaves, Uncle Tom and Eliza, each formerly owned by a genteel Kentucky plantation owner fallen into financial difficulties, Mr. Shelby. The book's action spreads apart geographically.[10] After the untimely death of his second master, Uncle Tom is "sold down the river" to the immoral and tyrannical cotton plantation owner Simon Legree. At the same time, threatened with the loss of her only child, Eliza ventures north, facing various dangers presented by nature and human cruelty, and eventually reuniting with her husband, George, another fugitive slave. As Stowe's scenes alternate between the North and the South, Stowe's slave characters present a spectrum of possible reactions to the Fugitive Slave Law, ranging from Tom's submission to Eliza's rebellion. Each change of scene shows various responses to Eliza's and Tom's chosen roles: some characters help and some hinder Eliza's escape; some characters show respect for and some impatience with Tom's compliance. The journeys of Eliza and Uncle Tom are not interrelated actions: Eliza ends up in Canada, surrounded by her family; Uncle Tom ends up murdered on a southern plantation. Nonetheless, despite the fact that Eliza in her flight and Tom in his submission represent different reactions to slavery and despite the fact that they travel in different directions, they do communicate Stowe's unified message:

> The totalizing effect of the novel's iterative organization and its doctrine of spiritual redemption are inseparably bound to its political purpose: to bring in the day when the meek—which is to say, women—will inherit the earth. (Tompkins, *Sensational* 139)

G. M. Goshgarian takes this concept of ideology's "ability" to unify action in "domestic fiction" and extends the idea to mid-nineteenth-century women's fiction: "ideology acquired the unifying power that unified scribbler fiction" (73). She thus implies a comfort that the mid-nineteenth-century reading public must have found in such narrative arrangement.

The ideology of *Uncle Tom's Cabin*, expressed through the medium of Stowe's rhetoric as well as through its overt subject matter, drew tumultuous public response:

> By the close of 1852 more than one million copies had been sold in America and England; editions and copies almost without number had been published in France; and it had been translated and published in the German, Italian, Spanish, Dutch, Danish, Swedish, Flemish, Polish, Magyar, Russian, and other languages. In the German language there were no less than twelve different translations. It was reviewed in all the journals in the land—receiving the most fierce and bitter denunciation and the highest possible eulogium. . . . above all, it was <u>read</u> as few books were read before. (Clark, Rev. D.W., D.D. 172)

"Uncle Tom's Cabin; or, the Man That Was a Thing" first appeared serialized from June, 1851, to April, 1852, in *The National Era*, an abolitionist Washington D.C. newspaper. Reactions to the tale, which appeared in book form as *Uncle Tom's Cabin; or, Life among the Lowly* (1852), varied according to the backgrounds and vested interests of readers. Favorable reviewers hailed the work as, "THE STORY OF THE AGE! . . . Testimonials of the strongest kind, numerous enough to fill a volume, have already appeared in the public journals" (Rev. of "Uncle," *The National Era* 62). The book also drew international acclaim:

> it is something to the credit of our National Literature, that it has produced the book of the age—a work which has gone through more editions and translations, been more widely circulated, and has created more sensation and discussion than any work issued during the present century. If it has covered Southern Slavery with odium, it has established beyond all question the power of American genius. ("Uncle Tom Abroad" 46)

Generally, Stowe's book had an immediate and powerful impact on readers in the North and abroad. Southern reactions were usually negative.[11]

Until recently, the tremendous political and social impact of *Uncle Tom's Cabin* on American culture had garnered comparatively more attention than had the book's rhetoric.[12] Nonetheless, in large part, Stowe created the book's impact through her play on the reader's multiple faculties and her use of sympathy.[13] Applying Campbell's *Philosophy of Rhetoric* to the work—exploring its appeals to the reader's understanding, imagination, passions, and will—may help explain the work's extraordinary rhetorical power and impact.

Campbell describes enlightening the understanding, the first of his ends of discourse, as proposing

> . . . either to dispel ignorance or to vanquish error. In the one, his aim is their *information*; in the other, their *conviction*. Accordingly the predominant quality of the former is *perspicuity*; of the latter, *argument*. By that we are made to know, by this to believe. (2-3)

Stowe presumes that her reader may err regarding law, religion, and gentility. Stowe addresses all three counts. From the first chapter of *Uncle Tom's Cabin*, the reader encounters a situation "not distinctly comprehended," a "position disbelieved or doubted" in opposition to the "law"—

represented by the lawful institution of slavery in general and The Fugitive Slave Law in particular. "The law considers all these human beings, with beating hearts and living affections, only as so many *things* belonging to a master," Stowe writes (19). In Chapter Two she applies the observation to George Harris: "This young man was in the eye of the law not a man, but a thing" (22). Yet, "the man could not become a thing" (24), she continues. The original subtitle of *The National Era* serial, "The Man That Was a Thing," points to the law's error, as do such chapter headings as "Showing the Feelings of Living Property on Changing Owners," "The Property Is Carried Off," and "In Which Property Gets into an Improper State of Mind." "In *Uncle Tom's Cabin* the central perception . . . is how humans may overcome reification—reduction to the status of a thing" (25), explains Josephine Donovan (1991); she continues, "Stowe recognizes that the phenomenon of objectification was at the heart of slavery's evil" (36). Stowe recognized evil not only in the objectification of slaves, but also in their use as commodities that wear out through use. Slave owner Legree explains his agricultural economics:

> "The yellow woman I got took in. I rayther think she's sickly, but I shall put her through for what she's worth; she may last a year or two. I don't go for savin' niggers. Use up, and buy more, 's my way;—makes you less trouble, and I'm quite sure it comes cheaper in the end." (395)

As she uses the character of Legree to expose the error of complacency with the custom and body of law that defines human beings as material commodities, Stowe enlightens her reader's understanding.

Stowe's reader faces similar errors regarding nineteenth-century assumptions about religion. Augustine St. Clare, Tom's second benign owner, and Marie St. Clare, Augustine's vain and treacherous wife, voice sharply differing religious views. Marie takes the view of her theological mentor that the Bible supports the institution of slavery as God "'hath made everything beautiful in its season' . . . some were born to rule and some to serve" (216). Augustine challenges the popular view pointedly, "Religion! . . . Is that which can bend and turn, and descend and ascend, to fit every crooked phase of selfish, worldly society, religion? . . . No!" Augustine's argument challenges both Marie St. Clare and the view popularized by such publications as *The Southern Literary Messenger*.

The reader may respond to this and other similar "sketches" with a change of conviction that enlightens his or her understanding. The reader might also recognize errors in cultural assumptions regarding the nature of gentility. The stereotypical Marie St. Clare epitomizes the appearance of gentility as she prepares for church. Her gorgeous dress, "in full force,—diamonds, silk, and lace, and jewels, and all" like the "fashionable church" where she could "be very religious . . . and very pious on Sundays" (213) contrasts sharply with Stowe's own evangelical views of modesty, represented by the stereotypical (model) child, Evangeline. "Eva" readily gives her gold vinaigrette to the slave, Mammy, and would welcome the ailing slave to her own more comfortable bed. As the mother represents aristocracy in an unfavorable light, the daughter shines with Christian and democratic spirit. The tension and contrast between Marie's and Eva's differing senses of gentility may serve to highlight errors in the reader's own assumptions and so enlighten his or her understanding.

Augustine St. Clare later compares the English gentility to the American—the aristocratic capitalist to the slave-owner. Each nation's ruling class appropriates lower classes "body and bone, soul and spirit," for its own use and convenience. "The slave-owner can whip his refractory slave to death,—the capitalist can starve him to death" (269). As St. Clare differentiates between the English capitalist/aristocrat and the slave-owner, he redeems the American oppressor somewhat: slave-owners mingle with the class they degrade, whereas the English capitalists/aristocrats do not. St. Clare argues that since the slave-owners' families and children "cling to and assimilate with" (272) the families and children of slaves, American laws are wrong to "forbid any efficient general educational system" (272). Further, Stowe has her readers understand that should one generation of slaves be educated, "the whole thing would be blown sky high" (272). Stowe seeks to "vanquish the error" of those who believe "it is the educated, the intelligent, the wealthy, the refined, who ought to have equal rights, and not the canaille" (314), and so to enlighten her reader's understanding.

As Stowe corrects the reader's unfounded assumptions about the nature of gentility, she offers a "disbelieved or doubted" (Campbell), or at least unusual, position. She writes:

> it is you considerate, humane men, that are responsible for all the brutality and outrage wrought by these wretches; because, if it were not for your sanction and influence, the whole system could not keep foot-hold for an hour (395-96).

The brutality of such slave traders and owners as Mr. Haley and Simon Legree is made possible and sustained by those who remove themselves from such lowlife and who reflect the genteel character of Senator Bird. Again, Stowe's "sketches" showing the reader social "wrongs" (9) enlighten the reader's understanding.

Stowe further enlightens her reader's understanding by providing new information that dispels ignorance. Nineteenth-century Northern readers and others unfamiliar with the character and nature of Negroes discovered in *Uncle Tom's Cabin* much new information about them: their psyche, their socioeconomic situation, and their ability (and willingness) to embrace Christianity. Stowe provides this new information by contrasting the characters of the black and the white races[14] and implicitly paralleling the character and status of Negroes to that of women: "women and Negroes are almost interchangeable when it comes to their natural virtues" (Herzog 115-16).[15] Carole Pateman puts this parallel between women and slaves into a contractual context, showing that both "domestic contracts between a master and his (civil) slave" and the marriage contract were "labour contracts":

> The civil master of a family attains his right over his wife through contract, his right over his servant was contractual and, according to some classic contract theorists and defenders of American slavery, so was his right over his slave. (116)

Identifying slaves with women, Stowe utilizes the psychological principles of association and sympathy (Campbell 132-33) to open her reader's mind (and heart) for receiving understanding. Further, identifying slaves with women enables Stowe to enlighten her white reader's understanding of the Negro as being human, as opposed to being an object.

When Stowe provides a picture of the African as "an elevated and cultivated race" having "a gorgeousness and splendor of which our cold western tribes faintly have conceived" (212), she dispels her reader's ignorance. She characterizes "the negro race" by

their gentleness, their lowly docility of heart, their aptitude to repose on a superior mind and rest on a higher power, their childlike simplicity of affection,
and facility for forgiveness. (213)[16]

The reader learns that the Anglo-Saxon race is "a 'masculine' race, the
Negro a 'feminine' and childlike people" (xviii), adds James M. McPherson. Stowe's women and blacks share the same spiritual superiority and
position from which to "save society from patriarchy, commercialism, and
injustice," a view known as "romantic racialism" (Herzog 114). Certainly, these sexist and racial characterizations may seem offensive to
twentieth-century readers.[17] However, "to attribute to someone the simplicity of a child . . . especially in the middle of the nineteenth century,
was a compliment of the first order" (Fredrickson 103). Herzog observes
Stowe

> to celebrate the intuitive strengths and communal instincts of women and
> slaves who expressed the "sympathies of Christ" as opposed to the
> "sophistries of world policy" (457).

> It was from the lowly of her society that she expected a new religious and
> political order to emerge. (120)

Immersed in a Christian ethic, the nineteenth-century reader was more
inclined to attribute superiority to one who was gentle, meek, and submis-
sive.[18] Stowe reinforces that understanding, specifically dispelling any
ignorance on the part of the reader about the Christian identity of the meek
as women, children, and Negroes.

This nineteenth-century sense of "difference" extended to the very methods by which the genders were thought to exercise their faculty of understanding.[19] Stowe enlightens her reader's understanding beyond issues of
gender and ethnicity to the issues of how all people might come to "feel
right" through their cognitive methods.[20] Eighteen-fifties readers held
assumptions different from those of twentieth-century readers regarding
masculine and feminine cognitive habits.[21] The influential editor of
Godey's Lady's Book, Sarah J. Hale (1858), quotes Henry Thomas
Buckle of *Frazer's Magazine* to describe the differences between men's
and women's thinking:

"Now, there are several reasons why women prefer the deductive, and if I
may so say, ideal method. They are more emotional, more enthusiastic, and
more imaginative than men; they therefore live more in an ideal world; while
men, with their colder, harder, and austerer organizations, are more practical
and more under the dominion of facts, to which they consequently ascribe a
higher importance." (463)[22]

Stowe's thoughts on this matter reflect those of Hale; Mrs. Bird criticizes
her husband's cognitive processes:

"I hate reasoning, John,—especially reasoning on such subjects. There's a
way you political folks have of coming round and round a plain right thing;
and you don't believe in it yourselves, when it comes to practice." (102)

Our good senator in his native state had not been exceeded by any of his
brethren at Washington, in the sort of eloquence which has won for them im-
mortal renown! How sublimely he had sat with his hands in his pockets, and
scouted all sentimental weakness . . . .
   He was as bold as a lion about it, and "mightily convinced" not only himself, but everybody that heard him;—but then his idea of a fugitive was only
an idea of the letters that spell the word . . . . He had never thought that a fugitive might be a hapless mother, a defenceless child . . . . (110)

Hale's and Stowe's observation that men and women have fundamental
differences in thought patterns parallels Stowe's information about ethnic
differences, politely maligning the "nature" of the Anglo-Saxon male.[23]
Stowe thus adheres to Campbell's dictum to dispel ignorance and so enlighten the reader's understanding about the cognitive and cultural under-
pinnings of slavery. Further, she instructs her reader to shun elements of
induction, organizational austerity, and cool, logical, practical methods in
a book that works heavily through appeals to the imagination and passions
and through the vehicle of sympathy.
   Stowe extends her reader's enlightenment of an understanding of race
into lessons about religion: "the negro is naturally more impressible to
religious sentiment than the white" (270). Elsewhere, Stowe jars the
reader by juxtaposing Marie St. Clare's racist brand of religion with the
sentence preceding that sketch: "they [Negroes] will exhibit the highest
form of the peculiarly *Christian life*" (213). She interweaves information
about the Negro's native Christian sentiment together with information
about the Negro's courage to maintain a sense of justice and Christian

duty. As he protects his wife, Eliza, and their child during their escape to Canada, George proclaims:

> But you have n't got us. We don't own your laws; we don't own your country; we stand here as free, under God's sky, as you are; and, by the great God that made us, we'll fight for our liberty till we die." (232)

In this sketch Stowe compares George's brave defense to the heroism of Hungarian youth, and then directly addresses the reader, challenging him or her to "dispel ignorance":

> it was a youth of African descent, defending the retreat of fugitives through America into Canada, of course we are too well instructed and patriotic to see any heroism in it . . . When despairing Hungarian fugitives made their way, against all the search-warrants and authorities of their lawful government, to America, press and political cabinet ring with applause and welcome. When despairing African fugitives do the same thing,—it is—what *is* it? (232)

Unlike Tom, whose southward progression exemplifies Christian humility and submission, George, on his journey North, exemplifies the "Christian soldier," replete with courage and heroism in the face of injustice. Providing her reader with new information about Negroes' character and place in history, Stowe dispels the reader's ignorance about the Fugitive Slave Act and so enlightens her reader's understanding.

The extent to which Stowe's writing reflects any one of Campbell's four ends of discourse illuminates her intent. In a broad sense, she intends primarily to appeal to her reader's understanding and will. She has written an overtly abolitionist book that begins by clearly and pointedly appealing to her readers' faculties of understanding that in a Christian culture people cannot be bought and sold and ends by appealing to her Christian readers' faculties of will to "see to it that *they feel right*" (515). In order to activate these faculties in her readers, however, Stowe relies heavily on those faculties that "spur" (Campbell's term) them: the faculties of imagination and passions. Although Stowe's main intent is to change the law through understanding and willful action, her method reflects her belief that one should base such action on those faculties closer to the feelings: the imaginative and impassioned (qualities she associates with women and slaves). Her object may derive from the cold, hard, dominant logic she attributes to Anglos and males,[24] but her process (or means of persuasion) derives from appeals to the reader's imagination and passions.

Campbell's second of four ends of discourse, pleasing the imagination, involves fixing the reader's attention. Touching on Campbell's ideas, the article, "Novels: Their Meaning and Mission" (*Putnam's Magazine*, 1854), discusses the dependence of literary discourse on its "relation to the *imagination* and the *fancy*"[25] (390). From the beginning in her first chapter, Stowe fixes the reader's attention with her sketch of the two "*gentlemen*" (emphasis Stowe's), Mr. Haley and Mr. Shelby. She immediately sets up a tension in the reader's mind between laughing at Haley or fearing his evil foreshadowing. The reader experiences what Campbell calls "vivacity": "Nothing contributes more to vivacity than striking resemblances in the imagery, which convey, besides, an additional pleasure of their own" (73). Haley strikes the reader, in part pleasurably, as a buffoon:

> He was much over-dressed, in a gaudy vest of many colors, a blue neckerchief, bedropped gayly with yellow spots, and arranged with a flaunting tie, quite in keeping with the general air of the man. (11)

The vivacity of Stowe's description draws her reader to her narrative's abolitionist argument: "its main object was to kindle and purify the imagination, while fanning into a livelier flame the slumbering charities of the human heart" (Rev. of *Uncle*, Dec. 1852). Thus she answers Campbell's call to present "qualities in ideas which principally gratify the fancy . . . [succeeding in] awakening and preserving the attention . . . " (Campbell 73).

Having secured the reader's attention initially through the images of Haley, Mr. Shelby, Eliza, and her son, Harry, Stowe keeps that attention fixed through her use of "resemblance," which, according to Campbell, contributes to vivacity. Campbell shows that "resemblance" in a reader's mind has rhetorical "connexions" both to style and to sentiment (294). Stowe's appeals to the imagination in terms "pictorial rather than cerebral" have been treated elsewhere, although not with reference to Campbell:

> Her imagination and writing style are pictorial rather than cerebral; she imagined these characters as a three-dimensional picture—or a vision, as she

would have put it—and somehow managed to transfer the picture to the reader's imagination. These visual images, like the musical leitmotiv in an opera, become associated with themes of love, suffering, loss, death, power, subordination, courage, salvation. (McPherson xiv)

Campbell's discussion of imagination—and its elements of resemblance and metaphor—has more to do with an association of ideas than an association of images.

Stowe shares with her reader a concept similar to the one Campbell terms "resemblance":

> The psychologist[26] tells us of a state, in which the affections and images of the mind become so dominant and overpowering, that they press into their service the outward senses, and make them give tangible shape to the inward imagining. (*Uncle Tom's Cabin* 457)

Similarly in the rhetorical philosophy of Stowe's brother, Henry Ward Beecher, "spiritual evolution occurred through the imagination," and involved a person's "experience, his heart, and his imagination" (Gabler-Hover 57). Stowe presents to her reader a sense of how the imagination works in an immediate theological context, showing Uncle Tom to resemble Christ. Not only would Tom "lay down his life for" his master (47), but he knowingly martyrs himself to enable all others, slaves and owners, on the Shelby place to continue living in peace and safety:

> If I must be sold, or all the people on the place, and everything go to rack, why, let me be sold. I s'pose I can b'ar it as well as any on 'em. . . . I never have broke trust . . . It's better for me alone to go, than to break up the place and sell all. (55)

Stowe continues to build the resemblance between Tom and Christ throughout the tale.[27] Shortly after his owner, Legree, had ordered Tom's whipping, Tom, reminiscent of Jesus at His crucifixion, prays: "O Jesus! Lord Jesus! have you quite forgot us poor critturs?" (420). The analogy between Tom and Jesus continues, as the whipped Tom reads from his Bible:

> Tom opened, at once, to a heavily marked passage, much worn, of the last scenes in the life of Him by whose stripes we are healed. . . . "Father forgive them, for they know not what they do." (421)

Finally, Tom experiences a comforting vision:

> Suddenly everything around him seemed to fade, and a vision rose before him of one crowned with thorns, buffeted and bleeding. . . . gradually, the vision changed: the sharp thorns became rays of glory; and, in splendor inconceivable, he saw that same face bending compassionately towards him, and a voice said, "He that overcometh shall sit down with me on my throne, even as I also overcame, and am set down with my Father on his throne. (456)

Stowe then has Tom offer "his own will [as] an unquestioning sacrifice to the Infinite" (456). Thus Stowe places her own views within a mid-nineteenth-century rhetorical context in which appeals to the understanding (which may well be her prime concern) best function through appeals "that are the transcendent production of the imagination," so tying the imagination to "everything that is in *rapport* with the infinite in man" ("Novels" 391). In Campbell's terms, through the element of imagination, "resemblance," Stowe fortifies her appeal to the reader's understanding.

In addition to presenting Tom as a Christ figure, Stowe also plays on the reader's imagination through biblical references. Of Eliza's escape northward, crossing the frozen Ohio River, a slave messenger reports to Mrs. Shelby, "Wal, she's clar 'cross Jordan. As a body may say, in the land o' Canaan" (91). With the reference here to the Eliza's crossing the Ohio, Stowe uses "popular imagery which rang certain bells in the average reader's mind" (Herzog xx), connecting Joshua's crossing of the Jordan to the "underground railroad."

Stowe also creates a resemblance between the fugitive slave, Eliza, and the refined white senator's wife, Mrs. Bird by establishing their joint identities as mothers. Mrs. Shelby pleads with her husband, "Am not I a woman,—a mother? Are we not both responsible to God for this poor girl?" (91). Stowe implicitly appeals to her reader's (Christian) reverence for motherhood[28] with this rhetorical question. Stowe reinforces the association between abolition and motherhood. Having crossed the Ohio on the ice, the fugitive slave, Eliza, finds herself in the kitchen of Senator and Mrs. Bird. In replying to Mr. Bird's questions, Eliza, noting Mrs. Bird's mourning dress, asks: "Ma'am . . . have you ever lost a child?" The two women realize a bond that they offer to share with the reader: "Then you will feel for me" (105).[29] Readers, domestic and foreign, responded to what Campbell calls "resemblance in imagery." Reporting from Europe, for example, George Sand (1853) writes:

> little white and black angels, in which every woman recognizes the object of her love, the source of her joys and her tears. In taking form in the mind of Mrs. Stowe, these children, without ceasing to be children, take also ideal proportions, and come to interest us more than all the personages in love romances. (15)

The identity, "mother," shared among the fugitive slave, the aristocratic white woman, and the reader creates a "resemblance in imagery" that awakens the reader's attention. While she appeals to the reader's respect for Eliza's motherhood, Stowe also appeals to the reader's sense of Christian responsibility for one's sisters and brothers. By sharing an identification as Christians, through the principle of "resemblance," the reader should feel a resemblance to Stowe's Christian characters and so feel "responsible to God for this poor girl." Further, by implicitly asking the reader to feel responsible to Eliza, Stowe asks the reader to feel responsible for other fugitive slaves.[30]

General references to Christian doctrine such as Eliza's comment on her crossing the ice floes of the Ohio, "The Lord helpd me; nobody knows how much the Lord can help 'em, till they try," (104) link the text to the nineteenth-century reader's typical theological training. Stowe pleases her contemporary reader's imagination through religious association by having Eva recognize the image of "a bright angel" in Topsy (336) and having George Shelby knock "Legree flat upon his face": "he would have formed no bad personification of his great namesake triumphing over the dragon" (488). Certainly, the hymn lyrics sprinkled throughout *Uncle Tom's Cabin* create in the reader's mind a resemblance between personal theological memories and the book's words.

In addition to more general resemblances, Stowe uses more specific metaphors to please her reader's imagination. Speaking of Henry Ward Beecher, Stowe's brother, however, Gabler-Hover argues that very general concepts can be thought of as metaphors as well. Claiming the central metaphor in Mark Twain's *Adventures of Huckleberry Finn* to be slavery itself, Gabler-Hover's explanation extends to *Uncle Tom's Cabin* as well:

> . . . the message of Henry Ward Beecher [is] that truth implies an openness to the experience of suffering . . . . The largest metaphor for suffering in the novel is the institution of slavery, which hides behind a lie of purported benevolence and the myth that blacks are lesser beings who do not suffer . . . . (50)

Stowe does show the suffering of blacks and so may (in Gabler-Hover's terms) use such suffering as a metaphor for slavery. Questions of which concept is a metaphor for which (or whether this likening might be more properly termed a synecdoche) point to the usefulness of Campbell's term, "resemblance."

Augustine St. Clare speaks of slavery using the metaphor of a steam engine: "put on the steam, fasten down the escape-valve, and sit on it, and see where you'll land." To which his brother, Alfred, replies, "I'm not afraid to sit on the escape-valve, as long as the boilers are strong, and the machinery works well." Augustine St. Clare mixes the steam engine metaphor with an analogous historical situation: "The nobles in Louis XVI.'s time thought just so; and Austria and Pius IX. think so now; and, some pleasant morning, you may all be caught up to meet each other in the air, *when the boilers burst*" (315).[31] Elsewhere, St. Clare speaks metaphorically of whipping slaves, using simile to liken the cruelty to a numbing and addictive drug: "Whipping and abuse are like laudanum; you have to double the dose as the sensibilities decline" (288).

Describing "heart" as playing a central part in *Uncle Tom's Cabin*, Donovan says: "Stowe's use of the metaphor of the heart throughout helps us to understand the nature of this [moral] revolution: it requires a mass change of heart" (45). To help foster this "mass change of heart," Stowe uses rhetorical appeals to the heart—in Campbell's terms, "to move the passions." Also perhaps confounding Stowe's use of the metaphor, heart, with her rhetorical appeal to the passions, Gabler-Hover quotes John Henry Newman to show a connection between the heart, the metaphor, and the imagination: "the heart is commonly reached, not through the reason, but through the imagination" (56). Gabler-Hover continues making such connections, again speaking of the rhetorical philosophy of Stowe's brother, Henry Ward Beecher:

> The perfect man in his search for truth uses his experience, his heart, and his imagination . . . For Beecher, spiritual evolution occurred through the imagi-

nation. Beecher's religion shared this conviction with the aesthetics of the time. (57)

Stowe's writing demonstrates such an aesthetic, interweaving resemblances and metaphors and religion with her appeals to the reader's imagination to establish her end of discourse: the abolition of slavery through what John R. Adams (1989) calls "fervent prayer" (40).

Even more than enlightening her reader's understanding and pleasing the reader's imagination, Stowe's *Uncle Tom's Cabin* is perhaps best known for moving the reader's passions, Campbell's third stated end of discourse.[32]   Campbell advises that "sympathy is one main engine by which the orator operates on the passions. . . . With them who mourn, we sympathize in tears" (96).[33]   *Uncle Tom's Cabin* was read tearfully by Stowe's contemporaries: "Editions of all sizes have appeared, and everybody devours it, and covers it with tears," writes Stowe's contemporary, George Sand (15). *The National Era* reviewed the work noting its ability to move the reader's passions:

> Its appeal to our sympathies is genuine. It . . . pictures facts, and the facts make us feel. We have never read a story of more power. We doubt if anybody has. The human being who can read it through with dry eyes, is commended to Barnum. (Rev. of *Uncle*, 15 April 1852: 62)

Well should the critics recognize sympathy at work in *Uncle Tom's Cabin*, for Stowe states in her Preface:

> The object of these sketches is to awaken sympathy and feeling for the African race, as they exist among us; to show their wrongs and sorrows, under a system [so] necessarily cruel and unjust . . . . (9)

It is largely through sympathy for her characters that Stowe appeals to her reader's passions and ultimately to her reader's will.

As delineated in Chapter III, above, Campbell describes seven "circumstances" (81) by which an author may operate on the reader's passions:

> probability, plausibility, importance, proximity of time, connexion of place, relation of the actors or sufferers to the hearers or speaker, interest of the hearers or speaker in the consequences. (81)

Stowe establishes the probability of *Uncle Tom's Cabin* in her Preface, promising "what personal knowledge the author has had, of the truth of incidents such as here are related, will appear in its time" (10). Indeed, one year after the publication of *Uncle Tom's Cabin*, true to her word, she published her *Key*—more than 500 pages of careful documentation to warrant her story's probability. Reaching beyond affirming her story's earthly probability, Stowe, in her Preface, calls on an even higher affirmation: one who, after all, holds "the great cause of human liberty" in His hands (10).

As an author establishes a story's probability by relating it to situations outside of the story itself, an author establishes a story's "plausibility," Campbell's second "circumstance" that operates on the passions, by keeping the narrative internally consistent. That is, while probability— "the aim of the historian" (82)—comes from proofs (such as found in Stowe's *Key*), plausibility—the aim of the poet (82)—comes from the internal consistency of the work itself. Despite the different directions in which her events proceed, despite her slave characters' different reactions to the Fugitive Slave Law, and despite her white characters' tremendously varied reactions to and senses of slavery, Stowe's message remains internally consistent: slavery is unconscionable and Christians are responsible for its abolition.

Campbell's third "circumstance" by which an author might move a reader's passions, "importance," fixes "the reader's attention more closely, to add brightness and strength to the ideas" (86). Campbell lists three ways in which a writer may accomplish establishing the "importance" that moves the reader's passions: "An action may derive importance from its own nature, from those concerned in it as acting or suffering, or from its consequences" (86).

Chapter Four, "An Evening in Uncle Tom's Cabin," demonstrates how Stowe moves a reader's passions using the circumstance of importance. In this chapter, Stowe, using what Campbell calls the lively idea, draws the (presumably white) reader into a sense of community with young George Shelby as he enjoys the earthy joys of "his" Uncle Tom, Aunt Chloe, and their children. The scene moves from description, through wonder and humor, to the characters' passionate call to Glory. Stowe writes that so much did [Uncle Tom's] prayer always work on the devotional feelings of his audiences, that there seemed often a danger that it would be lost altogether in the abundance of the responses which broke out everywhere around him. (43)

The language of the "meetin'" does more than describe the scene; rather, the words spoken at the meeting are spoken directly to the reader. Thus, the reader becomes the target of the passionate scene. As if the crescendo of firsthand involvement in a singing, exhorting, festive "meetin'" were not enough to move the reader's passion, Stowe abruptly breaks from its uplifting spirit and turns the reader's attention to a table in "the halls of the master," covered with documents, bills of sale, money, and the writing utensils necessary for assigning lives to unknown terrors (43-44). Each of these adjacent scenes is (in Campbell's terms) important by virtue of its "own nature" and "from those concerned in it as acting or suffering." By virtue of its "consequences" the scene of Uncle Tom's sale derives an importance that moves the reader's passions. Further, the juxtaposition of the two scenes and the reader's involvement in them appeal to the reader's passion by virtue of "importance."

Stowe establishes importance from "its own nature" by presenting the "nature" of "life among the lowly." According to Campbell, an author creates a sense of importance if a situation's result is uncommonly great (good or bad): what is godlike or what "in respect of atrocity is diabolical" (86). The activities during "an evening in Uncle Tom's cabin" and the simultaneous events in the "halls of the master" indeed foreshadow diabolical atrocities. Campbell continues, showing that actions derive importance from "those concerned in it, when the actors or the sufferers are considerable, on account either of their dignity or of their number, or of both" (86). Certainly the actor, Uncle Tom, epitomizes dignity:

Uncle Tom was a sort of patriarch in religious matters, in the neighborhood. Having, naturally, an organization in which the *morale* was strongly predominant, together with a greater breadth and cultivation of mind than obtained among his companions, he was looked up to with great respect, as a sort of minister among them . . . . (43)

And the number of people at the "meetin'" represents a vibrant religious community, indeed a circumstance of importance for Stowe's readers.

Finally, an event's importance, according to Campbell, moves the reader's passions from its consequences:

> when these [events] are remarkable in regard to their greatness, their multitude, their extent, and that either as to the many and distant places affected by them, or as to the future and remote periods to which they may reach, or as to both. (86)

Shelby's and Haley's business dealings foreshadow the extent of the book's events, the distances from the Shelby homeplace to which the slaves would be exiled, and the characters' futures—freedom and education for George, and death by whipping for Uncle Tom. Stowe's depiction of the slave trade was indeed "remarkable in regard to [its] greatness, multitude, and extent." With this sort of rhetorical narrative strategy, the text reflects Campbell's criteria for establishing "importance" and so moving the reader's passions.

Campbell's fourth "circumstance" by which an author may move a reader's passions, "proximity of time," points to the greater relevance of *Uncle Tom's Cabin* for the nineteenth-century reader than for the twentieth-century reader. During the nineteenth-century, the book dealt with current events; the twentieth-century reader encounters in the book events and "circumstances" that are past.

Campbell further explains that an author may move a reader's passions using "local *connexion*":

> the fifth of the above enumeration, hath a more powerful effect than proximity of time. . . . [We are] alarmed and agitated on being informed that any such accident hath happened in our neighbourhood. (88)

Stowe's scenes move through many neighborhoods where her readers might live. Her story begins in Kentucky, ground pivotal between North and South, and unfolds as far north as Canada and as far south as the New Orleans slave market. After scenes as far west as Legree's plantation off the Red River, Louisiana, and promises for George's education as far east as Europe, the book concludes where it all began, on the Shelby farm in Kentucky. Throughout the text, locations of scenes dot the map, maximizing chances that readers hearing Stowe's plea for abolition might identify with the locale of one scene or another.

The "Relation to the Persons concerned" (89), according to Campbell, has even greater power of association than "local connexion" to move a reader's passion. With a rationale similar to that for her strategy of putting her scenes in multiple locations, Stowe also introduces her characters within a variety of social situations with which a reader might associate. She offers characters of diverse classes: one reader might identify with the economically privileged Northerners, Senator or Mrs. Bird; another reader might identify with the economically privileged Southerners, the St. Clares; still another reader may identify with the economic pressures facing Mr. Shelby. Stowe offers a variety in her characters of diverse religious beliefs: one reader might identify (or yearn to identify) with the innocent sanctity of Eva or the vehement sanctity of Uncle Tom; another reader may identify with the domestic Christianity of Mrs. Shelby or Mrs. Bird; still another reader may identify with the spectrum of the unconverted—ranging from the intellectually agnostic (Augustine St. Clare) to the mischievous (Topsy) to the despondent and fallen (Prue).

Stowe also offers her reader the option for establishing a relation with various characters by virtue of their diverse cognitive habits: a reader might identify with the rational induction of Senator Bird, or with the intuitive deduction of Mrs. Bird.[34] A reader might identify with the cold common sense of Vermonter Miss Ophelia, or with the warm sensitivity of Augustine St. Clare. A reader might identify with the innocence and fresh young wisdom of Eva St. Clare or with the wisdom that comes with the age and experience of Uncle Tom. A reader might identify with the mechanical genius of the fugitive slave George Harris, or with the dynamism and perseverance of Eliza Harris. "Mrs. Stowe's fictional record of the inquisition by eternity becomes dense and persuasive," writes Barbara M. Cross (1971), "through the voices of Negro and white, Kentuckian and Vermonter, adult and child" (397). Each of Stowe's characters offers some human characteristic(s) by which to move a reader's passions.

Finally, Campbell's seventh and last circumstance by which an author may move a reader's passions, "interest in the consequences," brings "the object very near," enlivening "that sympathy which attacheth us to the concerns of others . . . [making] the mind cling to it as a concern of its own" (89). Through sympathy—interesting her reader in the "consequences" (81, 89) of her characters and their activities—Stowe interests her reader in the consequences of slavery and so brings the reader near her object: that regarding "the matter" of slavery, "the man or woman who *feels* strongly, healthily and justly, on the great interests of humanity, [becomes] a constant benefactor to the human race" (515).

Stowe implements her appeal to the reader's passions through the vehicle of sympathy: the "one main engine by which the orator operates on the passions" (Campbell 97). Although Stowe is best known for acting on the sympathies of mothers, she takes every opportunity to act also on the sympathies of other readers: legislators, clergymen, land owners, the old, the young, and slaves among others. Stowe interweaves an appeal to the reader's sympathy for her characters with an involvement of the reader in the consequences of both the characters' activities (within the book) and the nation's activities (regarding abolition, outside the book). By enlivening the reader's sympathy, Stowe attaches her reader's concern for her characters to concern for actual slaves and players in the fight for freedom.

Campbell names the appeal to a reader's will as the fourth and last end of discourse. He calls this final appeal, "calculated to influence the will and persuade to a certain conduct," "the most complex of all" because it results from "an artful mixture of that which proposes to convince the judgment, and that which interests the passions" (4). In other words, he holds that by incorporating together the argumentative and the pathetic, an author can produce in the reader a "*vehemence* of contention," which should, after all, be the author's goal.

According to Campbell, an author may mix reason with different types of pathos and so influence the reader's will in three ways. First, mixing reason with a pathos of sorrow, fear, shame, and/or humility can dissuade a person from some action. Stowe uses this formula both to describe Augustine St. Clare's views about slavery and to dissuade her reader from supporting slavery. Augustine confides to his cousin his inability to help his brother manage the family plantation. He explains how his brother Alfred had shamed him, calling him a "womanish sentimentalist" and humiliating him:

> Alfred scolds me, every time we meet; and he has the better of me, I grant,— for he really does something; his life is a logical result of his opinions, and mine is a contemptible *non sequitur*. (271)

Augustine tells Miss Ophelia (and the reader) his sense of shame regarding slavery: "The fact was, it was, after all, the THING I hated,—the using these men and women, the perpetuation of all this ignorance, brutality and vice,—just to make money for me!" (270). That is, Stowe couples her argument from reason for abolition with a sense of Augustine's shame at having to live with the slavery system whether or not he participates in it. Stowe takes this formula, combining reason and shame to influence a reader's will, beyond Augustine's immediate pain:

> many men . . . in their heart, think of it just as I do. The land groans under it [slavery]; and, bad as it is for the slave, it is worse, if anything, for the master. . . . a great class of vicious, improvident, degraded people, among us are an evil to us, as well as to themselves. (272)

Thus Augustine appeals to the will of the reader who may support the slave system by custom and/or economic necessity, but not by heart, to gather strength through Christian morality—"up to heaven's gate in theory, down in earth's dust in practice" (273)—to do as he sorrows he has not done in his own life: I had plans and hopes of doing something in this world . . . yearnings to be a sort of emancipator" (272). Combining reason and shame, Stowe appeals to the reader who identifies with Augustine's self-disgust at floating and drifting "instead of being actor and regenerator in society" (271), providing an association with the potential to influence the reader's will as well.

Campbell shows that an author may mix reason with "an intermediate kind of passion, . . . such as, joy, love, esteem, compassion," which could, depending on the author's intent, either persuade or dissuade a reader's will (5). Certainly, Stowe uses this sort of passionate appeal as she sketches the episodes of the good Christians; she calls on the reader to feel this "kind of passion" for characters such as Eliza, Uncle Tom, Eva, and Augustine St. Clare. As the reader then mixes those feelings with the "reason" Stowe has established in her initial arguments regarding slavery, the reader's passions are moved.

An author, according to Campbell, may mix reason with a third type of pathos, that of "hope, patriotism, ambition, emulation, anger," to "elevate the soul, and stimulate to action" (5). Through the sympathy she has already established for Eliza and George, Stowe uses this formula to move the reader's passions. Stowe mixes the argument that a person cannot be a saleable commodity with the gripping story of the Harris's ambition to hold their family together as a Christian unit. George presents a picture of anger, emulation, and patriotism—my blood is "about up to the boiling point" (139)—as he stands

> with clenched hands and glowing eyes, and looking as any other man might look, whose wife was to be sold at auction, and son sent to a trader, all under the shelter of a Christian nation's laws. (222)

Eliza presents a picture of hope and ambition as she flees northward with babe in arms, crossing the ice floes of the Ohio to save her child. Through sympathy with George, the reader feels anger at laws that perpetuate human suffering. Through sympathy with Eliza, the reader feels the ambition to challenge such legislation.

Stowe presents Uncle Tom's story, also mixing arguments for abolition with this type of pathos. From his early instinct to martyr himself for the good of his loved ones (55) to his dying words, "I forgive ye, with all my heart!" (481), Uncle Tom clearly emulates Christ. With his actions Stowe appeals to her reader's "anger" at the indignity of the circumstance. By consistently showing Uncle Tom's undying ambition and hope for Christian salvation, Stowe offers her reader a model for "emulation." Stowe concludes by addressing her reader, "See, then, to your sympathies in this matter! Are they in harmony with the sympathies of Christ?[35] or are they swayed and perverted by the sophistries of worldly policy?" (515). She seeks to influence her reader's will by imploring each to pray; to extend to fugitive slaves "refuge, . . . education, knowledge, Christianity"; and to make "reparation for the wrongs [of] the American nation," opening to Negroes "the doors of churches and school-houses" (516) and, eventually, politics (518).

Campbell's appeals—"to enlighten the understanding, to please the imagination, to move the passions, or to influence the will" (1)—work within *Uncle Tom's Cabin* in two ways. First, the four appeals work in an integrated manner within each episode. Each episode presents a rationale for abolition and proceeds through appeals to the imagination and passions to influence the reader's will. Second, the book in its entirety

seems to begin in its early chapters with an appeal to the reader's understanding; it then appeals to the reader's imagination as he or she considers
what might become of Eliza and Uncle Tom; action and language then
play heavily on the reader's passions with the deaths of Little Eva, St.
Clare, and Uncle Tom; finally, the work concludes with George Shelby's
resolution on Uncle Tom's grave that George

> would never own another slave, while it was possible to free him; that no-
> body, through me, should ever run the risk of being parted from home and
> friends, and dying on a lonely plantation, as he died.

Stowe continues young George's proclamation with an appeal through
association to the reader's will:

> Every time you see UNCLE TOM'S CABIN . . . let it . . . put you all in mind
> to follow in his steps and be as honest and faithful and Christian as he was.
> (509)

Stowe appeals even more directly to the reader's will in her "Concluding
Remarks" and continues that tone two years later in her *The Key to Uncle
Tom's Cabin* (1853).

In Campbell's terms, Stowe's *Key* (more obviously than *Uncle Tom's
Cabin*) privileges appeals to the reader's understanding and will above
appeals to the reader's imagination or passions.[36] The *Key* states that

> The great object of the author in writing has been to bring this subject of slav-
> ery, as a moral and religious question, before the minds of all those who pro-
> fess to be followers of Christ in America. (vi)

That is, Stowe admits her principal object as (in Campbell's terms),
"intended to enlighten the understanding" (1). Stowe shifts the sense of
her intent, however, to conclude her preface,

> The book is commended to the candid attention and earnest prayers of all true
> Christians throughout the world. May they unite their prayers that Christen-
> dom may be delivered from so great an evil as slavery ! (vi)

Stowe here moves the sense of her intention from enlightening her reader's
understanding to influencing her reader's "will." Veiling her directive in

third person, Stowe tells her reader to act—implicitly both to pray individually and to unite *en masse* in prayer to deliver Christendom (which evangelists see as the entire world through all of time) from slavery.

Similarly, *Uncle Tom's Cabin* professes appeals to the understanding and the will, but does so through the vehicle of sympathy, an element of the passions. Stowe begins her preface,

> The object of these sketches is to awaken sympathy and feeling for the African race, as they exist among us; to show their wrongs and sorrows, under a system so necessarily cruel and unjust as to defeat and do away the good effects of all that can be attempted for them, by their best friends, under it. (9)

Stowe proposes, therefore, to create within her reader, through sympathy, a passionate response to the evils of slavery. The book's conclusion, however, states Stowe's intention to influence her reader's will: "Think of your freedom . . . and be as honest and faithful and Christian as he [Uncle Tom] was" (509). Stowe admonishes her reader to emulate the Christian spirit and behavior of Uncle Tom, just as he emulated the spirit and behavior of Christ. Stowe moves specifically to influence the reader's will and behavior toward The Fugitive Slave Law, requesting her reader to make "some effort at reparation for the wrongs that the American nation has brought upon" the "poor unfortunates" who "seek a refuge . . . education, knowledge, and Christianity" (516).

Each of Campbell's appeals has a place in building Stowe's case. Certainly, her "reasoning is conclusive" (Campbell 78) and acquired an extra boost of credibility with the publication of *A Key to Uncle Tom's Cabin* in 1853. Her language carries that "reasoning" beyond indifference as she does "awaken sympathy and feeling for the African race" (Stowe 9), thereby demonstrating Campbell's statement that "thus passion is the mover to action, reason is the guide. Good is the object of the will, truth is the object of the understanding" (78). Stowe's reader comes to know the truth or reality of slavery by understanding her "sketches." Moving her reader's passions regarding the difficult realities of unjust murders, children sold beyond their mothers' arms, marriages ripped apart, great minds wasted, women sold into degradation—moving her reader's passions, in short, regarding the truth surrounding the law that "considers all these human beings, with beating hearts and living affection, only as so many *things* belonging to a master" (19), Stowe moves her reader from understanding to action. Good, the object of Stowe's will, becomes, likewise, the object of her reader's will.

NOTES

[1] To prevent another such catastrophe as the Holocaust, the Jewish community admonishes us to "never forget." Just so, we should never forget America's human catastrophe, slavery, and its legacy of ensuing racism. Few fail to recognize the horrors of genocide; the insidious nature of racism, however, leads some to shun African-Americans' grim history. The answer to questions of whether such literature as Stowe's *Uncle Tom's Cabin* describes nineteenth-century racial stereotyping and racism or proscribes those realities for current readers should be as obvious as reactions to viewing gas chambers. Facing the history of slavery head-on can only help black and white progeny declare, "never again." Offensive stereotypes characteristic of European-American mid-nineteenth-century writings should instruct us of the length to which racism extends—even to the discourse of abolitionists.

[2] Child's abolitionist works include *An Appeal for that Class of American called Africans* (1833), which John S. Hart (1852) describes as "the first work that appeared in this country in favour of immediate emancipation. It made a profound impression at the time" (117). Later, beginning in 1841, Child wrote extensively for the "Anti-Slavery Standard." (Hart 118)

[3] This description comes from Madeleine B. Stern, 272.

[4] As Stowe has her characters explain, "Faculties is different in different peoples, but cultivation of 'em goes a great way" (66).

[5] Discussing such "great American authors," Gabler-Hover writes that "Mark Twain befriended and read the work of Henry Ward Beecher, an influential exponent of American rhetoric in the 1860s" (5) and speculates about Henry James's awareness of Campbell, but does not mention that Harriet Beecher (Stowe) could have become aware of Campbell through her brother's interests and work.

[6] As some nineteenth-century women writers felt more comfortable emulating the arrangement of the Bible than the arrangement of the novel, the reception of *The Wide, Wide World* and *Uncle Tom's Cabin* (first and second million sellers in American literary history) suggests that readers, too, felt comfortable with books resembling compilations of biblical parables.

[7] Herzog quotes Leslie Marmon Silko.

[8] One might observe also that Stowe composes her book's action in a manner resembling a call and response or dialectic arrangement.

[9] John R. Adams hesitates to provide the customary plot summary (conventional literary material) as he introduces the book to his readers:

Although the skeleton of the story is now before the reader, the substance of the book eludes such tabulation, for the power and individuality of *Uncle Tom's Cabin* consist less in this conventional literary material . . . than in the special vitality infused into it. (26)

[10] Using Stowe's bifurcated plot as an occasion to dismiss the work, *The Southern Literary Messenger*, Jno. R. Thompson, editor and proprietor (1852), notes,

> Mrs. Stowe's events have many of them no connection with each other whatever. She has two principal characters, for whom the reader's sympathy is enlisted, whose paths never lie within a thousand miles of each other. . . . Mrs. Stowe reminds us of the ventriloquial vaudevilles . . . Perhaps, indeed, Mrs. Stowe has proceeded upon the principle laid down by Puff in the Critic—

> "O Lord, yes; ever while you live have two plots to your tragedy. The grand point in managing them is only to let your under-plot have as little connection with your main plot as possible." (631)

[11] Child, points out in one of her letters:

> It is really droll to see in what different states of mind people read "Uncle Tom." Mr. Pierce, Senator from Maryland, read it lately, and when he came to the sale of "Uncle Tom," he exclaimed with great emotion, "Here's a writer that knows how to sympathize with the South! . . . She knows how to feel for a man when he is obliged to sell a good honest slave." In his view the book was intended as a balsam for bereaved slave-holders. (Child 69-70)

Southern journals, such as *The Southern Literary Messenger*, printed scathing reviews, one of which called *Uncle Tom's Cabin* one of "the most reprehensible specimens of the tribe" that seeks "to delude . . . to produce discontent, to be the herald[s] of disorder and dissension . . . " (Rev. of "Uncle," *Southern* 721).

The negative Southern reaction to *Uncle Tom's Cabin* can be seen also in reviews of other 1852 books that editors overtly or implicitly compare to Stowe's popular work. *The Southern Literary Messenger* favors J. Thornton Randolph's *The Cabin and Parlor: Or Slaves and Masters*:

> Good in all respects. The style is that of a well educated and practised writer; the incidents are striking and told with spirit: pathos alternates with humor throughout the story, and the argument is manly and unanswerable. We can only regret that by similarity of title and the time of its publication, it should be associated, in any way, with Mrs. Beecher Stowe's volumes, of the very name of which the public are getting heartily tired, for "The Cabin and Parlor" is excellent enough to have won for itself a wide popularity, in the ab-

sence of that surfeit of 'nigger' literature, which now sickens the popular taste. (703)

In her 1853 *Key*, "Chapter III of Part III," Stowe quotes and discredits Randolph's representation of "the patriarchal stability and security of the slave population in the Old Dominion" (257). She describes the publishing situation: "every publisher and every press pours out anti-slavery books of every form and description, lectures, novels, tracts, biographies" (Mary Kelley 250).

Ironically, in its "Notices of New World," October, 1852, *The Southern Literary Messenger* placed directly beside its review of *Uncle Tom's Cabin*, a notice for the book, *Plantation and Farm Instruction, Regulation, Record, Inventory and Account Book. For the use of Managers on Estates*, that includes Negroes among the items in a list of farm equipment:

> it contains formulas for a daily record of plantation work; for an inventory of negroes with the quantity of clothing, tools and medicines given them, and a register of their births, deaths and marriages; for a list of stock, for a statement of produce made by the proprietor, &c., &c. . . . The book is well gotten up and is offered at a very moderate price.

The "Notice" also draws on scripture to discredit both Stowe and the recurrent theme in her work that women should teach men to live by a Christian ethic:

> as we find it recorded in the second chapter of the First Epistle to Timothy—
>
> "Let the woman learn in silence with all subjection."
>
> "But I suffer not a woman to teach, nor to usurp authority over the man, but to be in silence." ("Notices" 631)

Such pro-slavery reviews appearing in Southern newspapers and journals usually attacked *Uncle Tom's Cabin* for ". . . fallacy and . . . falsehood . . . false conclusions . . . false assertions . . . untruth . . . insinuation of untrue and calumnious impressions." They characterized Stowe's work as "pernicious . . . most erroneous . . . criminal and false . . . scandalous [and] . . . entitled to unmitigated censure and reprobation" (Rev. of "Uncle," *Southern* 726). Stowe responded to personal attacks and to attacks on the verity of her work by writing what she originally intended to be a short appendix to the tale. The short appendix to *Uncle Tom's Cabin* developed into her book of explanation, *A Key to Uncle Tom's Cabin; Presenting the Original Facts and Documents upon which the Story is Founded. Together with Corroborative Statements Verifying the Truth of the Work* (1853).

The explanatory key divides into four parts: "Part I" documents the nature and predicaments of each of the tale's characters, "Part II" explains the history and nature of slavery, "Part III" discusses the practice of American slavery, and "Part IV" puts slavery in the light of Christianity and concludes answering the question, "What is to be Done?" In Campbell's terms, Stowe's *Key* (unlike *Uncle Tom's Cabin*) privileges appeals to the reader's understanding and will over appeals to the reader's imagination or passions. As will be seen later in this chapter, the nineteenth-century reader may have taken Stowe's *Key* to have been the more "masculine" appeal needed to augment the more "feminine" appeal of *Uncle Tom's Cabin*. Stowe's *Key* documented and elaborated on the specifics, principles, and substance of *Uncle Tom's Cabin*.

In retaliation, *The Southern Literary Messenger* again reacted sharply to Stowe's 500+ page rebuttal of its previous scolding:

> Mrs. Stowe obtrudes herself again upon our notice, and, though we have no predilections for the disgusting office of castigating such offenses as hers, and rebuking the incendiary publications of a woman, yet the character of the present attack, and the bad eminence which she and her books have both won, render a prompt notice of the present encyclopaedia of slander even more necessary than any reply to her previous fiction. . . . She was then [at the time of her first book] an obscure Yankee school-mistress, eaten up with fanaticism, festering with the malignant virus of abolitionism, self-sanctified by the virtues of a Pharisaic religion, devoted to the assertion of woman's rights, and an enthusiastic believer in many neoteric heresies, but she was comparatively harmless, as being almost entirely unknown. ("A Key to Uncle Tom's Cabin" 321-29)

Northern reviews opposed the Southern reviews, "commenting upon the judgement" the Southern press pronounced "against *Uncle Tom's Cabin*" ("Slavery and its Abuses—Mrs. Stowe and the N. York Courier and Enquirer" 170) with pages of meticulously argued positive "comments." For more than a year, Northern editorials continued to comment both on the book and on the South's reaction to it: "The book of Mrs. Stowe is still doing its work as a missionary of Christianity and Humanity. It is read at the South, and indications multiply of its good influence" ("Uncle Tom's Cabin at the South" 335).

[12] Twentieth-century critics have recently begun to examine the rhetorical strategies of mid-nineteenth-century narratives. For example, Tompkins approaches Stowe's language in terms of its intentions:

> In modernist thinking, literature is by definition a form of discourse that has no designs on the world. It does not attempt to change things, but merely to represent them . . . . works whose stated purpose is to influence the course of history . . . such as the sentimental novel . . . make continual and obvious appeals to the reader's emotions" (125).

[13] "Its appeal to our sympathies is genuine" (Rev. of "Uncle," *National* 62)

[14] In retrospect Stowe may provide current readers with what may be new information about mid-nineteenth-century stereotyping of all characters, white or black.

[15] Herzog here quotes George M. Fredrickson, 113

[16] Later, in *The Key*, Stowe differentiates among ethnic natures:

> psychology with regard to the negro race . . . how very different they are from the white race. They are possessed of a nervous organization peculiarly susceptible and impressible. Their sensations and impressions are very vivid, and their fancy and imagination lively. . . . The fact is, that the Anglo-Saxon race—cool, logical, and practical—have yet to learn the doctrine of toleration . . . ." (45-46)

[17] Current readers may not readily see that "spiritual superiority" over patriarchal "organizations" was foundational and important to Stowe and her readers. Current readers who accept men's "colder, harder, and austerer" economic and cognitive "organizations" (Hale 463) may see the idea of "spiritual superiority" to have retarded women and African Americans' entry into the market economy and corporate capitalism. Warner and Stowe, however, clearly advocated an economic system based on Christian charity and denigrated the entrepreneurship and capitalism practiced and characterized by the likes of landowner Miss Fortune, slave trader Haley, capitalist Alfred St. Clare, etc. Warner's and Stowe's writings do not mean to retard women's entry into capitalism, but to prevent such "colder, harder, and austerer organizations" from developing.

[18] This view conflicts with such twentieth-century critics as J.C. Furnas, who chastise Stowe for her "assumption of the superiority of the white race" (287) or James Baldwin who claims "that the novel is activated by a 'theological terror' in which 'black equates with evil and white with grace'" (Sundquist 4). I do not attempt to "explain away" Stowe's racism, but to put her views within their historical-cultural and rhetorical context.

[19] Tompkins points out the importance to Stowe in recommending "not specific alterations in the current political and economic arrangements, but rather a change of heart" (132).

[20] Tompkins addresses this issue of cognitive methods as "sentimental power" in her chapter by that name.

[21] Twentieth-century feminist psychologists, Mary Field Belenky, Blythe McVicker Clincy, Nancy Rule Goldberger, and Jill Mattuck Tarule (1986) provide a related explanation in their theory of "procedural knowledge":

> Procedural knowledge is "objective" in the sense of being oriented away from the self—the knower—and toward the object the knower seeks to analyze or understand. In Piagetian language, procedural knowledge is tilted toward "accommodation" to the shape of the object rather than "assimilation" of the object to the shape of the knower's mind. (123)

Perhaps current cultural demands to think in such an "objectifying" manner helps some twentieth-century and current critics denigrate those literary works that appeal to the reader's more "subjective" faculties: imagination, passions, and will.

[22] More recently, Robin Lakoff's *Language and Woman's Place* presents a similar view: ". . . women are person-oriented, interested in their own and each other's mental states and respective status; men are object-oriented, interested in things in the outside world" (82).

[23] Taking women's exclusion from American legislative and judicial arenas and Hale's gender-specific description of cognitive patterns into account, Stowe continues in *The Key* to show the relationships among cognitive methods, gender, ethnicity and so explain Anglo-Saxon (male) complicity with slavery:

> the reason why the slave-code of America is more atrocious . . . is that the Anglo-Saxon race are a more coldly and strictly logical race, and . . . work out an accursed principle, with mathematical accuracy, to its most accursed results. The decisions in American law-books show nothing so much as this severe, unflinching accuracy of logic. (155)

[24] Stowe characterizes both Mr. Shelby and Senator Bird as fundamentally benign, but doomed to consider issues only within the confines of their own logic. Even the passionate and august St. Clare entrusts his passionate instincts to his rationality:

> What can a man of honorable and humane feelings do, but shut his eyes all he can, and harden his heart? I can't buy every poor wretch I see. I can't turn knight-errant, and undertake to redress every individual case of wrong . . . . The most I can do is to try and keep out of the way of it. (259)

[25] Chapter III explains that Campbell, too, often uses the terms, "imagination" and "fancy" interchangeably (81).

[26] Stowe does not reveal the identity of "the psychologist" to whom she refers. Of the rhetoricians informing 1850s rhetoric (and that of her brother, Henry Ward Beecher), Campbell was known as "the psychologist." After speaking of Beecher and Campbell in the same sentence, "The eighteenth- and nineteenth-century rhetorical renaissance was impelled by ministers such as Hugh Blair, George Campbell, and Henry Ward Beecher" (5) (and elsewhere, 39, 48, etc.), Gabler-Hover names Campbell as the primary true faculty psychologist (55).

[27] Stowe's use of Uncle Tom as a Christ-figure approaches Tompkins's idea of "typology." By typology, Tompkins refers to fiction in which characters, organization, and language can be "typed" (stereo-"typed") elements. Tompkins uses the term as a compilation of such elements ("typological narrative," 134) or as referring to a work's stock arrangement ("typological organization" 135). Stowe's use of Uncle Tom as a Christ figure can be thought of as an element of such typology; in Tompkins's words, *"Uncle Tom's Cabin* retells the culture's central religious myth—the story of the crucifixion—in terms of the nation's greatest political conflict—slavery . . . " (134). Rather than seeing him as an element of a larger typological system, Herzog sees Uncle Tom as more of a "type" in and of himself: "He is more a type than an individual . . . he is intended to be a type or symbol . . ." (106).

[28] Ann R. Shapiro shows "that *Uncle Tom's Cabin* was intended as a *woman's* protest against slavery" quoting from one of Stowe's letters:

> I wrote what I did . . . because as a woman, as a mother, I was oppressed and broken—with the sorrows of injustice I saw. . . . I must speak for the oppressed—who cannot speak for themselves. (20)

Shapiro also points out Stowe's feeling that women and mothers should lead the men who control legal and cultural situations (21), quoting from Stowe's *My Wife and I* (1871):

> The woman question of our day as I understand it is this—Shall MOTHERHOOD ever be felt in the public administration of the affairs of state? . . . I am persuaded that *it is not till this class of women feel as vital and personal responsibility for the good of the State, as they have hitherto felt for that of the family, that we shall gain the final elements of a perfect society.* (38-39).

[29] Stowe, too, shares this bond of motherhood; she lost her own infant son during a cholera epidemic in 1849.

[30] Stowe moves this appeal from the reader's imagination to the reader's will by the end of "her jeremiad" (Goodman 328), directly addressing the white woman reader:

> I beseech you, pity those mothers that are constantly made childless by the American slave-trade! And say, mothers of America, is this a thing to be defended, sympathized with, passed over in silence? (*Uncle* 515)

[31] Turn of the century Ph.D. in Rhetoric, Gertrude Buck, rescues the mixed metaphor from censure: "metaphor is not a mechanical device as rhetoricians had assumed but instead a 'biologic organism'" (Kitzhaber 180). "She rejected the notion of mixed metaphors, which she said were never mixed in the mind of the person who

produced them" (Horner 143). Campbell also condones the mixed metaphor when the incongruity of the expression does not "hurt the perspicuity of the sentence" (267).

[32] Within an explanation of this faculty, Campbell refers to the appeal to the heart. The extent to which a theologian or Christian writer should appeal to the reader's (or listener's) passions greatly concerned eighteenth- and nineteenth-century rhetoricians. Gabler-Hover, Johnson (*Nineteenth-Century Rhetoric*), and Winifred Bryan Horner (*Nineteenth-Century Scottish*) have clearly shown principles of moving the reader's passions as discussed in Campbell's *The Philosophy of Rhetoric* were no doubt familiar to nineteenth-century theological writers, including Stowe's father and brother. Acknowledging the usefulness of rhetorical appeals to the passions, Alan Brinton shows that well-published sermons such as those of Adam Batty propose that "the passions are, however, represented by their nature inferior to reason or the understanding, which ought to govern them" (60). Philosopher and humanist associate of Campbell, David Hume (1739) acknowledges,

> Nothing is more usual in philosophy, and even in common life, than to talk of the combat of passion and reason, to give the preference to reason, and to assert that men are only so far virtuous as they conform themselves to its dictates. (413)

Showing the fallacy of preferring reason to passion or of even posing reason against passion, Hume continues,

> reason alone can never produce any action, or give rise to volition . . . reason is, and ought only to be the slave of the passions, and can never pretend to any other office than to serve and obey them. (415)

Campbell believes that the four ends of discourse—appeals to the understanding, imagination, passions, and will—should have "connexion and dependency" on each other in a loosely hierarchical sense:

> Knowledge, the object of the intellect, furnisheth materials for the fancy; the fancy culls, compounds, and by her mimic art, disposes these materials so as to affect the passions; the passions are the natural spurs to volition or action, and so need only to be right directed. (2)

Stowe's contemporary, Emerson, reflects Campbell's sense that human faculties should have such a "connexion and dependency": "For Emerson, the one term, Mind, suggests an integrated, self-organizing Whole, not a series of separate mechanical faculties" (Teresa Toulouse 121). Contemporary (and as Kathryn Kish Sklar points out, 13) theological opponent of Stowe's father, William Ellery Channing, thought similarly about the connections between the understanding and the passions with regard to a theological audience. He linked the truth of belief to its reasonableness and to its emotional persuasiveness. If the 'best' minds in his audience must be rationally convinced of religion's value, they must also be moved. (Toulouse 79)

Principles of rhetorical persuasion

providing scientific insight into human nature and the organic principles that governed communication inspired a legion of supporters among nineteenth-century rhetoricians in North America who regarded *The Philosophy of Rhetoric* as an authoritative commentary on the philosophy and practice of rhetoric

reports Johnson (20-21), regardless of the various moral philosophers/theologians' religious stance.

[33] In her discussion of *Uncle Tom's Cabin*, Tompkins refers to "the sentimental novel ['s] . . . obvious appeals to the reader's emotions" (125) and "the tears of Topsy and of Miss Ophelia . . . [as] the sign of redemption" (131). Tompkins concentrates her discussion of weeping more in terms of the characters' action of weeping than in terms of Stowe's appeal to the passions to cause weeping as reader-response (131, 132).

[34] Mrs. Bird challenges her husband, "I hate reasoning, John,—especially reasoning on such subjects. There's a way you political folks have of coming round and round a plain right thing; and you don't believe in it yourselves" (102). She later counsels him, "Your heart is better than your head, in this case, John" (108).

[35] Stowe's appeals to enliven what readers already knew might not translate to the current multi-cultural or individualistic reader. Comparing the discourse and cultural mores of mid-nineteenth-century readers to those of current readers reveals some important differences in terms of moral and theological identities. A comparatively much greater number of Stowe's mid-nineteenth-century readers shared a Christian education and lived within a Christian belief system. By association, Christian references brought reader affirmation of new (shared) ideas and reinforced reader participation in a Christian community. This important foundation to Stowe's persuasion may be lost on current readers who consider themselves individuals distinct from community and/or who favor cognitive methods of analytical induction to cognitive methods of deriving answers and truths from some prescribed source such as Christian scripture. Stowe writes for readers whom she trusts identify themselves as members of and contributors to a community of shared beliefs.

[36] Throughout *The Philosophy of Rhetoric* Campbell presents some mixed messages. He specifies that any one discourse should admit "only one of these ends as the principal" (1). He also shows that the four ends of discourse are fundamentally interdependent and should "ascend in a regular progression" (2) from an appeal to the

reader's understanding, through those to the imagination and passions, to a final appeal to the reader's will.

Ann S. Stephens

V

ANN S. STEPHENS'S *MARY DERWENT*:
FROM THE FOLD TO THE INDIVIDUAL

"The feminine fifties"[1] saw a gradual transition in literature's purpose and rhetorical appeal. The decade's earlier bestsellers, Susan Warner's *The Wide, Wide World* (1851) and Harriet Beecher Stowe's *Uncle Tom's Cabin* (1852) functioned generally to instruct readers. Warner's and Stowe's evangelical works implicitly and explicitly ask the reader to infuse Christian consciousness and gentle behavior into personal, domestic, and (in the case of *Uncle Tom's Cabin*) national daily life. The subject matter of these early 1850s works overtly instructs readers to accept Christianity "to overcome evil with good" (*The Wide, Wide World* 21, 270) and "to see to it that *they feel right*" as Christians regarding slavery (*Uncle Tom's Cabin* 515). Rhetorically, these works appeal directly to the reader's understanding and will, using more indirect appeals to the reader's imagination and passions (usually through the vehicle of sympathy) to do so.

In contrast, while certainly providing instruction for the reader both by direct authorial voice and by more subversive means, the decade's later popular works, Ann S. Stephens's *Mary Derwent* (1858) and E.D.E.N. Southworth's *The Hidden Hand* (1859), sought primarily to tell a good story.[2] *Mary Derwent* tells a romantic and exciting tale based on historical events; *The Hidden Hand* presents the escapades of a madcap "damsel-errant in quest of adventures" (270). Like the decade's earlier works, these narratives appeal to a reader's multiple faculties, but as writers began to turn from religious evangelism to story-telling, Stephens and Southworth turn their primary appeals to the reader's imagination and passions. Appealing to these faculties, Stephens and Southworth more indirectly appeal to the reader's understanding and will to reevaluate woman's personal and social identity.

The beginnings of Stephens's *Mary Derwent* (1858) reach back to May, 1838, when *The Ladies' Companion* announced and began serializing its

"$200 Prize Article," Ann S. Stephens's "Mary Derwent. A Tale of the Early Settlers." Stephens, who had formed a resolution never again to connect her name with a prize article, nor indeed with any species of magazine literature, "had submitted the story under the pen name 'Catharine Rogers.'"[3] "Mary Derwent" thus claimed the award on its own merits and not by virtue of its author's reputation.[4]

Stephens's literary reputation was well earned. She began as an editor at the *Portland Magazine*, where she gained the literary recognition that secured her position at *The Ladies' Companion* before she arrived in New York. She edited *Peterson's* (in competition with *Godey's Ladies Book*) and *The Ladies' Companion* for years (quickly raising the latter's circulation from 3,000 to 17,000 subscription copies) and contributed as a writer to *Graham's* and *The Ladies' National Magazine* (*The American Literary Magazine* 336).

So well did the reading public receive the serialized article, "Mary Derwent," that *The Ladies' Companion* subsequently reported:

> We are happy to inform our readers that a proposal has been made our associate, Mrs. Stephens, by the Harpers, to make the Prize Tale of "Mary Derwent," published in our last volume the ground-work of a two-volume novel. ("Editors' Table," 50)

Despite a sustained reader interest that caused *The Ladies' Companion* to reprint the serialized work in 1840, eighteen years were to intervene before the story, reworked and expanded, would appear as the historically based volume, *Mary Derwent*.

Set in the lands occupied by the Six Nations Indians, predominantly the Wyoming Valley, Pennsylvania, during the years leading up to the Wyoming Valley Massacre of 1778, *Mary Derwent* tells the story of a sensitive, deformed young girl, Mary Derwent, as she observes life around her. In that valley on the small,[5] lush Monockonok Island in the Susquehanna River near the town of Wilkes-Barre, Pennsylvania, Mary lives peaceably amid natural beauty in a charming log cabin with her (supposed) family: a loving father, sister Jane, and grandmother. She interacts with other school children, a fatherly Zinzendorfian[6] missionary, and various Shawnee who consider the kyphotic[7] girl "the white bird . . . our prophet" (29).

Stephens begins her narrative in its chronological middle. In order to understand Mary's story, the reader must first learn the circumstances leading up to Mary's (and the book's) present—the story of Catharine Montour, who is revealed at the book's end to be Mary's mother. Stephens presents Catharine's personal narrative as a response to the kindly missionary's early query: "Lady . . . . Your speech is refined, your manner noble. Lady, what are you?" (70). Having transformed into the mysterious white Shawnee queen, Catharine replies, describing her life in England as the spirited and "warm of heart" daughter (then named Caroline) of a scholarly village pastor. At her father's death, she had married his student, a promising young minister, Varnham, who roomed with the family. By him she had borne a daughter, and shortly thereafter, at the death of a relative, had become a peeress in her own right, changing her name from Caroline Varnham to Lady Granby, "possessor of one of the finest estates in England, for the Granby honors descended alike to male and female heirs" (88-89). Flourishing in her new cosmopolitan lifestyle and embracing her peerage with pride and an "almost masculine consciousness of power, a sense of personal dominion," Caroline Varnham/Lady Granby subsequently had fallen in love with her husband's friend, Grenville Murray. Later, when Murray, unaware of her concealed affection for him, married, Caroline, Lady Granby had gone mad. After a year of dementia, she had "awakened" to discover that she had "destroyed" her child and her husband's life.

Overwhelmed at this realization, Lady Granby had resolved to leave her life in England and to live her remaining years in self-imposed exile. After staging a false suicide and disguising herself, she had sailed to America, taking with her a portion of her family's money and jewels. Entering the valley of the Mohawk from New York, she had entrusted her wealth to the agency of Sir William Johnson by whose influence she was adopted into the Shawnee tribe at the head of Seneca Lake, New York, where she received the cast-off English name of her new guardian, the feared and respected Queen Esther. Thus, Caroline Varnham, Lady Granby, had became Catharine Montour.

In *Mary Derwent* Stephens interweaves fictitious elements with events and characters she draws from history. During her time among the Shawnee, Catharine (drawn from an actual historical character) saves Grenville Murray (a fictitious character), her former British lover, and his family from death by submitting to marry Queen Esther's son, Gi-en-gwa-tah. Catharine's daughter from this marriage, the wild and beautiful light-skinned Shawnee princess, Tahmeroo (fictitious), loves and marries Captain Walter Butler, historically the most treacherous of the Tories associated with the Wintermoots and their Dutch allies at their suspicious fort nearby.[8]

Throughout the tale, the deformed Mary feels inexplicably drawn to the mysterious Catharine Montour. Mary and Tahmeroo sense an unrealized sisterhood and unknowingly shape their respective lives to reflect those of their parents: Mary to pursue spiritual purity as had her father (the Zinzendorfian missionary), and Tahmeroo to pursue obsessive desire as had her mother (Lady Granby/Catharine Montour). At the Wyoming Valley Massacre (an actual historic event) Tahmeroo helps Mary (her then unrevealed half-sister) and Jane Derwent escape. During that battle, both Murray and Catharine are stabbed by Queen Esther; Catharine recovers, but later dies after Queen Esther drives her out of the Shawnee tribe as "a traitress and a craven" (392). The kindly Zinzendorfian missionary, identified at last as Catharine's first husband, Varnham, appears at her death to reveal himself to Mary as her natural father and discloses to Mary the identity of her natural mother, Catharine Montour, who had in madness inadvertently caused Mary's deformity. The story ends with Mary and her missionary father, Varnham, and Jane and her husband, Edward Clark, living peaceably at the family estate in England. As her mother had done long ago, Tahmeroo flees that family estate to pursue unrequited love. Finding her treacherous husband, Butler, dead, she resolves to lead her people in rebuilding the Shawnee Nation from the ruins left by Sullivan's avenging troops.[9]

Whereas *The Wide, Wide World* and *Uncle Tom's Cabin* appear as compilations of stories and parables each reinforcing Christian ideology,[10] *Mary Derwent* appears "a tale." That is, the movement of Stephens's plot demands at least as much attention as do the book's more specifically stated lessons. From *Mary Derwent*'s plot the reader derives lessons or insights into cultural possibilities differing substantially from those offered by Warner's and Stowe's works. For example, Stephens challenges the taboo, miscegenation.[11] Also, the reader learns the cultural possibility of matrilineal inheritance,[12] for Stephens's tale depicts matriarchy in two cultures: the English[13] and the Shawnee.[14] Further, Stephens emphasizes

the importance of matrilineal inheritance beyond the material, as her female characters control and bequeath legacies of refinement, passion, and
power.

Unacknowledged by twentieth-century (and current) scholars, *Mary
Derwent* unfolds the fact that one of America's first European-American
leaders was a woman, the historical Catharine Montour. The body of evidence documenting Catharine Montour as an important historical figure
includes eighteenth- and nineteenth-century historians Witham Marshe
(1744, 1801, 1884), William Leete Stone (1841, 1865), Charles Miner
(1845), George Peck (1858), and John G. Freeze (1879).[15] These now
rare historical sources document Catharine Montour as the daughter of the
first governor of Canada, Count Frontenac, and his Native American wife.
From the her settlement at Catharinestown (now Montour Falls, New
York), Catharine Montour (sometimes in history confounded with Queen
Esther) guided the Six Nations of the Iroquois, who inhabited a large area
of what would later be claimed the United States. Despite Stephens's efforts at publicity, Montour's accomplishments to develop harmony among
various ethnic communities are unfortunately eclipsed in history by more
aggressive men such as those who sent Sullivan's troops to destroy her
seat of power.

Perhaps not recognizing the extent to which Stephens bases her characters, scenes, and incidents in *Mary Derwent* on history or perhaps led by
Harper's malicious curse (explained later in this chapter, 137-38), some
scholars ironically have accused Stephens of too much fantasy. Nina
Baym (*Woman's*), for example, criticizes: "Because these romances were
set in a clear fantasy world, these undomestic women could not serve as
models in the way that heroines of realistic fiction might" (181). More
recently, specifically referring to the situation and characters Stephens
depicts in *Mary Derwent*, Paola Gemme reports,

"... it is not surprising that Stephens would create in her novels alternative,
compensatory worlds in which women are the heads of the state. Stephens's
novelistic world is populated by heroines who are chiefs among men, though
the latter have to be racial Others (in most novels Native Americans) for
women's sway to be considered admissible" (51).

Actually, the matrilineal culture of the Six Nations provided quite a natural circumstance for the "celebrated . . . well educated . . . lady of com-

parative refinement" (Stone 187) French Canadian and Native American Catharine Montour to develop her prosperous settlement.

Perhaps because of Stephens's efforts to dramatize women's historical leadership roles, her work takes more the form of narrative than do such compilations of parables as *Uncle Tom's Cabin* and *The Wide, Wide World*. Even though *Mary Derwent* differs from *The Wide, Wide World* and *Uncle Tom's Cabin* in the prominence and function of its plot and its message, as with the earlier works, one can better appreciate the impact of Stephens's text[16] and its early impact by seeing how George Campbell's (1778) four appeals play on the reader's faculties of understanding, imagination, passions, and will. Campbell specifies of his first end of discourse, a writer's appeal to the reader's understanding, that effectiveness derives from presenting information that lies in the sphere of the reader's knowledge. Ideas should be no longer, nor more complex, nor more intricate than those to which the reader is accustomed (73). *Mary Derwent* demonstrates the first of Campbell's rhetorical principles in its use of elements familiar to her nineteenth-century reader. General issues of the strife between Indians and settlers, the hardships facing orphaned children, the opulence of the aristocracy, and the challenges to the physically disabled were all part of ordinary nineteenth-century life. Even the single contentious element Stephens offers her reader, the morality of miscegenation, would have been a well-known and controversial matter.

Similarly, Stephens's biblical references and allusions would not have been "more complex, or more intricate, than" those to which the reader was accustomed. She consistently likens Mary to an angel (27, 33, 36, 120, 166). The missionary's language is very like Christ's in the New Testament: "It is a beautiful love, Mary, that which strength gives to dependence, for it approacheth nearest to that heavenly benevolence which the true soul always thirsts for" (25).[17] Mary repeatedly refers to herself as alone in the "wide world" (82, 184, 205) a phrase that would certainly have called to the reader's mind the title of Susan Warner's *The Wide, Wide World*.

Stephens further appeals to her reader's understanding in her method of presentation, as she interweaves her own plot with historically documentable characters, scenes, and events. As Campbell stipulates that one should, Stephens captures her reader's attention through appeals to memory (73, 76). The number of history books describing the circumstances of the Wyoming Massacre, their availability, their repetition among themselves, the numerous reviews of Peck's concurrently published *Wyoming*,[18] and the sixty-two foot extant monument erected in May, 1841, provide evidence of the era's infatuation for the battle. As Miner describes, "so early as 1809, 36 years ago, several essays were published intended to awaken public attention to . . . the battle"(69). The story of the Wyoming Massacre, its heroes and heroines and surrounding events were part of the nineteenth-century cultural memory. Touching her reader's memory with details of historical events to form contextual associations and to foreshadow episodes in her plot, Stephens assures her reader's understanding.

In addition to appeals to her reader's a priori understanding, Stephens writes "to dispel ignorance or to vanquish error" (Campbell 2) by offering her reader new perspectives of several social issues. For example, she challenges the common stereotype of Indian as savage, by showing that much of the Native Americans' savage behavior was taught to them by the Tories. A conversation between the Tory, Butler, and the Mohawk, Brant, for example, indicates that the Tories paid Indians to collect human scalps: "It is a better business than trapping mink, and so you take it" (240). In this way, Stephens confronts Thomas Campbell's famous portrait of Brant as "monster" by showing the Tory Butler as instigator, a view corroborated by history.[19] Indeed, the research that Stephens did between the first publication of her "article" in 1838 and her later book led her to remove Brant from the Wyoming Massacre altogether, correcting her own error as well as that foisted on the public by the acclaimed poet, Thomas Campbell. Likewise to "vanquish error," Stephens characterizes Queen Esther's historic and well-known (to the nineteenth-century reader) savage massacre of the settlers at Queen Esther's Rock as a mother's anguished response to the killing of her beloved son (364). Both women, Catharine Montour and Queen Esther, have aristocratic European blood. By contrasting Queen Esther's increasing savagery to Catharine Montour's gradual softening, Stephens appeals to her reader's understanding of savagery as a human rather than an ethnic phenomenon.

Through Catharine's recitation to the missionary of the details of her life before she came to the Wyoming Valley, Stephens offers the reader new perspectives regarding women's potentials: ". . . my mind . . . became stronger, more methodical, and far more capable of reasoning" (81). English heiress turned Shawnee queen, Catharine serves "to dispel ignorance and to vanquish error" as she reveals how a woman can effectively (politically and culturally) lead her people.[20] With her charismatic figures, Stephens offers her woman reader leadership role models drawn from history.

Opening her tale with a positive and realistic portrayal of the "misshapened" character, Mary Derwent, Stephens also offers to enlighten her reader's understanding of the physically challenged. Laughed at by her playfellows (20-21), Mary expects that she will always be solitary and isolated from the company of others: an expectation any of Stephens's readers might have found quite reasonable for someone with Mary's injury. As Stephens offers new insight into both Indian belief and the nature of deformity itself, she appeals to her reader's understanding:

> "No, my child, it is not pity[21] with them but homage, adoration. That which you feel as a deformity, they hold to be a sacred seal of holiness which the Great Spirit sets upon his own. With them you, and such as you, are held only as little lower than the angels." (206)

To a reader in Stephens's time, such an appeal would have been doubly enlightening. The reader would gain new perspectives "to dispel ignorance or to vanquish error" both regarding the nature of the physical body, and nature of the "savage" as well as Stephens here commingles Native American spirituality with Christianity.

Campbell specifies that an orator may address a hearer's imagination, the second faculty to which a discourse might appeal, by exhibiting to it a lively and beautiful representation of a suitable object. He likens the task of the orator to that of the painter: each deals with imitation. Although Stephens takes much of her own inspiration from historical sources,[22] she paints in *Mary Derwent* scenery to engage her reader's imagination. She creates "resemblances" (Campbell's word) predominantly in terms of plant life and landscapes. Mary is consistently presented in harmonious and ordered natural surroundings, just as Tahmeroo consistently appears in nature's wild settings. The Indian village under the reign of Queen Esther and later Catharine Montour was

> rich with corn and fruit. Her apple orchards blossomed and cast their fruit on the edge of the wilderness. The huts of her people were embowered with peach trees, and purple plums dropped upon the forest sward at their doors. (136)[23]

Stephens describes that same scene after Tahmeroo's Christian wedding as "trampled grass, extinguished torches, and torn vines [that] betrayed a sense of silent devastation" (181). Here, Stephens uses nature, and her characters' relations to it, to inform her reader through appeals to the imagination, presenting a picture of a damaged landscape that foreshadows Tahmeroo's life with the villainous Butler.

All of the flowers and gardens Stephens depicts in connection with Catharine Montour are untamed. Catharine describes the progression of her early life as a series of botanical scenes:

> "never yet have I known a spot so quiet and lovely as my own birth-place. . . . There was something picturesque and holy in the little stone church, with its porch overrun with ivy, and its narrow gothic windows half obscured by the soft moss and creeping foliage which had gathered about them from age to age . . . the rank grass beneath the dark solemn shadows of yew trees. . . .
>
> Back from the church stood the parsonage . . . surrounded by a grove of magnificent oaks . . . . a rich, viny foliage had been allowed to blossom and luxuriate year after year, unpruned and abandoned to its own profuse leafiness . . . . masses of leaves and flowers [that] clung . . . wherever a tendril could enweave itself or a bud find room for blossoming." (75)

When Caroline (later Catharine Montour) was fifteen, Varnham came to live with her family as her father's ward. She describes,

> "I gave up for his use my own little sitting room, opening upon a wilderness of roses and tangled honeysuckles that had once been a garden, but which I had delighted to see run wild in unchecked luxuriance, till it had become as fragrant and rife with blossoms as an East India jungle." (77-78)

Campbell shows how these descriptions appeal to the reader's imagination:

> Now, as by the habitual use of a language . . . the signs would insensibly be-
> come connected in the imagination, wherever the things signified are con-
> nected in nature; so, by the regular structure of a language, this connexion
> among the signs is conceived as analogous to that which subsisteth among
> their archetypes. (259-60)

In these terms Stephens extends Warner's use of floral references from
occasions for didactic lessons (Warner elaborately explains a biblical parable by means of analogy to the white camellia; see above 62-63) to de-
pend comparative more heavily on the power of signs.

Stephens continues her use of botanical references as linguistic signs as
Catharine describes her grief at her father's death:

> "The passion-flower was in bloom, and hung in festoons of starry blossoms
> from the balustrades. The solitary white rose tree . . . had spread and shot
> upwards over the front of the balcony in profuse leafiness. A host of pearly
> blossoms, intermingled with the passion-flowers, and hung in clustering
> beauty . . . .
> An agonizing conviction of my loss struck upon my heart . . . . While the
> pang was keenest, I gathered a handful of roses from the tree which my
> mother had planted; carefully selecting the half-blown and most delicate
> flowers . . . ." (83-84)

Stephens likewise has Catharine use floral references to describe her year
of madness to the missionary:

> "But an atmosphere soft and bland as that which broods over a bed of water-
> lilies, when they unfold their pearly hearts to the evening breeze, received a
> rainbow light from the glowing trees and delicate flowers that burst to blos-
> som everywhere. . . .
> Oh! how happy I fancied myself in this ideal region! How I loved to inter-
> lace my wings . . . among the vines, or lay on the odorous flowers . . . ."
> (118)

Then, Catharine's reason returns at the expense of the very flowers that
had sustained her:

> "I can never describe the cold, hopeless struggle of my heart to retain the de-
> lusions which haunted my insane moments, when my intellect began to re-
> sume its functions. . . . my spirit clung with intense longing to its own wild
> ideal." (121)

Catharine wants to be an eternal flower; Stephens communicates this idea using appeals to the reader's imagination again by means of floral references:

> ". . . bury me beneath the balcony, and let that lone, white rose-tree blossom over me for ever and ever.
> . . . so my spirit shall stay among those pure flowers in patient bondage . . . . (124-25)

Analyzing *Mary Derwent* principally in terms of characterizations, plot, and the literal meaning of words, these descriptions of floral scenes might seem at best merely descriptions of floral scenes or at worst "flowery." In the light of Campbell's theory, however, these botanical references form "resemblances" in a reader's mind: signs insensibly connected in the imagination (Campbell 259-60).   A nineteenth-century reading of Stephens's floral imagery reveals a layer of meaning currently lost.   Images that might seem worn or stereotypical to a twentieth-century reader communicated directly and specifically to the nineteenth-century reader's imagination; in Campbell's terms, such images serve to awaken and preserve the reader's attention (73).   "Stereotypes were often turned into powerful symbols . . . popular imagery which rang certain bells in the average reader's mind" (xx), explains Herzog.   Prominent poet of the age and close friend of Stephens, Lydia H. Sigourney, illustrates this principle in her "Flora's Party" (1834), a lengthy poem that characterizes a multitude of flowering plants and neatly associates each with an encoded message presumably known to the nineteenth-century reader (93-97).   Corroborating Herzog's observation that "a favorite source of imagery is the world of flowers" (xx), Harris (*19th-Century*) discusses nineteenth-century use of floral metaphors as hermeneutic codes (79-80):[24]

> Almost any female reader in nineteenth-century America (and many male readers as well) would have had at least a passing familiarity with the language (the symbolic use) of flowers: They were a universal symbol . . . .
> Guides to them abounded. (80)

Flower images were not clichés, but as Johnson[25] (*Nineteenth-Century*) describes, acted to "intensify impression of experience and thus affect the emotions and the imaginative responses that spur belief and action . . ."

(42). Referring to Campbell in a discussion of appeals to the imagination, Johnson explains how nineteenth-century authors were taught "to stimulate the associative processes of the faculties" using "similitude and resemblance" (42). In this way, Stephens appeals to her reader's imagination to add to her reader's understanding. That is, Stephens communicates information through her appeal to the reader's imagination; as Campbell claims, "we really think by signs as well as speak by them" (259-60).

Flora's Dictionary, by a Lady, (Mrs. E. W. Wirt, 1831)[26] and Sarah Josepha Hale's Flora's Interpreter (1865)[27] offer the twentieth-century reader insight into common associations that a nineteenth-century reader might have made to particular flowers. "As is common with flower books," explains Harris, "each flower is paired with an association, usually reflective of an emotion or state of being" (81). Ivy, which overruns Catharine's birthplace, refers to matrimony, according to Wirt. Hale's reference reveals that ivy for the nineteenth-century reader referred to "wedded love" (Flora's 97). Stephens has Catharine Montour describe her birthplace as overrun with ivy, obscured by moss, foliated with grass, shadowed by yews, and surrounded by oaks; at this very spot she would eventually marry Varnham and live with him. Appropriately, Wirt explains moss as associated with the recluse. Hale shows it associated with "ennui" (Flora's 130); in this mossy place Caroline Varnham (Catharine Montour) spends her year of solitary madness. Grass, in the nineteenth-century reader's imagination, according to both Wirt and Hale, evoked "submission" (Flora's 79). Yew trees, according to Wirt, evoked pensive introspection; according to Hale, the yew meant "penitence" (Flora's 230). Catharine Montour reports to the missionary her own period of submission, pensive introspection, and penitence as she recounts the gradual return of her sanity after her year of madness (121). In this same account, Montour mentions the starlight that shone on the acacia in her garden (121-22) with reference to her concealed love for Grenville Murray; according to both Wirt and Hale (Flora's 13), acacia, for the nineteenth-century reader denoted "concealed love." Oaks, according to both Wirt and Hale (Flora's 136), meant "bravery," emphasizing Caroline Varnham's bravery in leaving behind all she had known as an English aristocrat to face whatever lay ahead in an unknown land.

When Varnham joins Caroline's family as her father's ward, she gives him her sitting room, which opens upon a wilderness of honeysuckle. As the story progresses, the two young people fall in love and marry, but Caroline eventually leaves civilized England for wild America. Nineteenth-century associations to honeysuckle mirror Stephens's imaginative appeal. First, Wirt states, honeysuckle means, "the colour of my fate." Hale specifies that coral honeysuckle denotes "fidelity" (*Flora's* 89). Caroline's fate was to love Varnham, leave him, but find him again before her death. Wirt's second association with honeysuckle as "I would not answer hastily," and Hale's explanation of it in its wild state as denoting "inconstancy" (*Flora's* 90) reflect Catharine's lengthy emotional suffering over abandoning one love (Varnham) and submitting to marriage with Gien-gwa-tah to save another (Murray). The honeysuckle in the garden Caroline relinquishes to young Varnham runs wild, much as Caroline herself runs wild.

Catharine associates the passion-flower with grief; according to Wirt, it meant "susceptibility"; to Hale it meant "religious fervor" (*Flora's* 143). Caroline's father was a religious figure; his death left her vulnerable to the temptations of an aristocratic world where she succumbs to her unrequited passion for Murray. Twice Caroline refers to the white rose tree as she describes her grief. Hale associates the white rose with "sadness" (*Flora's* 185) and the withered white rose with "I am in despair" (*Flora's* 186); with both references Stephens compounds her message without resorting to literal language.

Stephens uses a similarly encoded flower association that appeals to her reader's imagination and so imparts information about Mary. In a dialogue between Mary and the minister, Stephens makes it clear that Mary will never experience a man's sexual love:

> "But there is another love, my father; I have seen it at the school and in the cabins, I have watched it as I have the mountain flowers, and thought that God meant this love for me, like the rest; but when I go among other girls, no one will ever think that I am one of them . . . to all the rest I am a hunchback."
> . . . "my child it is true, this love must never be yours." (25)

Mary acknowledges the missionary's caution that her physical shape will prevent her from marrying and resigns herself to go beyond the earthly joy and grief that marriage might bring to enter the realm of heavenly love. In recognition of her fate, Mary's eyes "were pure and serene as violets that have caught their hue by looking up to heaven" (267). Wirt shows violets associated with love generally; Hale shows the blue violet associated with "faithfulness" (*Flora's* 218). Martha Barnette, however, is far more specific. She explains that, "the pansy itself is, after all, simply a cultivated variety of violet" (148). Barnette continues that from the sixteenth century on, men and women have "signaled their intent never to marry by wearing sprigs of violets . . ." (148).[28]

Although Stephens appears to encode Catharine Montour and Mary Derwent by means of different sorts of flowers, she also uses a single flower-related image to link them. Stephens first describes Mary as a girl " . . . swaying as she walked like a flower too heavy for its stem" (13). When, two hundred pages later in the book, Mary finally meets Catharine and finds herself inexplicably drawn to this strange Indian woman, Mary's head bends under the weight of Catharine's hand, "like a flower on its stalk" (205). Stephens appeals to the reader's imagination within her text using the word "like" to denote association. The floral references, known to the nineteenth-century reader, through their appeal to the reader's imagination, spoke for themselves.

Stephens appeals also to her reader's imagination by using a serpent image. When Mary first encounters Indians, they surround her "like a flock of tropical birds surrendering themselves to the charms of a serpent" (28). This allusion appeals to the reader's curiosity, for Mary is in no way serpentine. Later in the story, however, at Mary's first meeting with Catharine Montour, Stephens returns to the image of the serpent and clarifies it:

> Mary touched the clasp pointed out, and directly one of the serpent bracelets uncoiled from Catharine's wrist, as if it had been a living thing, and she wound it on Mary's arm, above the elbow, shutting the spring with a noise that sounded like a hiss.
> "It will guard you," she said, eagerly. "There is not a Shawnee savage who does not hold that sign sacred, nor one among the Six Tribes who will not protect its wearer . . . ." (210)

Stephens draws her allusion of the protective serpent directly from histories of the Wyoming Valley. For those readers acquainted with the

Wyoming Valley's historical lore, this allusion created a "resemblance" (Campbell) to the (then) well-known story of Zinzendorf. Isaac Chapman (1830) tells the story of the first white person known to visit the Wyoming Valley, the Moravian "Revivor," Count Zinzendorf. An anecdote that appears in several histories available to nineteenth-century readers describes Zinzendorf as he sat in his tent one night by the light of a small fire. Several Shawnee, intending Zinzendorf's assassination, found the minister engrossed in his writings and oblivious to a large rattlesnake that "passed over one of his legs undiscovered" (21). The Indians abandoned their murderous scheme and spread the word that with the snake the Great Spirit had protected the white man.[29] As the serpent protected Zinzendorf from the Indians, so does the serpent bracelet guard and protect its wearers, Catharine Montour and Mary Derwent. Stephens here appeals to her reader's probable memory of the Wyoming Valley's protective serpent, to remind the reader, through the faculty of the imagination, of the Indians' innate spirituality. Stephens thus "excites both the imagination and the sympathy of the reader," states an 1858 review of *Mary Derwent*, (*Harper's* 407), and illustrates the importance in the mid-nineteenth century of rhetorical appeals to a reader's imagination and sympathy.

"Sympathy," argues Campbell, "is one engine by which the orator operates on the passions" (96). Moving the passions, according to Campbell, is the third of a hearer's faculties to which an author may appeal. Campbell describes seven "circumstances" (81-90) by which an author may move the passions of a reader. The first of these, "probability," Stephens creates with her choice of a known historic context for her tale. Stephens's settings, characterizations, and incidents were common lore to the nineteenth-century reader[30] as prominent historian of the age, Elizabeth F. Ellet, reports:

> The name of Wyoming is celebrated from its association with events of thrilling interest. Its history from its first settlement is well known to the American reader, nor is there needed another recital of the catastrophe of July, 1778, . . . The pen of the historian—the eloquence of the orator—the imagination of the poet and novelist—have by turns illustrated the scene . . . . (193)

Despite Stephens's extensive use of historical material in *Mary Derwent*, however, the story was vindictively reported to have been improbable by

Harper's. Unfortunately, Nina Baym (*Novels* 80), Gemme (52), and other twentieth-century scholars have perpetuated *Harper's* criticism of the tale as defying "all sense of probability" apparently recognizing neither the work's close adherence to history nor *Harper's* ulterior motives for denigrating Stephens through their review.

Harper's had their own reasons to attack Stephens by denigrating *Mary Derwent* and went beyond the words of their review to insult her. "The Harpers" had earlier offered to publish a "two volume novel" version of *Mary Derwent*, an offer they publicized in *The Ladies' Companion*, November, 1838, (50).[31] When Stephens chose to publish with the Petersons, whose literary journal she edited, the August, 1858, *Harper's New Monthly Magazine* retaliated with a double insult to Stephens. In a fifteen-page article (306-22) replete with elaborate engravings, they celebrated Peck's *Wyoming: Its History, Romance, Stirring Incidents, and Romantic Adventure*, which had been published concurrently with *Mary Derwent*. Hidden in the back of that issue among "Literary Notices" is the editors' short review of Stephens's work, with its attack that "the plan of the work is bold—not to say audacious—involving demands on the faith of the reader which defy all sense of probability" (407). Despite *Harper's* public tiff, Stephens, by using available historic references— indeed, those used by Peck—created probability for her contemporary readers that, according to Campbell, "begets belief. Belief invigorates our ideas. Belief raised to the highest becomes certainty" (81).

The second of Campbell's "circumstances," "plausibility," refers to an internal coherence that arises "chiefly from the consistency of the narration, from its being what is commonly called natural and feasible" (82). Stephens maintains Campbell's recommended consistency through her development of her characters' interrelationships in the progress of the tale. Stephens links her characters in two ways: through their biological ties—both known and unknown to them—and through the emotional and spiritual connections they develop as part of the story's movement. The internal consistency of Stephens's tale (like its probability) reflects the historical consistency with which actual events unfolded in around the time of the Wyoming Valley Massacre. Readers aware of those events would consider the tale more plausible than readers who (like most twentieth-century readers) are unaware of the tale's historicity.

Campbell's third "circumstance," "importance," adds ". . . brightness and strength to the ideas" in three ways. An action may derive importance "by its own nature," if it "be stupendous in its kind," or if its "generosity is godlike . . . its atrocity is diabolical" (86). Stephens creates importance in the character of the generously Godlike missionary, Varnham: "a wonderful influence . . . a strong, pure soul" (17). Conversely, Stephens creates importance in her portrayal of the Wyoming Valley Massacre; "its atrocity is [as] diabolical" as the actual historical accounts of it. Or as Ellet describes, "the scene—the realities of which transcend the wildest creations of fiction" (193).

Campbell argues that "an action may derive importance . . . from those concerned in it as acting or suffering . . . " (86). By painting characters who brave physical hardships, emotional suffering, and ostracism from their fellows because of physical differences, Stephens, through the vehicle of sympathy, creates importance for her reader, and so moves his or her passions. Stephens's characters gain importance in her reader's mind by evincing "dignity"—for example, Stephens characterizes Catharine Montour as an aristocrat and as ruler of the Shawnee—and by making manifest their "number"—the actual Wyoming Valley Massacre involved great numbers of both settlers and Indians. An action may also "derive importance . . . from its consequences" (86), Campbell states. By constantly foreshadowing and suggesting later developments in her plot, Stephens builds a sense of importance for her reader.

Campbell's next two "circumstances" meant to move the reader's passions—"proximity in time" (87-88) and "connexion of place" (88)—refer to the immediacy of the tale for the reader. Although Stephens writes of a massacre that occurred before her own historical time and outside the geographical locale of many of her readers, various writers of the time have shown the great extent to which Indian affairs galvanized the attention of the nineteenth-century reading public.[32] Stephens moves the passions of her nineteenth-century reader by creating what Campbell terms "relation to the persons concerned" (89), the sixth of the "circumstances" by which an author can engender sensation through language. Using the vehicle of sympathy, Stephens draws her reader to exotic characters of a past era. These exciting characters have a "relation" to the reader not by virtue of their shared identity with the reader, but by virtue of their difference from the reader. The nineteenth-century readership had a particular

fascination for (relation to) "Exotics."[33]   So popular in the nineteenth
century was "Indian literature" that Madeleine B. Stern speculates *Mary
Derwent* "might well have become the first Beadle Dime Novel had it not
been reprinted before the eventful year of 1860" (34). Stern situates and
describes Stephens's contemporary readership:

> When the frontier had receded to the line of the Missouri and the Arkansas,
> when the Far West had been settled, and adventure was no longer just around
> the corner, arm-chair pioneers and Indian fighters could revel vicariously . . .
> (46)

in the historic frontier tale. That is, although she sets her tale outside the
"proximity in time" and "connexion of place" of her reader, by playing on
a nineteenth-century vicarious involvement with exotics, Stephens can
move her reader's passions.[34]

The final "circumstance," according to Campbell, by which an author
may move a reader's passion involves creating in the reader an "interest in
the consequences" (89). The writer enlists the reader's sympathy by
blurring the distinction between the reader's interest and that of the character. She uses particular instances of danger to draw her reader's interest to what outcomes may be. Situated on Monockonok Island in the
middle of the Susquehanna River in a valley peopled by Indians, the Derwent cabin sits: serene, but vulnerable and unprotected. In the famous
battle that extended to the Derwent cabin on the island, Catharine Montour tries to save the missionary, Mary, and Mary's Derwent family: Jane
and Grandmother (356ff). Clinging to a log with the current rushing
around them, Jane and Mary and their grandmother flee toward possible
safety at Forty Fort (362-65).

Stephens further arrests the reader's sympathy by constructing literary
situations drawn from history. The reader who was cognizant of the actual Wyoming Valley Massacre wonders if Stephens's characters will escape a massacre that so many others in history did not escape. For example, Stephens places Mary in a historical scene in which brother kills
brother during the massacre:

> "Brother—brother ! In the name of her who bore us, do not kill me !"
> shrieked the wretched man, looking with horror on the uplifted tomahawk. "I
> will be your slave—anything, everything, but do not kill me, brother !"
> "Infernal traitor !"

The words hissed through his clenched teeth ; the tomahawk whirled in the
air, and came down with a dull crash ! . . .
Mary turned sick with horror. (361)[35]

Stephens similarly situates Mary at the well-known massacre of "The
Bloody Rock." Doing so, Stephens creates in her reader an interest in
Mary's consequences and so moves her reader's passions:

A huge fragment of stone lay in the centre of a ring . . . . Around this rock
sixteen prisoners were ranged, and beneath them a ring of savages, each
holding a victim pressed to the earth. And thus the doomed men sat face to
face, waiting for death.
. . . With her son's tomahawk gleaming in her hand, she [Queen Esther]
struck into a dance, which had a horrid grace in it. With every third step, the
tomahawk fell, and a head rolled at her feet! . . .
Queen Esther's death-chant increased in volume and fury as the chain of
bleeding heads lengthened and circled along her tracks. Life after life
dropped before her, and but two were left, when Mary Derwent forced herself
through the belt of savages and sprang upon the rock.
"Warriors, stop the massacre—in the name of the Great Spirit, I command
you!" (364-65)[36]

The reader, in whom Stephens has established a sympathy for Mary, fears
for her as she enters a historical scene in which all settlers became victims.

Campbell's fourth and final appeal is to the hearer's faculty of will.
Admitting that this end of discourse is "the most complex of all" (4),
Campbell specifies that to influence the reader effectively, one artfully
mixes "that which proposes to convince the judgement, and that which
interests the passions" (4). That is, to influence the reader's will, a writer
should incorporate "the argumentative and the pathetic" (4). A complexity arises because Campbell differentiates three kinds of pathos. Mixing
reason with a pathos of "sorrow, fear, shame, humility" (5) "deject[s] the
mind, and indispose[s] it for enterprise" (5). Mixing reason with a pathos
of "hope, patriotism, ambition, emulation, anger" (5) "elevate[s] the soul
and stimulate[s] to action" (5). Finally, mixing reason with a pathos of
"joy, love, esteem, compassion" (5) can either restrain or incite action.

Stephens mixes reason with Campbell's first sort of pathos, using the
characters of both Mary Derwent and Walter Butler, to dissuade her
reader from certain behavior. The portrait Stephens paints of Mary's

pure soul trapped in her kyphotic body appeals to the reader's sorrow that the girl must endure her physical sufferings. That Mary endures her deformity with exemplary fortitude should appeal to a reader's "sorrow" and "humility" to humble a reader inclined toward pride. Stephens thus mixes her initial appeals to the reader's understanding of physical deformities ("the poor deformed girl" 27) with shame for insensitive behavior to form an appeal to dissuade the reader from future callous actions toward the physically challenged.

Conversely, Stephens's (historically accurate) portrayal of Butler as consistently selfish, blasphemous, ungentlemanly, dishonest, unpatriotic, and base throughout the book demonstrates Stephens's mixture of reason and Campbell's second sort of pathos to dissuade her reader from emulating Butler's coarse behaviors. Butler acts undisturbed when Catharine confronts him for his secret meetings with Tahmeroo, and he does not address her with respect during their confrontation (148). He patronizes Catharine despite the generosity of the terms she offers him if he will agree to marry Tahmeroo in a Christian ceremony and take her back to England as his wife (160). When Tahmeroo discovers her new husband courting Jane Derwent, Butler lies, pretending his actions were his effort to teach Tahmeroo a lesson (176). Stephens describes Butler's behavior at Johnson Hall as representative of "low breeding . . . off-handed impudence" (213), calling him " selfish . . . coarse . . . revolting" (217).[37] Stephens associates this unsavory character with the Royalist Dutch—Wintermoots, Van Gardners, and Van Alstyns—who did not invest their energies in the growing American nationalism of the book's setting. Stephens uses the combination of Butler's character and his associates to dissuade her reader from following similar paths.

Stephens mixes reason with a pathos of "hope, patriotism, ambition, emulation, anger" (5) to excite the reader "to resolution and activity" (5). In several scenes, she shows that women, when so resolved, are capable of actively pursuing their own life interests. After Butler, Tahmeroo's wedded husband, vanishes, the pining young Indian, learning of Butler's incarceration in the Albany jail, pleads with several characters to help her free him: "No one could help me—our great medicine men could only pity me when asked for counsel. My father had power to revenge his loss but that did not bring him back" (275). Realizing that her husband's freedom would come only from her own will and activity, Tahmeroo, armed simply with a letter from the missionary to General Schuyler (280), tricks Butler's jailers and leads him to freedom.[38] As the episode unfolds, Stephens demonstrates for her reader that a woman can rely effectively on her own will—wit, activity, and perseverance—to accomplish her goals. As Stephens does so, she calls upon her reader to emulate Tahmeroo's strengths.

Stephens further uses her authorial voice to move her reader to action through hope, patriotism, and emulation. Drawing from historical sources (Stone 234, Miner 212, and perhaps Peck 31),[39] she lauds the strengths of the Wyoming Valley women:

> The women of Wyoming rose and took their places bravely upon the hearthstone, ready to defend the children who clung to their garments, when the son or father fell upon the doorstep. They worked like their husbands; impending danger gave them quick knowledge, and women whose ideas of chemistry had never gone beyond the ash leech and the cheese-press, fell to manufacturing saltpetre. . . . delicate women and fair young girls took to the field and worked, side by side, with the old men, whose strength was scarcely greater than their own. (288)[40]

Stephens appeals directly to her reader to emulate these brave (and willful) women: "It was a brave, beautiful sight, which the American woman of our nineteenth century will do wisely to remember" (288). She would have her reader know that action is often the only viable course.

In the relationship between the missionary and Mary Derwent, Stephens mixes reason with the pathos of "joy, love, esteem, and compassion" (Campbell 5) to move her reader both to act in accordance with spiritual teachings and, conversely, to dissuade that reader from following only earthly passion. The two are faithful in their resolve to lead Christian lives. No other characters maintain such faith; those who pursue earthly goods, as Butler does, seem doomed to pain and suffering.

Finally, Stephens appeals to her reader's several faculties through the language of *Mary Derwent*. Her notes of work with American Indian language, housed with some of her collected papers at the New York Public Library, show her concern for expanding her own sense of language and sound. Stephens presents her readers with possibilities for an American language that combines decorum she heard in British English with those sounds of the Native American tongue that echo the nature of what they signify. From the first page of her work, Stephens directs her reader's attention to the sounds of her words, especially those she draws from Indian languages: "The Indians have gathered up the music of these waters in a name that will live forever—Monockonok[41]—rapid or broken waters" (1). The sound, "monockonok," is a homophone for the sound of such waters. Reflecting a natural quality, the name stands in direct contrast to such awkward place-names that white men chose, such as the quantifying, Forty Fort.[42]

As the language of *Mary Derwent* is opulent in its description of the natural environment, so is it opulent in its description of the book's characters, especially those women characters who bridge the English and Native American cultures. For example, Tahmeroo is

> . . . of a mixed race. The spirited and wild grace of the savage was blended with a delicacy of feature and nameless elegance more peculiar to the whites. . . . Her moccasins were of dressed deerskin, fringed and wrought with tiny beads, interwoven with a vine of silk buds and leaves done in such needlework as was in those days only taught to the most refined and highly educated class of whites. . . . All the grace, but not the chilliness, of marble lived in those boldly poised limbs, so full of warm, healthy life. (43)

Stephens's concept of miscegenation reaches beyond mere coupling to present an ideal of identity featuring what she sees as the best of both cultures.[43] This concept extends beyond her characters and plot to the descriptions that fill her reader's senses. In Campbell's terms, she appeals to her reader's understanding that combining the best of two races could benefit each.[44] Certainly, her vivid, sensual, and aesthetic representations of Tahmeroo and Catharine Montour appeal to her reader's imagination, and the concern she develops for her characters' eventual circumstances play upon her reader's passions. Finally, Stephens's appeals culminate in an appeal to the reader's will. Having traced the harrowing life of physically challenged Mary Derwent, Stephens confers on her a heavenly peace on earth—and the Granby inheritance. Tahmeroo, a woman of mixed race, is shown at the book's conclusion on her way to lead her people to a civilization whose beauty, peace, bounty, and joy are left to the reader's imagination. The reader has learned that such rewards come only through activity and willful struggle. The reader exits *Mary Derwent* with that "passionate eviction, that vehemence of contention" (Campbell 4) that he or she can incorporate into his or her own life valuable elements of self-determination gleaned from people of differing cultures and abilities.

Stephens's lessons regarding self-determination split somewhat from those lessons Warner and Stowe offer. Warner advocates that a person determine one's self in alignment with God's will; readers willing themselves (ourselves) to Christian ideology could establish an earthly Christian community. Stowe advocates that her readers determine their lives such that each "feels right" vis-à-vis Christian doctrine. As illustrated by Uncle Tom, self-determination might include an individual's Christian martyrdom for the good of the "whole place." As illustrated by Eliza, self determination might include individual heroic efforts for survival that always end such havens of Christian community as motherhood, theological identity, family, etc.

Stephens's sense of self-determination allows her heroes to move outside the fold; her model characters embody Christian virtues and ideology, but they tend to live such virtues outside identification with an author-specified community. Setting her tale in the historical time and place of frontier settlers, Stephens introduces the Christian isolato.[45] Mary Derwent, for example, must meet the challenges of her disability outside the social mores of heterosexual married life. Catharine Montour determines and lives her life in self-imposed penance and exile, a leader of foreign people in a foreign land. Extending Campbell's sense of will (to which an author should make rhetorical appeals) beyond that of a Christian motivated psychological faculty, Stephens begins to shift her appeals to a will individually motivated and apart from the Christian community.

NOTES

[1] So named by Fred Lewis Pattee.

[2] Describing *Mary Derwent* in "Literary Notices," the editor of *Godey's Lady's Book* (presumably Sarah Josepha Hale) emphasizes elements of story-telling:

> Mrs. Stephens' tales . . . have generally been well told and are full of interest—characteristics that are well sustained in the present work, which claims to have its foundation in history . . . ." (181)

[3] *The Ladies' Companion*, vol. 9 (May, 1838) 39. Madeleine B. Stern also quotes this passage in *We the Women* (33). Before "Mary Derwent" appeared in serial form in 1838, Stephens had secured its copyright in New York, July, 1837.

[4] In addition, Stephens published with Maturin Murray Ballou, Publisher (Stern 27, 28); Beadle and Company (Stern 37, 41, 44); Gleason's Publishing Hall (Stern 137, 139, 142); F. M. Lutton Publishing Company (Stern 215); T. B. Peterson and Brothers (Stern 229, 230, 232); and Street and Smith's *New York Weekly* (Stern 277, 281). She also edited *Frank Leslie's Ladies Gazette of Fashion* (Stern 182). For biographical material contemporary to her era, see "Mrs. Ann S. Stephens," (*The American Literary Magazine* [1848] 335-43), John S. Hart [1852] 193-99), or Phebe A. Hanaford [1882] 217-18). For recent biographical material see Stern (29-54).

[5] Monockonok Island appears to be about one or two acres.

[6] William L. Stone's *The Poetry and History of Wyoming* (1841) describes the missionary work of founder and apostle of the Moravians or "United Brethren," Count Zinzendorf, with the Delaware and Shawnee in the Wyoming Valley, Pennsylvania, autumn, 1742, (94-95). The nineteenth-century reader was very likely acquainted with Zinzendorf's activities from sources literary and theological as well as historical; see, for example, Lydia H. Sigourney's *Zinzendorff and Other Poems* (1837) or Enoch Pond, D.D.'s *Memoir of Count Zinzendorf* (1839).

[7] Although she does not use the word, "kyphotic," Stephens devotes Chapters Three and Four (17-27) to showing the cruelty of using the taunt, "hunchbacked." Stephens reinforces the term's derogative use in the voices of the vicious Tories, Wintermoot (19) and Butler: "The Little Hunchback . . . Out of my path, lying imp, before I trample your shapeless carcass under my feet" (169).

[8] Charles Miner (1845) explains,

The Wintermoots, a numerous family, seeming to have extraordinary means
at command, had . . . erected a fortification, known as Wintermoot's fort.
This was looked upon with jealousy by the old settlers. (191)

Stone (1841) adds, "the suspected [Wintermoot] family had in fact been plotting the
destruction of their own neighbours" (232). Stone's *Life of Brant* (1838) adds, ". . .
a distinguished Tory named Wintermoot . . . was active in bringing destruction upon
the valley, and, after doing all the mischief he could to the settlement, removed to
Canada" (333). Although the characters, Murray, Mary, and Tahmeroo do not appear in the historical sources available to Stephens, she places them within historical
events and draws from history the personalities, situations, and activities of numerous other characters.

[9] Stephens draws her account of the Wyoming Valley Massacre—its characterizations,
settings, and actions—from historical sources. The descriptive language of those
sources appears almost indistinguishable from hers.

[10] See above, Chapter IV, pages 84-85. Stowe states her work is to be "understood to
be a parable—a story told in illustration of a truth or fact" (Kelley 250). Comparing
Stowe's narrative arrangement to that of a quilt, Showalter (*Sister's*) describes *Uncle
Tom's Cabin* as scenes stitched together to create a cumulative ideological effect
(155). Tompkins (*Sensational*) speaks of "the totalizing effect of the novel's iterative
organization" (139).

[11] Warner avoids interracial coupling in her books. Stowe portrays most of her interracial couples as white men exploiting black women, for example, "one young
woman, who had been sold by the traders for the worst of purposes" (*Key* 318).
"Stephens and some other women writers had no qualms about miscegenation," write
both Baym (*Woman's* 181) and Kristin Herzog (xxi).

[12] Neither Warner nor Stowe challenges patriarchal economic laws or mores; in the
worlds they paint, men (such as God, Christ, fathers, brothers, and husbands) are
supposed to care for and protect women.

[13] In Stephens's work the Granby peerage extends to women as well as to men.
Whether this inheritance line accurately reflects the history of the actual English
Granby family is speculation. See Rutland.

[14] Leadership roles in the Six Nations were determined according to a matrilineal
model. "The Iroquois Confederacy . . . gives women power in the political affairs of
the tribes," states Herzog (xvi).

[15] For their assistance in directing me to historical materials, I thank Elsie B. Russell,
Memorial Library, Montour Falls, NY, and The Wyoming Valley Historical Society,
Wilkes-Barre, PA.

[16] Largely due to the success of the book, *Mary Derwent,* expanded from the serialized "article" of the same name, Beadle and Company asked Stephens to expand to book length in a similar manner another of her serialized tales. In 1860 Beadle and Company then published *Malaeska; the Indian Wife of the White Hunter,* initiating their series of "Dime Novels—The Choicest Works of the Most Popular Authors."

[17] In the Gospel of John, Christ himself says, " . . . he that believeth in me shall never thirst . . . " (6.35) and " . . . if any man thirst, let him come unto me" (7.37).

[18] Other reviews of Peck's *Wyoming* appeared in *The National Era* (June 10, 1858), *Harper's New Monthly Magazine* (June, 1858), and *Ladies' Repository* (July, 1858).

[19] Thomas Campbell's poem, "Gertrude of Wyoming," (1809) popularized the idea of the American Indian as savage and of the Mohawk, Joseph Brant, as "monster." Several references (including the notes to revised editions of the epic poem, e.g., 1858: 93-94) relate that Brant's son confronted the poet who had so defamed both his father and his people:

> the son of Brandt, a most interesting and intelligent youth, came over to England . . . . He then referred me [T. Campbell] to documents which completely satisfied me that the common accounts of Brant's cruelties at Wyoming, which I had found in books of Travels, and in Adolphus's and similar Histories of England, were gross errors, and that, in point of fact, Brant was not even present at that scene of desolation.
> . . . the *New Monthly Magazine,* in the year 1822, [published] . . . an antidote to my fanciful description of Brant. (Stone *The Poetry* 323)

[20] Having through the time of the book followed Queen Esther and Catharine Montour as they governed their people, it seems quite natural that the book concludes with Montour's daughter, Tahmeroo, returning to her people to rebuild the culture after Sullivan's decimation of it. By the end of the book, Stephens has thus demonstrated for her reader woman's natural place in government.

[21] Stephens later deepens her reader's understanding of pity when she has Tahmeroo realize that only she can act to release her husband from jail: pity is a nonproductive luxury when circumstances demand action. Action, in Campbell's scheme, is the natural result when understanding has triggered imagination, which has in turn evoked emotions that finally engage the will.

[22] Descriptive scenes of the Wyoming Valley available to Stephens appear in Isaac Chapman's *History of Wyoming* (1830), Stone (1838, 1841), and Miner—especially, his "Preliminary Chapter."

[23] Although such "paintings" of nature may appeal to a reader's imagination, Stephens had discovered their fact from historical sources. For example, see Stone's *Life of Brant* (25).

[24] See above, Chapter III, (60-61).

[25] Johnson refers to Campbell's contemporary fellow Scottish theological rhetorician, Hugh Blair, here to describe nineteenth-century cognitive habits.

[26] Wirt's reference is alphabetically arranged and non-paginated.

[27] Hale's book of floral references sold more than forty thousand copies (Hart 94).

[28] "The color of which is traditionally associated with the gay community," continues Barnette (148).

[29] Stone (1841) draws from Chapman and presents the story (94-97); Miner copies Chapman's "original and well authenticated narrative entire" (38-41).

[30] Also, see above (127). Histories of the Wyoming Valley Massacre are found in popular literary sources, essays, and histories published before *Mary Derwent* such as those written by Chapman, Stone, and Miner, as well as in sources published after 1858.

[31] The announcement reads:

> We are happy to inform our readers that a proposal has been made our associate, *Mrs. Stephens*, by the Harpers, to make the Prize Tale of "Mary Derwent," published in our last volume the ground-work of a two-volume novel, and that at present all the leisure which can be obtained from her duties as one of editors of this magazine, will be devoted to the completion of the work. Consequently all the magazine writing emanating from her pen is secured *exclusively* to the *Ladies' Companion*.

Evidently, *The Ladies' Companion* did not afford Stephens much leisure; the completed *Mary Derwent* (in one volume) did not appear until twenty years later.

[32] "Captivity literature was enormously popular" states James D. Hart (1950) (40). Herzog discusses the "American Indian epic" (xvi) at length in her work. Like *Mary Derwent*, Grace Greenwood's *A Forest Tragedy* (1855) includes the specific circumstances of the Six Nations, 1775-1777 (2) for its setting. Ellet and other historians refer to the nineteenth-century public fascination with the Wyoming Valley Massacre and related events.

[33] Herzog so titles her book: *Women, Ethnics, and Exotics: Images of Power in Mid-Nineteenth-Century American Fiction.*

[34] The subject of Native Americans also finds positive reception in twentieth-century films such as *Dances with Wolves* and *Little Big Man* and in books such as John G. Neihardt's *Black Elk Speaks*, 1961, and Dee Brown's *Bury my Heart at Wounded Knee: An Indian History of the American West*, 1970.

[35] Stephens paraphrases this incident from historians Isaac A. Chapman, William L. Stone, and Charles Miner. Chapman (1830) relates the scene:

> "So it is you is it?" His brother finding that he was discovered, immediately came forward a few steps, and falling on his knees, begged him to spare his life, promising to live with him and serve him, and even to be his slave as long as he lived, if he would only spare his life. "All this is mighty good," replied the savage hearted brother of the supplicating man, "but you are a d***d rebel" . . . . (128)

Stone (1841), emphasizes that "the greatest barbarities of this celebrated massacre were committed by the tories (sic)":

> One of them was discovered by his own brother, who had espoused the side of the crown. The unarmed Whig fell on his knees before his brother and offered to serve him as a slave forever, if he would but spare his life. But the fiend in human form was inexorable; he muttered "you are a d—d rebel," and shot him dead. . . . The name of the brothers was Pensil. (194-95)

Miner (1845) tells the tale similarly:

> One of the fugitives by the name of Pensil sought security by hiding in a cluster of willows on the island. Seeing his tory (sic) brother come up, and recognize him, he threw himself at his feet, begged for protection, and proffered to serve him for life, if he would save him. "Mighty well!" was the taunting reply. "You d—d rebel," and instantly shot him, dead. (225)

[36] Stephens draws this passage from Stone and Miner. Stone writes:

> . . . the scene was that of horrible slaughter.
> . . . The place of these murders was about two miles north of Fort Forty, upon a rock, around which the Indians formed themselves in a circle. Sixteen of the prisoners, placed in a ring around a rock, near the river, were held by stout Indians, while the squaws struck their heads open with the tomahawk.
> . . . It has been said, both in tradition and in print, that the priestess of this bloody sacrifice was the celebrated Catharine Montour, sometimes called Queen Esther, whose residence was at Catharinestown at the head of Seneca

Lake. But the statement is improbable. Catharine Montour was a half-breed, who had been well educated in Canada. . . . she herself was a lady of comparative refinement. She was much caressed in Philadelphia, and mingled in the best society. (186-87)

Miner relates the story as follows:

Sixteen or eighteen [prisoners] were arranged around one large stone, since known as the bloody rock. Surrounded by a body of Indians, queen Esther, a fury in the form of a woman, assumed the office of executioner with a death maul or tomahawk, for she used the one with both hands, or took up the other with one, and passing round the circle with words, as if singing, or counting with a cadence, she would dash out the brains, or sink the tomahawk into the head of a prisoner. (226)

[37] Stone's *Life of Brant*, Vol. I, describes Butler: ". . . his temper was severe and irascible . . ." (369-70).

[38] Stone (*Life of Brant*, Vol. 1) describes:

The arrest of Walter N. Butler, at the German Flatts, in the summer of 1777; his trial, and condemnation to death; his reprieve; as also his subsequent imprisonment in Albany, and his escape; are facts.
. . . being either sick in reality, or feigning to be so, through the clemency of General Lafayette his quarters were changed to a private house, where he was guarded by a single sentinel. It appears that the family with whom he lodged were Tories at heart; and having succeeded in making the sentinel drunk, through their assistance Butler was enabled to effect his escape. (369-70)

Peck's *Wyoming*, published concurrently with *Mary Derwent* (1858), relates the event's history similarly (34-35).

[39] *Noble Deeds of American Women*, edited by J. Clement and introduced by Lydia Sigourney (1852), also quotes related passages from Miner's *History*, 142.

[40] Stephens's passage here is taken from historical sources almost verbatim (Peck 31, Miner 212, Stone 234). Whereas male historians use the passage to demonstrate that the government had virtually abandoned the settlers of the Wyoming Valley, Stephens uses it to celebrate pioneer women's strengths and ingenuity.

[41] The name of the now deserted Monockonok Island seems known only to a few local farmers and amateur historians in Wilkes-Barre, PA.

[42] In contrast to the Indian tendency to name the environment to reflect its qualities or describe its elements, early European-Americans tended to name their environment

to reflect themselves. Hence, Indian place names might resemble sounds and sights; European place names, (e.g. "Wilkes-Barre," "Catharinestown," "Pennsylvania," etc.) might be named for European founders.

[43] Like Sarah Josepha Hale (see Chapter I, 14-15 above), Stephens rejects the cold and austere element of European-American identity.

[44] In the figure of the evil Queen Esther, Stephens shows that combining European and Native American cultures could also produce a monster embodying the worst attributes of each civilization. Stephens, however, clearly guides her reader to value the cultural combination represented by Tahmeroo.

[45] Stephens does so with others of her era such as Thoreau writing of his solitary experience at Walden Pond.

THE WYOMING MONUMENT

Height 62's feet

Reprinted from Charles Miner's
History of Wyoming (1845). Appendix: 69.

E.D.E.N. Southworth

VI

E.D.E.N. SOUTHWORTH'S *THE HIDDEN HAND*:
AN ALTERNATE WAY OF BEING

By the beginning of the 1860s, E.D.E.N. Southworth's *The Hidden Hand* (1859) had, with her heroine, Capitola, challenged the feminine model and cultural ethos proffered in *The Wide, Wide World* (1850) by Susan Warner's heroine, Ellen Montgomery. "Indeed it is entirely possible that Southworth had Ellen, the ultimate sentimental heroine, in mind in the composition of this book, and intended Cap [Capitola] as a corrective to her" (234), speculates Joanne Dobson (*"The Hidden"*). Susan Coultrap-McQuin explains:

> Capitola, manages to overturn most of the popular nineteenth-century assumptions about womanhood . . . . The novel puts to rest the notion that all nineteenth-century heroines were Ellen Montgomerys; Capitola neither submitted to her fate nor cried about it. (Rev. 70-71)

Dobson elaborates on the contrast between Capitola and Ellen, concluding:

> In creating Cap, Southworth turns Ellen Montgomery on her head, and if in so doing she allows the reader to see past the petticoats and glimpse the saucy knickers, well, so much the better. (Introduction xxix)

Southworth indeed confronts stereotypical nineteenth-century mores.[1] She derides sentiment[2] ("Cap isn't *sentimental*! and if I try to be, she laughs in my face!" [175]), mocks domesticity[3] ("No one but himself to mend his poor dear gloves! Oh—oh, boo-hoo-oo!" [433]), and challenges nineteenth-century gender roles ("Demmy, you New York newsboy, will you never be a woman?" [376]). Further, Southworth raises questions having to do with minors' economic and civil rights, challenging the law which "invests the guardian with great latitude of discretionary power over the person and property of his ward" (303). Of criminals' civil rights, she states, "the fact and the law" should be in accordance "with justice and humanity! . . . so that the iron car of literal law should not always roll over and crush justice!" (423). Finally, she advocates women's rights: "When women have their rights, [Cap] shall be a lieutenant-colonel herself. Shall she not, gentlemen?" (348), and an anti-imperialist foreign policy: "if a foreign foe invaded [our] shores, yes; but what had [our country] to do with invading another's country?" (345).

Southworth, likewise, confronts stereotypical nineteenth-century literary mores. *The Hidden Hand* virtually parodies such earlier 1850s works as *The Wide, Wide World* (1851) and *Uncle Tom's Cabin* (1852) with its typically lost orphaned heiress who reacts to the stock situations in humorously anti-typical ways.[4] Even Southworth's narrative structure mocks the requisite conclusion of marriages promising that the good characters "all enjoy a fair amount of human felicity" (485).

The Hidden Hand features a plot that draws comparatively more attention to itself than do the patched-together (Elaine Showalter, *Sister's* 155) or parable-like[5] (Kelley 250) *The Wide, Wide World* and *Uncle Tom's Cabin*. As readers, scholars, and critics have long acknowledged, Southworth derives rhetorical power not only from her appeals to the reader's various faculties, but also from her art of story-telling[6] as she capitalized on her reader's eagerness to hurry on to "the secret mystery of the plot" (Kelley 220). Unlike *The Wide, Wide World's* almost institutionalized plot—stored in the nineteenth-century mind as part of the era's collective unconscious—and unlike *Uncle Tom's Cabin's* "non-plot"—lodged in the nineteenth-century reader's mind as reminiscent of collected biblical stories or parables—*The Hidden Hand* traces the adventures of a hero whose individuality can focus various contingent plots into a linear progression of action. Whereas *The Wide, Wide World* has drawn critical attention to its plot's stereotypicality and whereas *Uncle Tom's Cabin* has drawn critical attention to its plot's non-existence, *The Hidden Hand* has drawn attention by virtue of its hero's and plot's uniqueness.

Critics agree that writing a synopsis for Capitola's adventures poses difficulty. Coultrap-McQuin attributes the difficulty to the "multiple mysteries, innumerable moments of coincidence and suspense, and almost too many characters to explain" (Rev. 70). "The novel defies summary because of the sheer number of melodramatic incidents" (70), conclude Freibert and White. Papashvily attempts a summary from the angle of a single character:

Several complicated subplots arose from the machinations of a villain, Le
Noir, who murdered his brother, imprisoned his sister-in-law in a madhouse,
abducted their child and its nurse, sold them into slavery, confiscated the estate, mistreated his ward and schemed to have her fiancé dishonored and
sentenced to death by a court-martial. (126)

But these are the actions of only one of three villains.

Another attempt at synopsis might follow the escapades of the tale's
heroine, Capitola, later Capitola Black, eventually revealed as Capitola Le
Noir, the name of her abducted, captive, discovered, and restored mother.
The self-described "damsel-errant in quest of adventures" (270) is at her
birth smuggled away from her mother's villainous abductors by a kindly
midwife who raises her to girlhood in the slums of New York and who on
her deathbed confides to Major Warfield or "Old Hurricane" of Hurricane
Hall the circumstances of the girl's birth and the fact of her existence.
Young Cap, faced by social restrictions against girls and women making
their own money, in order to feed and protect herself in the city, cross-
dresses, thus enabling herself to sell papers, shine shoes, carry bags, etc.
When Old Hurricane comes to New York to search for the young heiress
who could unseat his rival, the villainous Le Noir, he at once encounters
her as "a very ragged lad, some thirteen years of age" (33). The two
meet, at first comically as the street-wise Cap attempts to protect the
blustery old major and then poignantly as the rural gentleman seeks to
protect his gender-switching ward. Once Cap is situated at the Warfield
family mansion, the story breaks into subplots complete with colorful
rogues, pious martyrs, and numerous comical characters. The author of
the various intrigues, however, through direct appeals to her reader's
various faculties, keeps her reader focused on the unifying plot: unravel-
ing who's who and rectifying the damage done by the villains.

Noticing appeals to the reader's faculties—in George Campbell's terms,
appeals to the understanding, imagination, passion, and will—within *The
Hidden Hand* can clarify how Southworth succeeds at telling a story that
ends up putting "designs" on her reader. Whether consciously or not,
Southworth uses rhetorical appeals to her reader's faculties[7] that have "a
hidden hand" in directing her contemporary cultural ethos.[8]   Attention to

Southworth's rhetorical appeals can begin to illuminate a turn in the 1850s when the self turned from a communal being living within a potentially benign patriarchal and domestic order to a self-reliant individual living within a potentially threatening patriarchal and domestic order. Importantly, attention to rhetorical appeals can illuminate such social changes without judging one author's message inferior to that of another.[9]

In *The Hidden Hand* Southworth appeals to the reader's understanding (the first of Campbell's ends of discourse) "either by explaining some doctrine unknown, or not distinctly comprehended by them, or by proving some position disbelieved or doubted by them" (Campbell 2). She writes, that is, "either to dispel ignorance or to vanquish error" (Campbell 2). Generally, Southworth proposes to dispel a reader's ignorance in the personal situations she presents; she proposes to vanquish a reader's error in the political situations she presents. As the personal and political aspects of situations begin to overlap, so do the aspects of dispelling ignorance and vanquishing error.

Southworth presents material to dispel her reader's ignorance in the personal situations of two groups of characters: those associated with the Willow Heights household—Marah Rocke; her adopted "son," Herbert Greyson; her son, Traverse Rocke; his betrothed, Clare Day; and her father, Dr. Day—and the pair characterized by "strength, courage, and spirit" (390), Capitola and Black Donald. Southworth uses these characters to offer lessons perhaps applicable to a reader's personal situations. For example, frustrated with their attempts to furnish Marah Rocke with a more meaningful life, Marah's friends Dr. Day and Clara suddenly realize that they can employ her as a housekeeper. Dr. Day presents a lesson to Traverse and to the book's reader:

> That's the way, Traverse, that's the way with us all, my boy! While we are looking away off yonder for the solution of our difficulties, the remedy is all the time lying just under our noses! (132)

Similarly, at the scene of Traverse's[10] life-threatening court-martial, his childhood adoptive brother/lover, Herbert Greyson, alluding to a scheme to save Traverse, offers to dispel Traverse's and the reader's ignorance: "It is a truth! Things difficult—almost to impossibility can always be accomplished! Write that upon your tablets, for it is a valuable truth!" (411). Traverse, himself, has occasion to offer a proverb to the reader in the guise of a letter to his mother, Marah Rocke. Newly a physician, Traverse gladly serves the poor without recompense: ". . . I should still have desired to serve the indigent; "for whoso giveth to the poor lendeth to the Lord" (322).

The pious messages to the reader coming from the characters associated with Willow Heights extend even to Capitola's comments at times. Through her, Southworth delivers to the reader a moving litany of Christian appeals during an exciting encounter between Cap and the dashingly handsome villain, Black Donald, whom Southworth has associated with Capitola in their like appearances, names, and characteristics.[11] Having concealed himself in Cap's secluded bedroom, Black Donald locks her in the room with him and hints at seduction or rape. Summoning her "faculties" (384), Cap coaxes the unsuspecting villain into a chair positioned over a trap door that could well lead to his death. With him thus in limbo she delivers in four pages a Christian sermon (389-93).

As Cap seeks to dispel the ignorance of Black Donald, Southworth enlightens her reader's understanding by using Campbell's implicit premise that some sermons are more effective than others. Black Donald, hearing Cap's words without sympathy, laughs off her pleas; the reader, both hearing Cap's words and feeling sympathy for Donald's impending doom, experiences a more compelling rhetorical appeal. Black Donald elsewhere delivers a sermon regarding social Darwinism:

> Every creature preys upon some other creature weaker than himself—the big beasts eat up the little ones; artful men live on the simple; so be it! the world was made for the strong and cunning; let the weak and foolish look to themselves! (148)

Although this principle is voiced in a den of villains, Southworth, by linking Capitola with Black Donald and by her characterization of Capitola herself, here dispels the reader's ignorance by legitimating for women personal attributes of artfulness and strength. Southworth qualifies such characteristics for the reader when Capitola admonishes Black Donald that the qualities that the two of them share, "strength, courage, and spirit" come not "from the Evil One, but from the Lord" and so should be "used for the good of man and the glory of God" (390).

Southworth's offers to dispel the reader's ignorance in personal situations overlap at times with her offers to vanquish culturally and/or politically accepted error. First, Southworth links dispelling the reader's ignorance in personal affairs of the heart with showing the reader errors in nineteenth-century marriage laws. On the one hand, Southworth bids the reader to be aware of love's misuse: the aptly named "Craven" regards love to be that "which is often only appetite" (349). On the other hand, Southworth alerts her reader to more positive aspects of love. Her authorial voice tells us, "there is a clause in the marriage service which enjoins the husband to *cherish* his wife. I do not believe many people ever stop to think how much is in that word" (94). This information, meant to dispel the reader's ignorance in personal areas, overlaps with information meant to vanquish what Southworth sees as an error in the law. As voiced by Craven,

> whatever power the law gives the husband over his wife and her property, shall be mine over you and your possessions! . . . Oh! to get you into my power, my girl! not that I *love* you, moon-faced creature! but I *want your possessions!* which is quite as strong an incentive. (300)

Thus Southworth alerts her contemporary reader to human (and, perhaps by association, specifically male) tendencies to ignore nurturing and to confound love with monetary greed as she implicitly asks her reader to challenge the economic aspects of marriage laws.

Southworth similarly links dispelling ignorance in personal affairs with vanquishing error in cultural affairs with respect to patience. Traverse must learn to overcome his own impatience:

> "Impatience! Doctor Day always faithfully warned me against it—always told me that most of the errors, sins and miseries of this world arose from simple impatience, which is want of faith. And now I know it!" (345)

Southworth warns her reader in no uncertain terms of the misery (which Southworth knew too well)[12] that could result from marrying without waiting patiently for maturity:

> No girl can marry before she is twenty without serious risk of life, and almost certain loss of health and beauty; that so many do so is one reason why there are such numbers of sickly and faded young wives. (228)

Southworth would have her readers evaluate their personal attitudes toward patience and collectively mend the cultural error of marrying young.

Southworth uses Traverse, similarly, to appeal to the reader to act without ignorance when making personal decisions. Traverse realizes he has acted out of ignorance "enlisting for a war the rights and wrongs of which [he knows] no more than anybody else does!" (345). In the same scene, Southworth appeals to the reader to understand an error in foreign policy: military defense may be justified, but military aggression has no justification (345).

One of Southworth's greatest appeals to her reader's understanding in *The Hidden Hand* has to do with the nineteenth-century woman's economic situation. The book opens with a narrative scene depicting the cultural constraint against an orphan girl feeding and protecting herself; Cap must impersonate a boy in order to survive. Elsewhere, referring to her "eccentric little friend Capitola's ways" (326), Clara presents alternative economic possibilities for women. Southworth, through Clara, states, "I stand upon the broad platform of human rights, and I say I have just as good a right to work as others" (326). Southworth here dispels the nineteenth-century reader's probable ignorance—by showing that a woman can develop the ability to function economically in the rising market economy. Here, the rhetorical appeal to dispel her reader's ignorance in the area of economics overlaps with the rhetorical appeal to vanquish the cultural error of refusing women the right to sustain themselves.

Finally, Southworth appeals to her reader's faculty of understanding regarding the subject of gender. By showing a woman engaged in activities generally associated with men, Southworth attempts to broaden her reader's concept of what may be considered women's sphere. Through Capitola's identity, Southworth dispels her reader's ignorance of women's possibilities and communicates the importance of a woman's self-actualization. In addition to delimiting possibilities for women's identities through the character of Capitola, Southworth challenges nineteenth- (and twentieth-) century personal views of maleness with the androgynous Traverse:[13]

> If masculinization is the remedy for women, then this good young man, Traverse Rocke, reveals Southworth's remedy for men—desexualization. Traverse is obviously a sissy.[14] (Habegger 207-08)

When he denounces Traverse as "sissy," Habegger reveals a view of ideal manhood very different from Southworth's. Through dialogue, Southworth says:

> "Traverse, you talk like a dandy, which is not at all your character. Effeminacy is not your vice."
> "Nor any other species of weakness, do you mean?" (343-44)

Here Southworth proposes a concept of effeminacy that is neither vice nor weakness.[15] Taking this concept a step further, Southworth shows that although an effeminate man might feel uncomfortable as a soldier (as Traverse does), he can function well in the military. Southworth shows her reader the ironic gender-based error of admitting to the service someone as sentimental as Traverse, while denying admission to a woman as capable as Cap.

Southworth appeals to her reader's understanding to vanquish error in social and/or political terms usually having to do with law. For example, in the case of Traverse's court-martial, Southworth reveals the disparity between law and justice. The evil Colonel Le Noir, in an effort to eliminate Traverse, assigns him to duties day and night, thus depriving him of sleep. At the end of several sleepless days and nights, Traverse is set on guard, "where a few hours later he was found asleep upon his post" (423), a capital offense. Southworth thus shows her reader the error of a legal system in which fact and law lead to a verdict out of "accordance . . . with justice and humanity" (423). That is, she writes to vanquish her reader's error in supporting such a legal system.

Of imagination, the second of Campbell's ends of discourse, Southworth, directly addressing her reader, says "there is some advantage in having imagination, since that visionary faculty opens the mental eyes to facts that more practical and duller intellects could never see" (444). Southworth informs her reader, also, that appealing to the imagination is more powerful than providing realistic description in the scene where Capitola reveals she has dashed the Le Noir plan to secure Clara's fortune by a forced marriage. Here Southworth says in an authorial voice: "The effect of this outburst, this revelation, this explosion, may be imagined but can never be adequately described" (315). Southworth elsewhere acknowledges the part a reader plays in creating a story, implicitly forewarning the reader of the authorial power to stimulate reader imagination. Southworth offers the introductory verse:

> Imagination frames events unknown,
> In wild, fantastic shapes of hideous ruin,
> And what it fears creates!
> —Hannah More (209)

Southworth, through More's verse, invites the reader to make use of that which lies in the memory (as fear) to help stimulate the imagination. Campbell addresses the interdependency of memory and imagination:

> Vivid ideas are not only more powerful than languid ideas in commanding and preserving attention, they are not only more efficacious in producing conviction, but they are also more easily retained. Those several powers, understanding, imagination, memory, and passion, are mutually subservient. . . . it is necessary for the orator to engage the help of memory . . . . (75)

What lies in a reader's memory can be summoned by an author to cause the reader to create ideas. Campbell explains the psycho-dynamics of memory and imagination in a way that parallels the workings of Southworth's rhetorical appeals:

> from experiencing the connexion of two things there results . . . an association between the ideas or notions annexed to them, as each idea will moreover be associated by its signs, there will likewise be an association between the ideas of the signs. Hence the . . . signs will be conceived to have a connexion analogous to that which subsisteth among the things signified. (259)

Campbell shows that presenting to the reader's imagination one image, through association (or connection) can produce in the imagination an analogous image. In such a way Southworth presents her reader with images of nature and architecture that by their common nineteenth-century associations were sure to "tell her reader something."

Chapter V demonstrates how the nineteenth-century reader's memory regarding flower-imagery helped the reader create the story of Stephens's *Mary Derwent*. Unlike Stephens, Southworth uses relatively few floral appeals to her reader's imagination. Southworth does, however, describe Traverse's impression of Clara Day as associated with violets: "There had been for him only a vague, dazzling vision of a golden-haired girl in floating white raiment, wafting the fragrance of violets as she moved . . ." (130). Sarah Josepha Hale's *Flora's Interpreter* (1832) explains that the white violet "has very odorous flowers" and associates this species with "modesty" (219). Traverse and Clara and their relationship are indeed characterized by modesty. As noted in the previous chapter (184), Martha Barnette (1992) explains the violet as an uncultivated pansy, associated historically with people who might choose not to marry (148). Despite the nod to convention in which Southworth ends *The Hidden Hand* with three marriages, including that of Traverse and Clara, the association of violets with Traverse and Clara reinforces for the nineteenth-century reader Traverse as a gender-neutral character. To Traverse, Clara's words sound "sisterly":

> It made him deeply happy to hear her call him "Traverse." It had such a *sisterly* sound coming from this sweet creature. How he wished that she really *were* his sister! (emphases Southworth's) (132-33)

By appealing to the reader's memory through the principle of association (here to violets), Southworth invites the nineteenth-century reader to help create Traverse's identity.

As Southworth draws on the image of violet held in the reader's memory to pique the imagination and so aid the understanding, she draws on images of architecture to help tell the story of *The Hidden Hand*. "In this," writes Harris,

> Southworth, like Warner [and Stephens], is drawing on cultural codes that were especially meaningful to her readers. . . . In using architectural associations as part of her narrative structure, Southworth was employing imagery that already spoke eloquently to a readership for whom domestic architecture had become an iconographically significant new art, and for whom ever-increasing mobility created a nostalgia for the imaginary virtues of their childhood homes. (*19th-Century* 137)

To help her reader solve the mystery of Cap's lineage, Southworth appeals to her reader's imagination, providing hints of architectural associations.

The story opens with a view of "Hurricane Hall": "a large old family mansion, built of dark, red sandstone, in one of the loneliest and wildest of the mountain regions of Virginia" (7). The reader learns that Major Ira Warfield is "the lonely proprietor of the Hall," living in seclusion "on this his patrimonial estate" (7). Here the images, "family mansion," "patrimonial estate," and "Hall" contrast with descriptions of Warfield as "lonely" and "in seclusion." The reader knows that a "mansion" or "estate" or "Hall" should accommodate many residents—namely, Warfield's family. That Warfield is "lonely" and "in seclusion" foreshadows the narrative's mystery: what has caused the emptiness of the "Hall."

The mystery of Hurricane Hall deepens with the author's description of Capitola's room. It

> belongs to the *oldest part of the house.* . . . a part of the grant of land given to the *Le Noirs*. And the first owner, old Henri Le Noir, was said to be one of the grandest villains that ever was heard of. . . . this very room was a part of the old pioneer hunter's lodge" (73).

Southworth here extends her appeal to the reader's imagination via architectural associations. Capitola, ostensibly an orphan, finds herself in a mansion described as both "family" and "patrimonial." Further, she is roomed in that part of the Hall, separated from the rest of the house, that dates back to a shady lineage. Since to the nineteenth-century mind, the character of houses had significance to the reader's imagination, the connections between Cap and some "old" event and between Cap and the Le Noirs' land grant created significance in the imagination that eventuated in information. The nineteenth-century reader read the passage not as mere description of a room, but as a sign of Cap's probable biological relationship to the Le Noirs and their "grant of land"—all of which is revealed in more literal words by the end of the book.

In other allusions to architectural iconography that most likely appealed to her nineteenth-century reader's imagination, Southworth introduces "Harriet, the Seeress of Hidden Hollow," better known as "Old Hat," a witch who lives in a "hut."[16] Southworth situates Hat's hut amid a fearful and threatening picture of nature:

> It was an awful abyss, scooped out as it were from the very bowels of the earth, with its steep sides rent open in dreadful chasms, and far down in its fearful depths a boiling whirlpool of black waters. . . . through a thicket of stunted thorns and over a chaos of shattered rocks, Capitola approached . . . to

the brink of this awful pit. . . . [Amid] this terrible phenomenon of natural
scenery . . . [appeared] in the thicket on her right a low hut . . . (271)

To the nineteenth-century mind a hut signified such threatening and untamed associations. At the scene of Old Hat's hut, Southworth delivers
not only a witch's prophesy, but also creates in the reader's imagination
connections to threatening metaphysical forces. Reading the palm of
Capitola on which appears a small red birthmark in the shape of a hand
("the hidden hand") and presumably seeing there Cap's genetic connection
to her mother,[17] Hat shrieks, "the curse of the crimson hand is upon you!"
(273); thus Southworth again prods her reader's imagination. The witch
and her hut denote to the reader an extant threatening power lying beyond
the apparent with which Cap will have to grapple.

Cap encounters the witch and her hut as she searches for "the Hidden
House." This structure, as its name implies, hides much of the story's
mystery. Here Cap was born to a mother of hidden identity. Shortly
thereafter, the infant Cap was smuggled away, hidden in her midwife's
scarf. Here Cap's mother is imprisoned, hidden for fifteen years by the
evil Le Noir usurpers. Cap seeks the Hidden House partly because she
wishes to meet its new resident, Clara Day, who is secluded there against
her will and away from her friends by Colonel Le Noir. Cap seeks the
Hidden House also out of curiosity. Southworth appeals to her reader's
imagination:

> The Old Hidden House, with its mysterious traditions, its gloomy surround-
> ings and its haunted reputation, had always possessed a powerful attraction
> for one of Cap's adventurous spirit. To seek and gaze upon the sombre house,
> of which, and of whose inmates, such terrible stories had been told or hinted,
> had always been a secret desire and purpose of Capitola. (269)

The Hidden House is, after all, a "house," connoting a building bereft of
the amenities and human touch that "make a house a home."[18]   To the
nineteenth-century reader, a sense of domestic human kindness could be
found present in a "home." A "house," however, denoted a lack of human
kindness, an empty shell—like the Hidden House. Thus, Southworth's
signifier brought to the reader's mind a sense of the coldness and unnatu-
ralness that would unfold in events at this place.

Southworth calls the residence of the long suffering, kind, faithful, martyr figure, Marah Rocke, a "cottage" (61, 62, 87, 103). "In Southworth's novels," Harris explains, "protective enclosures fit the spirits that own them: her grand women own mansions, her timid spirits own cottages" ("The House" 19). Just so, Southworth appeals to the reader's imagination with a description of Marah's "poor cottage" that enables the reader to guess the character of its inhabitants:

> Beside an old, rocky road, leading from the town of Staunton, out to the for-est-crowned hills beyond, stood alone, a little, gray stone cottage, in the midst of a garden enclosed by a low, moldering stone wall. A few gnarled and twisted fruit trees, long past bearing, stood around . . . . (61)

Here live two poor women and their sons, all as humble and honest as their shared abode. With the description of their dwelling, Southworth tells her reader that the women have lived "rocky" lives, and are exiled from their proper social place. Their personalities, reflecting their "little, gray stone cottage," are closed in on themselves, stalwart, and cold to the world. The abode provides the image that the women are "stone-walling" in life; its surrounding garden provides the image that the women are, by choice or by age, barren.

Marah's personal tragedy involves her early life, during which she lived in a "log cabin." The strength of the log cabin reflects the strength of the "handsome, strong, and ardent" man who built for his young wife her "woodland home." Marah describes: ". . . he built for me a pretty cabin in the woods below the Fort, furnished it simply . . . " (94). Southworth communicates Marah's "ruin" in the image of the log cabin. By trickery, Le Noir crosses the threshold of the log cabin. As he violates the cabin's strength, he violates that of Warfield and so disables Warfield from continuing to cherish and nurture Marah. She is cast out of the cabin's and Warfield's protection.

Southworth presents Marah's salvation again in terms of architectural imagery. When Marah's psyche and health deteriorate, the kindly and wise Dr. Day prescribes,

> your mother [Marah] should be in a home of peace, plenty and cheerfulness! . . . Your mother wants good living, cheerful company, and freedom from toil and care! The situation of a gentleman's or lady's housekeeper in some home

of abundance, where she would be esteemed as a member of the family, would suit her; but where to find such a place! (131)

Marah's mental and physical health return when she enters a home of Dr. Day's description: his own, Willow Heights.

Southworth implicitly describes the character of Dr. Day with appeals to the reader's imagination as she describes the architecture of Day's home, Willow Heights. Traverse's

> one great admiration was the beautiful Willow Heights, and its worthy proprietor. . . . an avenue of willows . . . led up to the house, a two-storied edifice of gray stone, with full-length front piazzas above and below. . . . The whole aspect of the man, and of his surroundings, was kindly cheerfulness. The room opened upon the upper front piazza, and the windows were all up to admit the bright morning sun and genial air, at the same time that there was a glowing fire in the grate to temper its chilliness. (101)

The name, "Willow Heights," however, carries with it a message extending beyond Southworth's actual description of the "place" and its inhabitants. Through the nineteenth-century language of plant life,[19] Southworth provides an image of foreboding. The place-name projects a concept of literal incongruity: willows are low-land trees; they do not do well on "heights." Further, the willow is known for its suppleness; it is vulnerable to being bent and swayed. Southworth hints through her reader's imagination that Willow Heights, despite all its apparent comforts, might prove to be a place where the inhabitants have difficulty taking root. When Dr. Day dies, Clara is carted off and Marah is sent packing. Later, the place becomes a prison for Capitola's captive mother. Southworth characterizes these three women as "willowy"; they are bent and swayed by the power of Le Noir. The nineteenth-century reader was likely to sense in the place's association to the willow the image of the "forsaken lover" (Hale 224). Marah, Traverse, and Clara are exiled from Willow Heights and estranged from each other at the death of Dr. Day. Further, Traverse becomes the forsaken lover as his communication with Clara is severed by Colonel Le Noir.[20]

As Southworth situates her pinnacle image of womanhood, Clara Day (bright day) on a "height," she situates her den of thieves first in the deserted "Old Road Inn" and then underground. Southworth alerts her reader's imagination to the characters she will introduce by describing a forsaken inn: "abandoned and suffered to fall to ruin" (140). She continues to characterize people in terms of their residences: "we have had to lie low—yes, literally—*to lie low*—to keep out of sight, to burrow under ground! in a word, to live in this cavern!" (339). Shady, low characters live as varmints, in a cave.

"Literary training," Harris admits (*19th-Century* 32), might cause the twentieth-century reader to consider such popular images or architectural iconography as "stereotyped." The mid-nineteenth-century reader, however, found such appeals to the imagination not literary problems, but "verbal codes" (Harris *19th* 32) or "powerful symbols," (Herzog xx), that "rang certain bells in the average reader's mind" (Herzog xx). "Easily recognized stereotypes," adds Dobson, "offered Southworth instantly recognizable vehicles of communication with which to reach and manipulate her numerous readers" ("Introduction" xxvii). Reading *The Hidden Hand* with attention to Campbell's views helps reestablish an appreciation for such overt appeals to the reader's imagination.

Southworth's architectural references thus foreshadow and communicate meaning to the reader before a scene unfolds. With these architectural details Southworth also gains the reader's attention: "The imagination must be engaged," according to Campbell, to assure an author the reader's attention. "The attention is prerequisite" (Campbell 73) to approaching the reader's faculty of reason. Through appeals to her reader's imagination, Southworth appeals to her reader to "reason out" the story's mystery. Combining such appeals to reason and imagination may well establish the secret of Southworth's story-telling prowess.

Southworth was termed an "impassioned" writer, known for her "power of her portraiture, and the spell which holds her readers" (Mary Forrest 216). Southworth's appeal to a reader's passion, the third of Campbell's possible ends of discourse, appears mostly through the sympathy Southworth builds between her reader and the character of her protagonist, Capitola. "Sympathy," Campbell posits, "is one main engine by which the orator operates on the passions" (96). With numerous depictions of Cap's antics, Southworth employs sympathy as a rhetorical appeal to urge her reader to emulate her heroine. Ironically, though, Cap exhibits characteristics other than those Southworth expects in her reader:

Now the soul of Capitola naturally abhorred sentiment! (123)

But you see Cap isn't *sentimental!* (175)

Cap listened very calmly to this story, showing very little sympathy, for there
was not a bit of sentimentality about our Cap. (305)

Nonetheless, Southworth uses sentiment and sympathy as rhetorical appeals to urge her reader to emulate Cap's character—a character bereft of
sentiment. Regarding another character, Marah, however, Southworth
has the wise and benign Dr. Day state "mental medicine [is] sympathy"
(131). These messages appear contradictory until one realizes that Cap
needs no such medicine. "The miserable need the aid and sympathy of
others; the happy do not," explains Campbell (131). Southworth urges
her reader through sympathy with Cap to rely on personal activity in life's
pursuits.

Through sympathy, "Our Cap" appears an irresistible figure. In her,
Southworth offers her reader "the long-lost twin sister of Huckleberry
Finn" (Habegger 201); she shows both that a woman *can* take care of herself and that ". . . liberty is too heavy a price to pay for protection and
support!" (175). With humor and authorial voice, Southworth uses the
character, Capitola, to present her own

> dedication to individual self-realization, especially for women . . . a dynamic
> that overrides all obstacles and [provides] . . . a vision of individual freedom
> at times strangely at odds with . . . cultural limitations" (xxv-xxvi).

Southworth appeals to her reader's sympathy to join in Cap's character
and spirit. The author creates situation after situation in which "by sympathy we rejoice with them that rejoice, and weep with them that weep"
(Campbell 131),[21] causing the reader to accept Capitola as "a model of
female autonomy" (Dobson, "Introduction" xxviii).

It is important to note, however, that although Southworth appeals to
her reader's passion through sympathy with Cap to develop "the saving
characteristics of self-reliance, irreverence, and active, rather than passive, courage" (Dobson, "Introduction" xxxi), Southworth presents these
characteristics to her reader in episodes that do not end in some moral.
That is, Southworth presents in the character of Cap an alternative way of
being. For example, in Chapters XV and XVI: "Cap's Country Capers"
and "Cap's Fearful Adventure," Cap breaks the rule of her well-meaning

guardian and crosses the river that marks her boundary for horseback-riding. Near sunset she realizes that she is six or seven miles or about three hours from home (112). As Cap contemplates "the loneliness of the woods, and the lateness of the hour, her own helplessness, and—Black Donald!" (113), she is overtaken by a villainous and threatening horse-man, Craven Le Noir, whom she eventually outsmarts. Southworth con-cludes the episode with Cap thumbing her nose both at danger and at pa-ternal authority (118).[22]

Should the reader look for a moral in this episode, he or she would learn either to do as one is told by a well-meaning authority or to question authority. Southworth intends neither, but through the vehicle of sympa-thy with her heroine, urges her reader to emulate Cap's "high degree of courage, self-control, and presence of mind" (114). Scene after scene of-fers circumstances that would be difficult for anyone to emulate, such as Cap challenging a villain to a duel or Cap springing a maximum security criminal from death-row. Southworth does not urge the reader to take ill-advised chances, but does (through sympathy) urge the reader to be true to him- or herself.[23]

At this point Southworth's rhetorical appeals to the reader's passions (through sympathy with Cap) begin to merge with her appeals to the reader's will. Campbell explains the will, his fourth and final end of dis-course, "is in reality an artful mixture of that which proposes to convince the judgment, and that which interests the passions . . . " (4). Rhetorical appeals to reason meet rhetorical appeals to passion in *The Hidden Hand* in Southworth's "design": challenging mid-nineteenth-century cultural roles for men and women.

The young men whom Southworth provides her male reader to emulate, Traverse Rocke and Herbert Greyson, embody virtues countering those necessary for success in a competitive and aggressive market economy. First, they do not need to enter that arena, because they both end up eco-nomically "kept" by women heiresses. Second, the two men lead lives in which they nurture others: Herbert always brings money and gifts back from the sea for Capitola and for his adoptive mother and brother; Trav-erse begins life working at odd jobs to support his mother, and pursues a medical profession in which he cares for the poor without economic remu-neration. Finally, the two young men enjoy a strong love for each other: Traverse allows himself "an almost girlish smile and blush" when alone with Herbert (428); as Herbert sees Traverse, tears "rush to his eyes—for the bravest is always the tenderest heart" (407). Indeed, the two experience "mesmerism . . . strange effects produced quite unconsciously by the presence of one person upon another" (407-08). At no time do Traverse and Herbert exhibit aggression or competition with each another.

The supporting women characters Southworth provides as possible models (such as Clara Day, Marah Rocke, and Capitola's mother, Madame Le Noir) fall in with those of whom Harris says, "unimaginative women are not villains in Southworth's novels, but they remain among the lower orders of human kind. Each of these three women lacks or has lacked a mother-figure and, coincidentally, each fails to develop the ability to keep from falling prey to Colonel and/or Craven Le Noir. Clara's father hires a mother-figure to guide his daughter to womanhood; under the terms of paternal guardianship, however, the foster mother-figure proves ineffectual, leaving Clara vulnerable. Marah Rocke is a child-bride whose husband cannot both care for her full-time and pursue his military career, creating a situation that leaves Marah vulnerable. The child-bride, Madame Le Noir, falls victim to her evil brother-in-law at the murder of her husband. Women, Southworth makes clear, must gain self-reliance and "cap-ability" while making the transition from a mother's home to that of a husband.

Of the young women's roles that Southworth provides her women readers to emulate, Capitola obviously steals the show. She has been mothered by a kindly mid-wife until she "was big enough to pay for her keep in work" (28) and by that time had learned (somehow) to live by her wits. Cap embodies the virtues necessary for surviving in a culture becoming progressively less benign to women as industry began to encroach on the economy of domesticity: "Of a naturally strong constitution and adventurous disposition, and inured from infancy to danger, Capitola possessed a high degree of courage, self-control, and presence of mind." In an emergency "all her faculties instantly collected and concentrated themselves on the emergency" (114). "The instinct of the huntress possessed her" (157). Cap can and does maintain her liberty whether she finds herself in an urban slum or a country mansion. "The heroine [such as Capitola] challenges her fate, conquers herself, creates and controls her world" (Harris, *19th-Century* 151). In short, concludes Harris, "Southworth's female protagonists see themselves as movers and shakers" (*19th-Century*

137-38). Creating ample sympathy in the reader for this "mover and shaker," Southworth appeals to the reader's passions and will.

Campbell's stipulation that an author appeal to the reader's will by convincing the judgment and interesting the passions helps explain *how* Southworth teaches male readers to expand their human characteristics beyond those engendered by a competitive and aggressive economic culture and *how* she teaches (as Harris, *19th-Century*, puts it) "female readers to become the heroines of their own lives" (135). Southworth establishes ties of sympathy between her model characters and the reader. At the same time, she convinces the reader's judgment that the model roles she sets up are not only viable, but are also desirable in both a personal and a community sense. This combination of appeals to the reader's judgment and passion (through sympathy), then plays on the reader's will. The female reader wants to be like Cap; should the reader opt to marry—perhaps as an afterthought to adventures as in Cap's case—the reader should seek for a mate someone with those characteristics of Traverse and Herbert.

In large part, it is through Southworth's rhetorical appeals that she was "influential in changing the possibilities of reality for women" as Dobson ("Introduction" xl) puts it. Southworth offers to enlighten her reader's understanding by providing new information—often alerting her reader to (dispelling ignorance regarding) the confines of social convention—and by challenging what she would have the reader see are social wrongs—especially in the realms of jurisprudence and marital-economic laws. Southworth draws her reader's attention to her instruction and keeps her reader's attention poised to receive further instruction by raising her reader's admiration for whatever ideas her narrative might hold. That is, by showing her reader recognizable images and letting her reader's imagination embellish those images, she "compounds" (Campbell 2) the understanding she imparts. Through sympathy (creating in her readership a virtual rooting-section) for her heroine, Southworth raises the reader's passions, transforming simple understanding in the reader's mind to conviction. Finally, Southworth succeeds in influencing the reader's will. The rhetorical appeals to understanding, imagination, and passion combine to persuade the reader to expand his or her identity in fundamental ways.

NOTES

[1] Southworth's refusal in *The Hidden Hand* to bow to stereotypical nineteenth-century mores and laws brought her into disfavor with such powerful critics as *Godey's* Sarah Josepha Hale who accused her of a "freedom of expression that almost borders on impiety," particularly for taking her characterizations "beyond the limits prescribed by correct taste or good judgment." Hale had some basic ideological differences with Southworth—notably in the areas of abolition and women's rights. Hale (*Biography*) describes herself as having

> no sympathy with those who are wrangling for "woman's rights;" (sic) nor with those who are foolishly urging women to strive for equality and compe- tition with men. . . . The Bible does not uphold the equality of the sexes. (xxxvii)

Interestingly, Hale's quotation critical of Southworth appears in the 1855 edition of John S. Hart's *Female Prose Writers of America* (215). Hart, too, must have felt un- comfortable with Southworth: although she had been published since 1847, refer- ence to her is conspicuously missing from his earlier (1852) volume.

Similarly, Henry Peterson of the *Saturday Evening Post* chastised Southworth for the "blunder" of her indelicate hand with moral issues (Coultrap-McQuin, *Doing* 65, Kelley 21). Undaunted by negative remarks from influential critics and editors, however, Southworth "considered herself to be a Christian woman with the best of moral intentions as a writer" (Coultrap-McQuin, *Doing* 65). In discussing her sense of self as a Christian novelist, Southworth declares,

> We must teach Christian lessons in parables as our Lord and Savior did. . . . The novelist—the popular novelist—has a hundred-fold larger audience than the most celebrated preacher, and, therefore, a tremendous responsibility." (Coultrap-McQuin, *Doing* 60)

Contemporary reviewers claimed Southworth's work "truly moral, religious, and elevating" (Rev. *The Lost Heiress*), "beautiful and instructive . . . with the most ele- vated sentiments of love and constancy" (Rev. *The Deserted Wife*), and "directed by a high sense of duty . . . in the defence of virtue, or in the denunciation of vice" (Rev. *The Two Sisters*). If some readers complained, Southworth countered "there were a 'half million readers who being satisfied, say nothing'" (Kelley 220). For all of Cap's and Southworth's own authorial impieties in *The Hidden Hand*, Southworth's message was "regarded as of high moral tone" (Phebe A. Hanaford 217). Even with- out "the patent piety of the other domestic novelists," Southworth's characters, ac- knowledged "a Divine Being" and recognized "His particular protection" (Papashvily 119-120). In the face of *The Hidden Hand's* irreverence toward social norms, and "infrequency of [soteriological] articulation," as Lynette Carpenter points out,

"Christian doctrine forms the book's implied context" (27). Cap may lack senti-ment, but she both espouses and acts on Christian ideology.

[2] Alluding to Southworth's work as a whole, James D. Hart calls her writing "no less sentimental" than Fanny Fern's (96). Lucy Freibert and Barbara White correct such statements: "Southworth was clearly not the 'domestic sentimentalist' she is classi-fied as in many literary histories" (70).

[3] Of Southworth's domesticity, Lucy Freibert and Barbara White remark, ". . . a home to Southworth is as good as its trapdoors and secret passages" (70).

[4] Unlike Warner's heroine, Ellen Montgomery, who must struggle painfully to develop her selfhood, Capitola enters the story with the same spunk and self-realization with which she exits; Cap grows to womanhood, but her character remains unchanged.

[5] For an explanation of these descriptions, see Chapter IV, (84-85).

[6] Critics and scholars have long identified Southworth as a storyteller. "Her name is familiar to story-lovers all over the land," writes Hanaford (217). "She was a superb storyteller" (Doing 60), affirms Coultrap-McQuin with additional allusions to Southworth's "storytelling ability" (Doing 61). "Her forte was not the mastery of stylistics nor the subtle delineation of human complexities," writes Dobson, "rather, it was storytelling" ("Introduction" xii). Of The Hidden Hand in particular Coultrap-McQuin says, "the book shows how great a storyteller Southworth was" (Rev. 71). In it "she relies on a mastery of storytelling," adds Dobson ("Introduction" xxvii). A "plot novel" Fred Lewis Pattee (1940) calls it (123).

Yet, with all these accolades, critics and scholars complain of The Hidden Hand's plot. Some critics note the "adherence to the conventional plot line" (Dobson "The Hidden" 227). Others cite the plot's excesses:

. . . there is only one murder, there are three kidnappings, three miraculous escapes from death, two duels, two prison outbreaks, two deathbed confes-sions, a carriage accident, and a shipwreck (70)

observe Lucy Freibert and Barbara White (1985). "Like all Mrs. Southworth's nov-els," writes Russell B. Nye (1975), The Hidden Hand "suffered from an excess of improbable plot, but no one cared" (12). Baym explains, "the need for probability was less strongly felt by readers than by critics . . . " (Novels 80).

[7] For the extent to which Campbell's rhetorical appeals shaped 1850s cognitive mores see Chapter II (27, 39) and elsewhere above as well as Johnson (Nineteenth-Century, 19-21, 173), Gabler-Hover (35), and others.

[8] Harris cites Hans Robert Jauss's work showing "that literary texts have the power to change readers' social and literary horizons, and therefore, ultimately, to change both literature and society" (*19th-Century* 32. See also "The House" 28).

[9] At this juncture it's safe to say that history has moved from a vision of Ellen Montgomery's communal self to a vision of Capitola's more self-reliant self. During the century and a half that has ensued since mid-1850s authors wrote, women have progressively accepted and entered men's (as Hale puts it) "colder, harder, and austerer organizations" (468). It is not my intention, however, to align critical comments with historical-economic observations. Granted that Southworth is subversive in depicting "Capitola a Capitalist" (465ff) as "freeing" women to join the market economy. Just so is Stowe subversive in depicting her women characters as free to "feel right" in the face of such men's economic dictums as The Fugitive Slave Law. Noting Campbell's theory at play in mid-nineteenth-century works can help current readers experience more closely authors' impacts on multiple faculties. Discussion of such rhetorical appeals, however, does not justify privileging one work to another as based on underlying economic assumptions.

[10] For an explanation of Traverse's sexuality (or lack thereof), see Habegger (270). Traverse and Herbert Greyson slept together throughout their youth. Southworth uses language to describe their relationship, such as: ". . . he [Herbert] had begged Traverse to let him have his photograph taken, and the latter, with a laugh, at the lover-like proposal, had consented" (347). In one of the book's few floral references, Southworth has Traverse mention violets (130), "the color of which," Martha Barnette points out, "is traditionally associated with the gay community" (148). See page 182, above. Perhaps the "back and forth" connotation of the name "Traverse" adds to Southworth's sense of gender reversal.

[11] "Black Donald is present in the text as Cap's double," explains Dobson in her "Introduction." "Both are linked with the spirit of misrule, associated with the dark possibilities of human energies uncontrolled by social restraints: he is *Black* Donald; she is Capitola *Black*" (xxxix). Similarly, she is called "Cap"; he is called "Cap'n" (142, 43, 44).

[12] "Southworth saw nothing funny in the situation of the young wife married to an old man," explains Habegger (207). Her own mother had married at the age of fifteen and became the widowed mother of two daughters at twenty. Within *The Hidden Hand*, Marah—meaning "bitter" (87)—marries at sixteen and is "discarded," pregnant, at seventeen (98). Capitola's victimized mother married as "a mere child . . . a creature so infantile—for she was scarcely fourteen years of age" (176-77).

[13] Traverse represents, as Cecelia Tichi (1992) says of Walt Whitman, "a figure who is alternatively female and transsexual" (225). Through Traverse, Southworth creates (as Tichi describes Poe's heroes): "androgynous, embodied pleas for the human wholeness that must encompass the male and the female" (225).

[14] By using the derogatory term "sissy," Habegger reveals his view that to lose machismo is to devalue maleness.

[15] Papashvily describes the androgynous Ishmael of Southworth's *Ishmael* or *Self-Made* (1863-64),

> if Capitola served as an ideal for the new woman, Ishmael was the model for the male. . . . He was obliging, docile and agreeable . . . he spoke in sweet, modulated tones. . . . It seems obvious he shared another attribute of the heavenly beings, neuter gender. (133)

Like Traverse, the character of Ishmael shows that effeminacy is not a vice or weakness, but a virtue.

[16] "Hat (who lives in a hut, not a hall or a house)," says Carpenter (17).

[17] At the time of Cap's birth, her mother's "right hand was sewed up in black crape" (20) as was her face and head to hide her identity. Southworth implies that the young mother's right hand is covered to hide an identifying mark that could well resemble Cap's: "in the middle of [Cap's] left palm was the perfect image of a crimson hand, about half an inch in length" (28). Habegger states the book's title refers to the young mother's hand, "swathed with 'black crepe'" (202). Most other scholars assume the book's title refers to Cap's birthmark; Carpenter points out how the cover of Rutger's reissue of the text even features "dozens of tiny red cartoon hands, outlined in black" (17).

[18] A cultural idiom.

[19] Harris defines the "language of flowers" as the "symbolic use" of flowers (*19th-Century* 80).

[20] Clara and her betrothed, Traverse Rocke, are victims to isolation from loved ones. Reminiscent of Ellen Montgomery of Warner's *The Wide, Wide World*, their mail is intercepted, opened, read, and withheld.

[21] See also Campbell (96): "With them who laugh, our social joy appears; With them who mourn, we sympathize in tears . . . —Francis"

[22] Although they more obviously accept the patriarchy of Christianity, Warner's Ellen Montgomery grows to have the ability likewise to challenge men's rule ("when by chance her will might cross theirs" [538]; "'I will do what I think right, come what may'" [541]) and Stowe's Eliza likewise certainly shuns both danger and men's laws as with her child she flees her new master and crosses the ice floes of the Ohio River.

BEYOND UNDERSTANDING

Exploring Susan Warner's *The Wide, Wide World,* Harriet Beecher Stowe's *Uncle Tom's Cabin,* Ann S. Stephens's *Mary Derwent,* and E.D.E.N. Southworth's *The Hidden Hand* evinces parallel transformations through the 1850s in theological assumptions, women's social roles, literary conventions, and cognitive methods. The decade that opened with Ellen Montgomery's struggles to align her will with a utopian Christian ideal closed with Southworth poising Capitola ready to join men's earthly organizations from the military to the economic. Whereas Warner and Stowe had appealed to reader will to promote Christian ideals though the supporting faculties of imagination and the passions and their vehicle of sympathy, Stephens and Southworth appealed comparatively more directly to the reader's imagination. Ellen ponders the meanings of images and so grows and changes; from the very beginning Capitola "thinks on her feet" and acts definitively. Thus the decade began with appeals to the reader to exercise understanding of Christian doctrine through the images of parable and ended with appeals to the reader to exercise personal autonomy sparked by the imagination of free will in a free market and free society. At the same time, literary arrangements transformed from parables (Mary Kelley 250) or quilt-pieces (Elaine Showalter 155) that reiterate an ideology of evangelical Christianity and Christian domesticity to a more linear plot, moving, as Kristin Herzog writes, "from point A to point B to point C" (177). That is, as evidenced by these four works, the decade saw an evolution from ideologically-based to plot-based fiction. Within those evolving narrative structures the earlier works showed model characters drawing conclusions from an a priori-established and commonly-held Christian-based belief system. The decade ends with Stephens's recognition that one needs to discover things for oneself: ". . . when did example save? When did the fall of one human being prevent the fall of another?" (325) and Southworth's Cap iconoclastically thumbing her nose at established male dominance (118).

In terms of George Campbell's theory that discourse intends "to enlighten the understanding, to please the imagination, to move the passions, or to influence the will" (1), all four works surveyed invoke a reader's understanding. Each author uses language clear enough to have been understood by, and so to have garnered, a very broad readership. Indeed, the language, plots, and characters of these works are so easily understood that scholars and/or critics have condemned them as cliché or stereotyped. The respective works, however, utilize the appeal to the reader's understanding variously. Warner provides her reader with numerous occasions meant to carry a clear Christian message. Through her episodes and parables, Warner appeals to her reader's understanding and will to pursue a Christian life. Stowe, likewise appeals to her reader's understanding and will to align personal and national decisions with Christian teachings. Stowe presents her reader with the clear abolitionist message that slavery is anti-Christian: a person cannot be a Christian and treat another person as a piece of property.

Although Stephens and Southworth certainly direct secondary messages to the reader's understanding and will, these authors' central message, a challenge to nineteenth-century gender roles, comes to the reader in large part through sympathy and appeals to the reader's imagination and passions. In *Mary Derwent* Stephens relies on appeals to the reader's imagination with extravagant scenes and characters drawn from history and with the use of floral iconography to help her reader understand that women can pursue their own destinies, rule nations, and live exotic lives. In *The Hidden Hand*, by establishing the reader's sympathy with the spunky heroine and through appeals to the reader's imagination and passions, Southworth offers the reader an understanding that women can be autonomous and self-sufficient by exercising their own wills with "courage, self-control, and presence of mind" (114).

All four authors appeal to the reader's sympathy: "by sympathy we rejoice with them that rejoice, and weep with them that weep" (Campbell 131). Warner and Stowe invoke the reader's sympathy, encouraging him or her to emulate the Christian behavior of Mrs. Montgomery, Alice, Ellen, and John, on the one hand, and Eva, Tom, Eliza, George, Mrs. Shelby, and Mrs. Bird, on the other hand, through "lessons" such as those resulting from the scenes of Ellen's peeking at the leather scraps, Ellen's overcoming her tendency to let Miss Fortune upset her, Eliza's crossing the ice floes, Uncle Tom's enduring the slings and arrows of slavery, etc. These instances draw on reader sympathy, implicitly asking the reader to reevaluate real life circumstances that might involve dishonesty, lack of control, defeatism, or weakness.

Stephens provides a mixed message regarding the reader's intended response to potential role models and lessons. First she directs the reader to emulate the bravery, wit, and strength of pioneering women: "It was a brave, beautiful sight, which the American woman of our nineteenth century will do wisely to remember" (288). Soon thereafter she reveals her frustration that humans can learn only from their own mistakes: "My own destiny . . . might be the salvation of many in its moral, but when did example save? When did the fall of one human being prevent the fall of another?" (325) This ambivalence hints that the reader might effectively emulate the good qualities of Stephens's characters, but might have difficulty deriving specific lessons from given episodes. Likewise, the reader comes away from *The Hidden Hand* perhaps willing to emulate Capitola's spunk and "individual self-realization" (Dobson xxv), but perhaps unwilling to engage in duels or send potential rapists down trap doors.

These theological, social, and rhetorical progressions have important implications. For example, the women characters in the earlier novels appear interchangeable once they align their will with that of God. Willingly pursuing a Christian ideal, these women accept a single life role, by which they act similarly. In *The Wide, Wide World* Alice easily replaces the dying Mrs. Montgomery and Ellen easily replaces the dying Alice. With these characters, Warner presents a sisterhood of women easily melding into each other as they embody identical values and life goals. In *Uncle Tom's Cabin* Stowe's model characters seek not differentiation, but conformity to cultural (theological) standards. The well-to-do Mrs. Bird and fugitive slave, Eliza, share the role of Christian motherhood, a role more vital to each of them than differences in class, ethnicity, or individual personality. Similarly, Uncle Tom and Eva share a Christian role— important as a model of social cohesion that transcends differences in ethnicity, class, and age.

As the 1850s progress, however, characters (especially women characters) move from an all-one-in-Christendom identity to an identity increasingly more individuated and necessarily self-reliant. Women characters, unsupported by patriarchal, domestic, or theological structures, begin to see opportunities for success outside those realms. By the middle of the decade, the reader discovers in Fanny Fern's *Ruth Hall* (1855), a heroine who, like Capitola and all four of the authors discussed here, must support herself by her own wit and industry. The domestic literature exemplified by *The Wide, Wide World* and *Uncle Tom's Cabin* gives way to a literature in which characters (especially women) play roles as diverse as the exotic English-American Shawnee queen, Catharine Montour, and the cross-dressing mad-cap heiress from Rag Alley, Capitola Le Noir.

Creating such unique and individual characters, Stephens and Southworth do, indeed, turn "Ellen Montgomery on her head." Southworth sets women free within a potentially threatening patriarchy to act as individuals. By the end of the "feminine fifties," Cap shows that women can well function by their own particular strengths and activities. "And," continues Dobson, "so much the better" (Dobson xxix). But the situation is more complex than Dobson's favorable nod at the historical evolution of gender roles suggests. At the same time that women gained in what Dobson terms "woman's 'power'" (xxii) or "individual self-realization" (xxv), women also lost the strength of sisterhood and communal identity that allowed characters and readers to cross ethnic, socio-economic, and gender-role boundaries. On the one hand, "so much the better" that men have become more benign and/or able to be civilized by women and that women have become more active in their own pursuits. On the other hand, so much the worse for the brotherhood and sisterhood engendered by Christian domesticity.

Summarizing these various progressions may add another perspective to historical views of the 1850s. Early literary works such as *The Wide, Wide World* and *Uncle Tom's Cabin* feature characters who share identities and a cultural ethos of communality. These works feature community-owned "over-plots" (Baym), which are known to and shared by their readership. Set within an economic system of domesticity, Warner and Stowe implicitly espouse Christian generosity and an economy based on such communal dynamics as sharing the raw materials for making Christmas gifts in *The Wide, Wide World* (291ff) or Uncle Tom's sense of responsibility to be sold rather than let the community surrounding "the place . . . go to rack" (55).

The later works of the decade, *Mary Derwent* and *The Hidden Hand*, present a sense of characters, action, economic assumptions, and rhetorical strategies that differ from those of the earlier works. Their characters portray and implicitly advocate a striking individualism. With action-packed plots Stephens and Southworth propel the reader journeying through exotic and/or Gothic landscapes and adventures. The later works feature individuals who take the initiative to "seize the day" and "make it" despite certain cultural, physical, and economic obstacles. In *Mary Derwent* Stephens comes out of her story to instruct her reader to emulate the strength and bravery of the pioneer women; at the same time Stephens presents a feminine hero whose windfall fortune initiates a tragedy that she confronts head-on. In *The Hidden Hand* Southworth shows explicitly how women may pursue economic enterprise (326) and shows through the model of Cap how women can protect themselves from being exploited in circumstances that range from threats of urban homelessness to threats of forced sex and marriage.

Mary Derwent and *The Hidden Hand* thus assent to a cultural move toward personal autonomy and survival within the developing market economy and communicate that assent through discourse that relies heavily on appeals to the reader's imagination and passions fueled in turn by rhetorical appeals to the understanding and will. On the one hand, *The Wide, Wide World* and *Uncle Tom's Cabin* advocate a personal and political domestic communality that their authors (with Hale) demonstrate as superior to men's colder and more austere organizations. On the other hand, by privileging individualism and self-sufficiency, *Mary Derwent* and *The Hidden Hand* demonstrate that women can enter into men's colder and more austere organizations and there flourish. Some current readers might favor (with Campbell's theoretical foundation in Christian theology) the Christian vision espoused by Warner and Stowe as opposed to Stephens's and Southworth's more earthly vision of human possibility. Other current readers (accepting Campbell's theoretical foundation in the human ability to think for one's self) might prefer Stephens's and Southworth's visions of self-determination to a personal and cultural ideal limited by a pre-determined patriarchal doctrine.

Campbell quite inadvertently provides a solution to this assumed critical dilemma. He advocates using rhetorical appeals to various faculties the function of which derives from what people know about people:

> With them who laugh, our social joy appears;
> With them who mourn, we sympathize in tears;

If you would have we weep, begin the strain,
Then I shall feel your sorrows, feel your pain.
                              Francis
                              (quoted in Campbell 96)

He advises writers to create appeals to please the imagination and move
the passions based on what he or she knows, intuits, or deduces regarding
discourse and what people have in common. Attributing this sort of deductive thinking to women, Hale quotes Henry Thomas Buckle to situate
the faculty of imagination as elemental to deductive thought:

> "In regard to women being by nature more deductive, and men more induc-
> tive, you will remember that induction assigns the first place to particular
> facts; deduction to general propositions or ideas. Now, there are several rea-
> sons why women prefer the deductive, and if I may so say, ideal method.
> They are more emotional, more enthusiastic, and more imaginative than men;
> they therefore live more in an ideal world; while men, with their colder,
> harder, and austerer organizations, are more practical and more under the
> dominion of facts, to which they consequently ascribe a higher importance.
>   Another circumstance which makes women more deductive is, that they
> possess more of what is called intuition." (463)

Like any good male described here, Campbell rejects the deductive syllogism. Yet his philosophy of discourse clearly advocates using appeals to
those faculties that foster deductive thought (as explained here). Working
with rather than against the grain of Campbell's apparent contradiction,
current readers, too, can have it both ways. We can admit equally to the
powers of inductive analysis and to (as Stowe puts it) the power of
"feeling right." We can rise above the false need to prefer plot to no plot
or no floral references to such references. Rising above the role of critical
judge, we can value mid-nineteenth-century fiction for its artistry and
well-wrought rhetorical appeals rather than succumbing to the urge to rate
such works hierarchically—canonizing or not canonizing—according to
the day's political fashion.

    Criticism contemporaneous to these authors affirms the importance in
the nineteenth century of appeals to a reader's several faculties; just so,
mid-nineteenth-century American women's literature experienced after the
era gains vibrancy when read beyond only understanding. Acknowledging
the power of these works to play on the reader's multiple faculties indeed
provides a twist to issues of canon by transferring the focus of admission

criteria from the subject of gender to the subject of rhetorical effectiveness: how authors manage to enlighten, please, move and/or influence readers. Such discussions can result in nineteenth-century women's texts admission to the canon not by virtue of the writers' and writings' gender identification, but by virtue of the texts' interactions with readers. Appreciating the rhetorical effectiveness of authors whose concerns may lie outside current political agendas or needs for linear plot, action, etc. may help explain the literary success of America's early prominent literature. Legitimating the rhetorical appeals of communally held images and passions that draw writers and readers together may well generate ties of sisterhood, brotherhood, and community, much needed as we approach the twenty-first century.

WORKS CITED

Adams, John R. *Harriet Beecher Stowe; Updated Version.* Boston: Twayne Pub., 1989.

Ahlstrom, Sydney E. *A Religious History of the American People.* New Haven: Yale UP, 1973.

Bakhtin, Mikhail M. *The Dialogic Imagination.* Trans. Caryl Emerson and Michael Holquist. Ed. Michael Holquist. Austin: U of Texas P, 1981.

Barnette, Martha. *A Garden of Words.* New York: Random House, 1992.

Baym, Nina. "Melodramas of Beset Manhood: How Theories of American Fiction Exclude Women Authors." *American Quarterly* 23 (Summer, 1981) 123-39.

———. *Novels, Readers, and Reviewers. Responses to Fiction in Antebellum America.* Ithaca: Cornell UP, 1984.

———. *Woman's Fiction: A Guide to Novels by and About Women in America, 1820-1870.* Ithaca: Cornell UP, 1978.

Belenky, Mary Field, Blythe McVicker Clinchy, Nancy Rule Goldberger, and Jill Mattuck Tarule. *Women's Ways of Knowing. The Development of Self, Voice, and Mind.* New York: Basic Books, Inc., Publishers, 1986.

Benet, William Rose, ed. *The Reader's Encyclopedia.* New York: 1948.

Berger, Peter. *Social Construction of Reality.* New York: Doubleday & Co., Inc., 1967.

Berlin, James A. *Writing Instruction in Nineteenth-Century American Colleges*. Carbondale: Southern Illinois UP, 1984.

Bevilacqua, Vincent. "Philosophical Origins of George Campbell's *The Philosophy of Rhetoric.*" *Speech Monographs* 32 (1965): 1-12.

Bitzer, Lloyd. Editor's Introduction. *The Philosophy of Rhetoric*. By George Campbell. Carbondale: Southern Ilinois UP, 1963. vii-li.

Bizzell, Patricia. "Opportunities for Feminist Research in the History of Rhetoric." *Rhetoric Review* 11 (1992): 50-58.

Bode, Carl. *The Anatomy of American Popular Culture 1840-1861*. Berkeley and Los Angeles: U of California P, 1959.

Brande, W.T., F.R.S.L. & E., of Her Majesty's Mint, ed. *Dictionary of Science, Literature, and Art: Comprising the History, Description, and Scientific Principles of Every Branch of Human Knowledge; with the Derivation and Definition of all the Terms in General Use*. New York: Harper & Brothers, 1850.

Brinton, Alan. "The Passions as Subject Matter in Early Eighteenth-Century British Sermons." *Rhetorica* (Winter, 1992): 51-69.

Brown, Dee. *Bury My Heart at Wounded Knee. An Indian History of the American West*. New York: Holt, Rinehart & Winston, 1970.

Brown, Herbert Ross. *The Sentimental Novel in America, 1789-1860*. Durham, NC: Duke UP, 1940.

Bruner, Jerome. *Actual Minds, Possible Worlds*. Cambridge, MA: Harvard UP, 1986.

Rev. of *The Cabin and the Parlor: Or Slaves and Masters*, by J. Thornton Randolph. *The Southern Literary Messenger* Nov. 1852: 703.

Campbell, George. *The Philosophy of Rhetoric*. Ed. Lloyd F. Bitzer. Carbondale: Southern Illinois UP, 1963.

Campbell, Thomas. *Gertrude of Wyoming*. New York: D. Appleton & Co., 1858.

Carpenter, Lynette. "Double Talk: The Power and Glory of Paradox in E.D.E.N. Southworth's *The Hidden Hand*." *Legacy* 1993: 17-30.

Cawelti, John G. *Adventure, Mystery, and Romance: Formula Stories as Art and Popular Culture*. Chicago: U of Chicago P, 1976.

Chapman, Isaac. *A Sketch of the History of Wyoming*. Wilkesbarre: Sharp D. Lewis, 1830.

Child, Lydia Maria. *An Appeal for that Class of Americans Called Africans*. Boston: Allen & Ticknor, 1833.

―――. *The Letters of Lydia Maria Child*. Boston: Houghton, Mifflin and Co., 1883.

Clark, Rev. D.W. "Literary Women of America. Number XII. Mrs. Harriet Beecher Stowe." *Ladies' Repository* (March 1858): 171-74.

Clement, J., ed. *[Eighth* (sic) *Thousand] Noble Deeds of American Women; with Biographical Sketches of some of the more Prominent*. Buffalo: Geo. H. Derby and Co., 1852.

Cogan, Frances B. *All-American Girl, The Ideal of Real Womanhood in Mid-Nineteenth-Century America*. Athens: U of Georgia P, 1989.

Cott, Nancy F., ed. *Root of Bitterness. Documents of the Social History of American Women.* Boston: Northeastern UP, 1972.

———. *The Bonds of Womanhood: "Woman's Sphere" in New England 1780-1835.* New Haven, CT: Yale UP, 1977.

Cott, Nancy F. and Elizabeth H. Pleck. *A Heritage of Her Own: Toward a New Social History of American Women.* New York: Simon and Schuster, 1979.

Coultrap-McQuin, Susan. *Doing Literary Business. Aemrican Women Writers in the Nineteenth Century.* Chapel Hill: The U of North Carolina P, 1990.

———. Rev. of *The Hidden Hand or, Capitola the Madcap*, by E.D.E..N. Southworth. *Legacy* (Fall, 1988): 70-71.

Cross, Barbara M. "Stowe, Harriet Beecher." *Notable American Women, 1607-1950.* Campbridge: Belknap P, 1971.

Dances with Wolves. Dir. Kevin Costner. Orion Pictures, 1990.

Davidson, Cathy N., ed. *Reading in America: Literature & Social History.* Baltimore: The Johns Hopkins UP, 1989.

———. *Revolution and the Word: The Rise of the Novel in America.* Oxford: Oxford UP, 1986.

Rev. of *The Deserted Wife* by E.D.E.N. Southworth. *Godey's Lady's Book.* Dec. 1855: 560.

Dobra, Susan. "Annie Besant: Orator, Activist, Mystic, Rhetorician." Conf. on Coll. Composition and Communication Convention. Grand Hyatt, Washington D.C. 23 March 1995.

Dobson, Joanne. "The Hidden Hand: Subversion of Cultural Ideology in Three Mid-Nineteenth-Century American Women's Novels." *American Quarterly* (1986): 223-42.

———. "Introduction." *The Hidden Hand or, Capitola the Madcap.* By E.D.E.N. Southworth. 1888. New Brunswick: Rutgers UP, 1988.

Donovan, Josephine. *Uncle Tom's Cabin. Evil, Affliction, and Redemptive Love.* Boston: Twayne Publishers, 1991.

Douglas, Ann. *The Feminization of American Culture.* New York: Alfred A. Knopf, 1977.

———. "The 'Scribbling Women' and Fanny Fern: Why Women Wrote." *American Quarterly* 23 (Spring 1971): 3-24.

"Editor's Easy Chair." *Harper's New Monthly Magazine* March, 1855: 550-51.

"Editors' Table." *Godey's Magazine and Lady's Book* Sept. 1851: 185-86.

"Editors' Table." *The Ladies' Companion* 9 (Nov. 1838): 50.

Ehninger, Douglas. "Campbell, Blair, and Whately: Old Friends in a New Light." *Western Journal of Speech Communication* 19 (October 1955): 263-69.

Ellet, Elizabeth F. *Women of the American Revolution.* Vol. 2. Philadelphia: George W. Jacobs and Co., 1900. 2 vols.

Elliott, Kenneth. "Rhetoric & Rhetorical Studies Chat (Pre/Text)." E-mail. 5 July 1995.

Rev. of *Female Prose Writers of America*, by John S. Hart. "Literary Notices." *Godey's Magazine and Lady's Book* Jan. 1852: 91.

Rev. of *Female Prose Writers of America*, by John S. Hart. "Literary Notices." *Godey's Magazine and Lady's Book* Dec. 1854: 554.

Rev. of *Female Prose Writers of America*, by John S. Hart. "Literary Notices." *Ladies' Repository* April, 1855: 251.

Fern, Fanny. *Fern Leaves from Fanny's Port-Folio.* Second Series. Buffalo: Miller, Orton & Mulligan, 1854.

Fetterley, Judith, ed. *Provisions. A Reader from Nineteenth-Century American Women.* Bloomington: Indiana UP, 1985.

Rev. of *The Floral Offering*, by Henrietta Dumont. "Literary Notices." *Godey's Magazine and Lady's Book* Feb. 1852: 165.

Rev. of *Flora's Dictionary*, by Mrs. E.W. Wirt. "Literary Notices." *Godey's Magazine and Lady's Book* Jan. 1856: 87.

Forrest, Mary. *Women of the South, Distinguished in Literature.* New York: Charles B. Richardson, 1866.

Fredrickson, George M. *The Black Image in the White Mind: The Debate on Afro-American Character and Destiny, 1817-1914.* New York: Harper and Rowe, 1971.

Freeze, John G. "Madame Montour." *Pennsylvania Magazine of History and Biography* 3 (1879): 79-87.

Freibert, Lucy M. Rev. of *The Wide, Wide World*, by Susan Warner with an Afterword by Jane Tompkins. *Legacy* 4 (Fall, 1987): 66-68.

Freibert, Lucy M. and Barbara A. White. *Hidden Hands, An Anthology of American Women Writers, 1790-1870.* New Brunswick, NJ: Rutgers UP, 1985.

Freier, Paulo. *Pedagogy of the Oppressed.* Trans. Myra Bergman Ramos. New York: The Seabury P, 1970.

Furnas, J.C. *Goodbye to Uncle Tom.* New York: William Sloane Associates, 1956.

Gabler-Hover, Janet. *Truth in American Fiction. The Legacy of Rhetorical Idealism.* Athens: U of Georgia P, 1990.

Gemme, Paola. "Legacy Profile: Ann Sophia Winterbotham Stephens." *Legacy. A Journal of American Women Writers* 12 (1995): 47-55.

Gilbert, Sandra M. amd Susan Gubar. *The Madwoman in the Attic. The Woman Writer and the Nineteenth-Century Literary Imagination.* New Haven: Yale UP, 1979.

Golden, James L. and Edward P.J. Corbett. *The Rhetoric of Blair, Campbell, and Whately.* New York: Holt, Rinehart & Winston, Inc., 1968.

Golden, James L., Goodwin F. Berquist, and William E. Coleman. *The Rhetoric of Western Thought.* Debuque: Kendall/Hunt Pub. Co., 1976.

Goodman, Charlotte. "From *Uncle Tom's Cabin* to Vyry's Kitchen: The Black Female Folk Tradition in Margaret Walker's *Jubilee.*" *Tradition and the Talents of Women.* Ed. Florence Howe. Chicago: U of Illinois P, 1990.

Goshgarian, G.M. *To Kiss the Chastening Rod: Domestic Fiction and Sexual Ideology in the American Renaissance.* Ithaca: Cornell UP, 1992.

Greene, Gayle. *Changing the Story, Feminist Fiction and the Tradition.* Bloomington: Indiana U P, 1991.

Greenwood, Grace. *A Forest Tragedy and Other Tales.* Boston: Ticknor and Fields, 1855.

Habegger, Alfred. *Gender, Fantasy, and Realism in American Literature.* New York: Columbia UP, 1982.

Hagaman, John. "On Campbell's *Philosophy of Rhetoric* and its Relevance to Contemporary Invention." *Rhetoric Society Quarterly* XI (1981): 145-55.

Hale, Sarah Josepha. *Biography of Distinguished Women; or Woman's Record, from the Creation of A.D. 1869.* 3rd ed., revised. New York: Harper & Bros., 1876.

————. *Flora's Interpreter, and Fortuna Flora.* 1832. Boston: Chase and Nichols, 1865.

Hanaford, Phebe A. *Daughters of America; or, Women of the Century.* Augusta: True and Co., 1882.

Harris, Susan K. "The House that Hagar Built: Houses and Heroines in E.D.E.N. Southworth's *The Deserted Wife.*" *Legacy* 4 (Fall, 1987): 17-29.

————. *19th-Century American Women's Novels. Interpretive Strategies.* Cambridge: Cambridge UP, 1990.

Hart, James D. *The Popular Book, a History of America's Literary Taste.* Berkeley: U of California P, 1950.

Hart, John S. *The Female Prose Writers of America.* Philadelphia: E.H. Butler & Co., 1852.

Hawthorne, Nathaniel. *Letters of Hawthorne to William D. Ticknor, 1851-1864.* Newark, NJ: Carteret Book Club, 1910.

Helsinger, Elizabeth K., Robin Lauterback Sheets, and William Veeder. *The Woman Question: Society and Literature in Britain and America, 1837-1883.* Vol. 3. New York: Garland Pub. Inc., 1983. 3 vols.

Herzog, Kristin. *Women, Ethnics, and Exotics. Images of Power in Mid-Nineteenth-Century American Fiction.* Knoxville: U of Tennessee P, 1983.

Holman, C. Hugh, William Flint Thrall, and Addison Hibbard. *A Handbook to Literature.* New York: The Odyssey P, 1960.

The Holy Bible. King James Version. New York: New American Library, 1974.

Horner, Winifred Bryan. "The Eighteenth Century." *The Present State of Scholarship in Historical and Contemporary Rhetoric.* Ed. Winifred Bryan Horner. Columbia: U of Missouri P, 1983: 101-33.

————. *Nineteenth-Century Scottish Rhetoric, The American Connection.* Carbondale: Southern Illinois UP, 1993.

————. "The Roots of Modern Writing Instruction: Eighteenth- and Nineteenth-Century Britain." *Rhetoric Review* 8.2 (Spring 1990): 322-45.

Howell, Wilbur Samuel. *Eighteenth-Century British Logic and Rhetoric.* Princeton: Princeton UP, 1971.

Ingpen, Ada M. *Women as Letter-Writers: A Collection of Letters Selected and Edited by Ada M. Ingpen.* London: Hutchinson & Co., 1909.

Johnson, Nan. "Innovations in Nineteenth-Century Pedagogy: The Rhetorics of Henry Day, M.B. Hope, and Franz Theremin." *The Rhetorical Tradition and Modern Writing.* Ed. James J. Murphy. New York: Modern Language Association, 1982. 105-18.

————. *Nineteenth-Century Rhetoric in North America.* Carbondale: Southern Illinois UP, 1991.

Jolliffe, David A. "The Moral Subject in College Composition: A Conceptual Framework and the Case of Harvard." *College English* 51.2 (Feb. 1989): 163-73.

Kaplan, Bruce Eric. Cartoon. *New Yorker.* 10 Aug. 1992: 59.

Keeney, Elizabeth B. *The Botanizers: Amateur Scientists in Nineteenth-Century America.* Chapel Hill: U of North Carolina P, 1992.

Kelley, Mary. *Private Woman, Public Stage. Literary Domesticity in Nineteenth-Century America.* New York: Oxford UP, 1984.

Rev. of *A Key to Uncle Tom's Cabin. The Southern Literary Messenger.* June, 1853: 321-25.

Kitzhaber, Albert R. *Rhetoric in American Colleges, 1850-1900.* Dallas: Southern Methodist UP, 1990.

Knickerbocker's Magazine. XLV. (1855): 525.

Kolodny, Annette. *The Land Before Her. Fantasy and Experience of the American Frontiers, 1630-1860.* Chapel Hill: The U of North Carolina P, 1984.

Lakoff, Robin. *Language and Woman's Place.* New York: Harper & Row, 1975.

Lanham, Richard. *A Handlist of Rhetorical Terms. A Guide for Students of English Literature.* Berkeley: U of California P, 1968.

"Letter to the Mohawk Chief Ahyonwaeghs, Commonly Called John Brant, Esq. of the Grand River, Upper Canada. From Thomas Campbell." *The New Monthly Magazine and Literary Journal* (Jan. to June, 1822): 97-101.

Levy, Anita. *Other Women. The Writing of Class, Race, and Gender, 1832-1898.* Princeton: Princeton UP, 1991.

Little Big Man. Dir. Arthur Penn. C.B.S./Fox Co., 1970.

Rev. of *The Lost Heiress* by E.D.E.N. Southworth. *Godey's Lady's Book.* Dec. 1854: 555.

Macpherson, C.B. *The Political Theory of Possessive Individualism; Hobbes to Locke.* New York: Oxford UP, 1962.

Marshe, Witham. *Journal of the Treaty at Lancaster in 1744, with the Six Nations.* Annotated by William H. Egle, M.D. 1744, 1801. Lancaster: The New Era Steam Book and Job Print, 1884.

"Mary Derwent." *The Ladies' Companion.* Vol. 9 (May, 1838): 39ff.

Rev. of *Mary Derwent* by Ann S. Stephens. *Godey's Lady's Book.* Aug., 1858: 181.

————. *Harper's New Monthly Magazine.* Aug., 1858: 407.

May, Caroline. *The American Female Poets.* Philadelphia: Lindsay & Blakiston, 1859.

Miller, Susan. *Textual Carnivals. The Politics of Composition.* Carbondale: Southern Illinois UP, 1991.

Miner, Charles. *History of Wyoming, in a Series of Letters, from Charles Miner, to his Son, William Penn Miner, Esq.* Philadelphia: J. Crissy, 1845.

Mott, Frank Luther. *Golden Multitudes: The Story of the Best Sellers in the United States.* New York: Macmillan Co., 1947.

"Mrs. Ann S. Stephens." *The American Literary Magazine* (June, 1848): 335-43.

Neihardt, John G. *Black Elk Speaks: Being the Life Story of a Holy Man of the Oglala Sioux.* Lincoln: U of Nebraska P, 1961.

"Novels: Their Meaning and Mission." *Putnam's Monthly Magazine* (Oct. 1854): 389-96.

Nye, Russel B. "The Novel as Dream and Weapon: Women's Popular Novels in the 19th Century." *Historical Society of Michigan Chronicle* 2 (4th quarter, 1975): 2-16.

Papashvily, Helen Waite. *All the Happy Endings: a Study of the Domestic Novel in America.* New York: Harper & Bros., 1956.

Pateman, Carole. *The Sexual Contract.* Stanford: Stanford UP, 1988.

Pattee, Fred Lewis. *The Feminine Fifties.* New York: D. Appleton-Century Co., 1940.

Pearson, Edmund. *Dime Novels; or Following an Old Trail in Popular Literature.* New York: Kennikat P, Inc., 1968.

Peck, George. *Wyoming: Its History, Romance, Stirring Incidents, and Romantic Adventure.* New York: Harper and Brothers, 1858.

Petter, Henri. *The Early American Novel.* Ohio State UP, 1971.

Rev. of *Plantation and Farm Instruction, Regulation, Record, Inventory and Account Book. For the use of Managers on Estates,* by a Southern Planter. *The Southern Literary Messenger.* Oct. 1852: 638-39.

Pond, Enoch, D.D. *Memoir of Count Zinzendorf.* Boston: Massachusetts Sabbath School Society, 1839.

Porte, Joel. *Emerson in his Journals.* Cambridge: Harvard UP, 1982.

Radway, Janice A. *Reading the Romance: Women, Patriarchy, and Popular Literature.* Chapel Hill: U of North Carolina P, 1984.

Railton, Stephen. "Mothers, Husbands, and Uncle Tom." *Georgia Review* (1984): 129-44.

"Religious Fiction: *The Wide, Wide World* by Elizabeth Wetherell; *Glen Luna* by Amy Lothrop." *The Prospective Review* 9: 314-39.

Reynolds, David S. *Beneath the American Renaissance. The Subversive Imagination in the Age of Emerson and Melville.* Cambridge: Harvard UP, 1989.

Reynolds, Moira Davidson. *Uncle Tom's Cabin and Mid-Nineteenth-Century United States; Pen and Conscience.* Jefferson, NC: McFarland & Co., Pub., 1985.

"The Romance of Wyoming." Rev. of and excert from George Peck, D.D., *Wyoming; Its History, Stirring Incidents, and Romantic Adventures. Harper's New Monthly Magazine* Aug., 1858: 306-22.

Rutland, Violet (Lindsay) Manners, Duchess of. *Portraits of Men and Women, by the Marchioness of Granby.* Westminister: A. Constable & Co., 1900.

Sand, George. "Uncle Tom's Cabin." *The National Era.* 27 Oct. 1853: 15.

Sandage, Allan. *The Carnegie Atlas of Galaxies.* Washington DC: Carnegie Institution of Washington, 1994.

Shapiro, Ann R. *Unlikely Heroines. Nineteenth-Century American Women Writers and the Woman Question.* New York: Greenwood Press, 1987.

Showalter, Elaine, ed. *The New Feminist Criticism. Essays on Women, Literature, and Theory.* New York: Pantheon Books, 1985.

――――. *Sister's Choice. Tradition and Change in American Women's Writing.* Oxford: Clarendon P, 1991.

Sigourney, Lydia H. *Letters of Life.* NY: D. Appleton & Co., 1866.

――――. *Poems.* Philadelphia: Key & Biddle, 1834.

――――. *Zinzendorff and Other Poems.* New York: Leavitt, Lord & Co., 1837.

Sklar, Kathryn Kish. *Catharine Beecher; A Study in American Domesticity.* New Haven: Yale UP., 1973.

"Slavery and Its Abuses—Mrs. Stowe and the N. York Courier and Enquirer." *The National Era* 21 Oct. 1852: 170.

Smith, Olivia. *The Politics of Language, 1791-1819.* Oxford: Clarendon P, 1984.

Southworth, E.D.E.N. *The Hidden Hand or, Capitola the Madcap.* Ed. Joanne Dobson. New Brunswick: Rutgers UP, 1988.

Starling, Elizabeth. "Female Eloquence." *Godey's Magazine and Lady's Book* April, 1852: 295.

Stephens, Ann S. *Mary Derwent.* Philadelphia: T.B Peterson & Brothers, 1858.
――――. *Malaeska; the Indian Wife of the White Hunter.* New York: Irwin P. Beadle & Co., 1860.

――――. "Mary Derwent. A Tale of the Early Settlers." *The Ladies' Companion* 9 (1838): 39-45, 89-142, 185-90, 235-46, 282-92.

————. Miscellaneous manuscripts and notes. New York: New York Public Library, Manuscript Division.

Stern, Madeleine B. *Publishers for Mass Entertainment in Nineteenth-Century America*. Boston: G.K. Hall & Co., 1980.

————. *We the Women. Career Firsts of Nineteenth-Century America*. New York: Schulte Pub. Co., 1963.

Stewart, Donald C. "The Nineteenth Century." *The Present State of Scholarship in Historical and Contemporary Rhetoric*. Ed. Winifred Bryan Horner. Columbia: U of Missouri P, 1983.

Stone, William Leete. *Life of Brant, (Thayendanegea) Including the Border Wars of the American Revolution*. 1838. Albany: J. Munsell, 1865.

————. *The Poetry and History of Wyoming*. New York: Wiley and Putnam, 1841.

Stowe, Harriet Beecher. *The Key to Uncle Tom's Cabin; Presenting the Original Facts and Documents Upon Which they Story is Founded Together with Corroborative Statements Verifying the Truth of the Work*. London: Clarke, Beeton, and Co.,

————. *My Wife and I: or, Harry Henderson's History*. New York: J.B. Ford and Co., 1874.

————. *Uncle Tom's Cabin or, Life among the Lowly*. New York: Vintage Books, 1991.

Sundquist, Eric J., ed. *New Essays on Uncle Tom's Cabin*. Cambridge: Cambridge UP, 1986.

Swearingen, C. Jan. *Rhetoric and Irony. Western Literacy and Western Lies*. New York: Oxford UP, 1991.

Tichi, Cecelia. "American Literary Studies to the Civil War." *Redrawing the Boundaries: The Transformation of English and American Literary Studies*. Ed. Stephen Greenblatt and Giles Gunn. New York: The Modern Language Association of America, 1992.

Tompkins, Jane. Afterword. *The Wide, Wide World*. By Susan Warner. New York: The Feminist P, 1987. 584-608.

————. "Indians": Textualism, Morality, and the Problem of History." *"Race," Writing, and Difference*. Ed. Henry Louis Gates, Jr. Chicago: U of Chicago P, 1986.

————. *Sensational Designs: The Cultural Work of American Fiction, 1790-1860*. New York: Oxford UP, 1985.

Toulouse, Teresa. *The Art of Prophesying*. Athens: The U of Georgia P, 1987.

Rev. of *The Two Sisters* by E.D.E.N. Southworth. *Godey's Lady's Book*. Nov. 1858: 468.

"Uncle Tom Abroad." *The National Era*. 24 March 1853: 46.

Rev. of *Uncle Tom's Cabin*. *The Southern Literary Messenger*. Dec. 1852: 721-31.

"Uncle Tom's Cabin at the South." *The National Era*. 2 June 1853: 86.

Rev. of *Uncle Tom's Cabin* by Mrs. Harriet Beecher Stowe. *The National Era*. 15 April 1852: 862.

Rev. of *Uncle Tom's Cabin; or Life Among the Lowly*, by Mrs. Harriet Beecher Stowe. *The Southern Literary Messenger*. Oct. 1852: 630-638.

Warner, Susan. *The Wide, Wide World*. Ed. Jane Tompkins. New York: The Feminist P, 1987.

Weaver, Richard M. *The Ethics of Rhetoric*. Chicago: Henry Regnery Co., 1953.

Wetherell, Elizabeth (Susan Warner). *The Wide, Wide World*. New York: G.P. Putnam & Co, 1851.

White, Isabelle. "Anti-Individualism, Authority, and Identity: Susan Warner's Contradictions in *The Wide, Wide World*." *American Studies* 31 (1990) 31-42.

Rev. of *The Wide, Wide World*. "Editors' Book Table." *Godey's Magazine and Lady's Book* March, 1851.

———. "Notices of New Works." *Southern Literary Messenger*. March, 1851: 189.

Wirt, Elizabeth Washington (Gamble). *Flora's Dictionary by a Lady*. Baltimore: Fielding Lucas, Jun., 1831.

Wolff, Janet. *Feminine Sentences. Essays on Women and Culture*. Berkeley and Los Angeles: U of California P, 1990.

Rev. of *Wyoming; Its History, Stirring Incidents, and Romantic Adventures* by George Peck, D.D. *Harper's New Monthly Magazine* June, 1858: 116.

———. *The National Era* June 10, 1858: 90.

———. *Ladies' Repository* July, 1858: 438.

Zwarg, Christina. "Fathering and Blackface in *Uncle Tom's Cabin*." *Novel: A Forum on Fiction* (Spring 1989): 274-87.

INDEX

Martha L. Henning holds a Ph.D. in Rhetoric and Composition. She currently teaches writing and literature at Portland Community College, Oregon, and co-chairs the annual Young Rhetoricians' Conference.

(Photo by Kendra Cott.)